invisibility

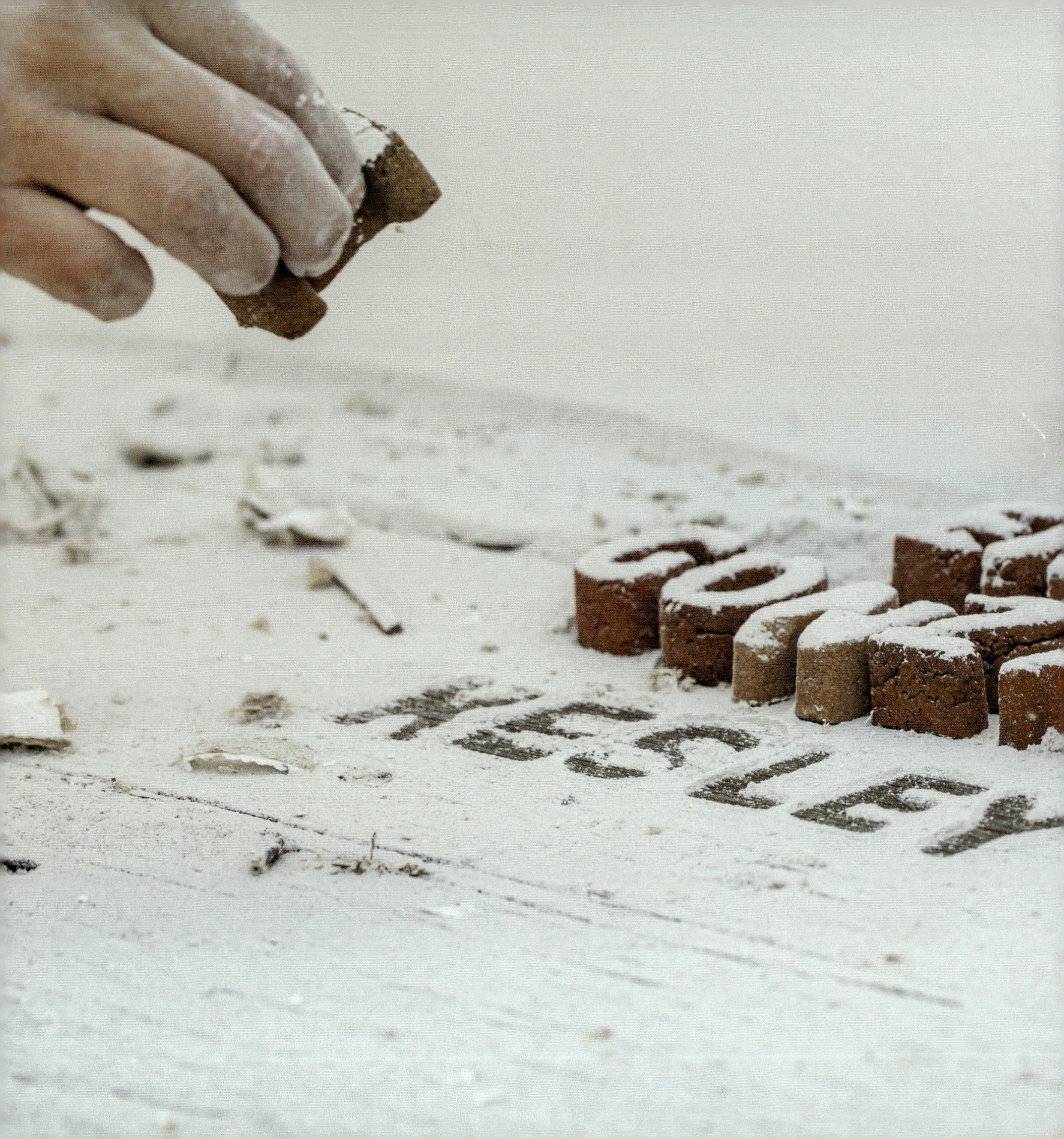

(in)visibility

aesthetics of undocumentedness

The Fowler Museum at UCLA

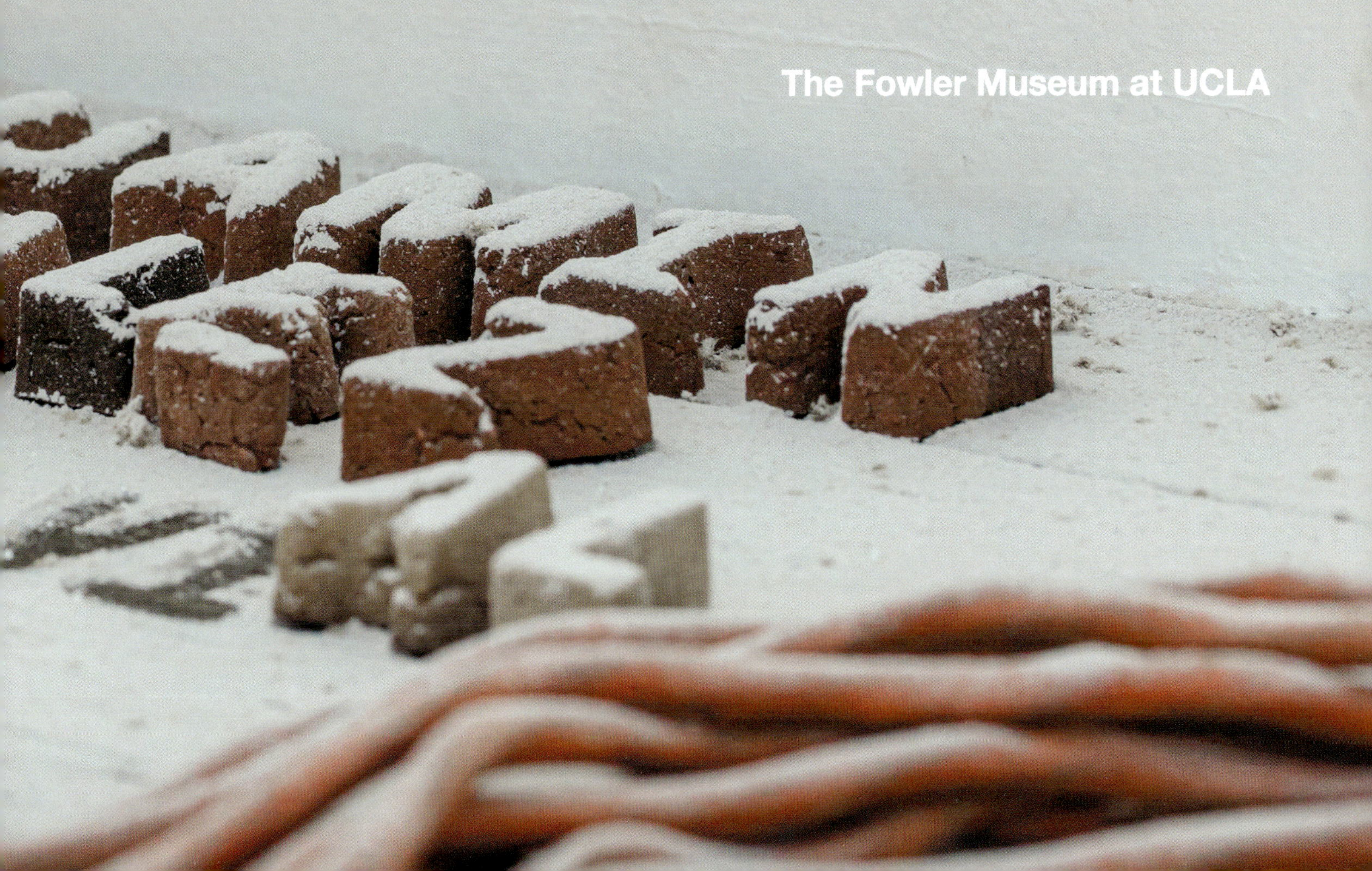

(COVER)
5 ▮▮▮▮▮▮▮▮
(b. 1984, México City, México)
Aquí Estamos (We are here),
2015–25
Mixed media (plaster, wood,
wire, concrete)
150 x 150 x 200 cm
Courtesy of the artist

(INSIDE FRONT COVER)
▮▮▮▮▮▮▮▮
(b. 1982, Santiago, Chile)
Weapon #30, 2022
Silkscreen, acrylic on collage
cardboard, and canvas
244 x 152 cm
Courtesy of the artist

(INSIDE BACK COVER)
▮▮▮▮▮▮▮▮
(b. 1982, Santiago, Chile)
Weapon #29, 2022
Silkscreen, acrylic on collage
cardboard, and canvas
244 x 152 cm
Courtesy of the artist

(TITLE SPREAD)
26C ▮▮▮▮▮▮▮▮
(b.1985, Quetzaltengo, Guatemala)
Gemidos de la Tierra (Wailings of
the land) (detail), 2024
Archival footage of political art
action
106 x 152 cm
Photograph by ▮▮▮▮▮▮
Courtesy of the artist, ▮▮▮▮, and
▮▮▮▮▮▮▮ Gallery

(RIGHT)
▮▮▮▮▮▮▮▮
(b. 1992, Leon, Guanajuato,
México)
Untitled (Kudzu) (detail), 2023
Archival ink-jet print mounted on
wood panel 81 x 101 cm
Courtesy of the artist

LIBRARY OF CONGRESS CATALOGING-IN-PUBLICATION DATA

Names: Fowler Museum at UCLA
Title: (In)visibility
Other titles: (In)visibility (Fowler Museum at UCLA)
Description: Los Angeles : Fowler Museum at UCLA, [2025] | Includes
  bibliographical references. | Summary: "This book features the artwork
  of individuals in the undoc+ spectrum (currently or formerly
  undocumented). The works visually explore the aesthetics of
  undocumentedness, the complexity of immigration journeys,
  hyperdocumentation, re-indigenizing in diaspora, immigrant labor,
  healing from immigrant trauma, imperfect solidarities with exile and
  refugee communities, and remembrance of those who perished in search of
  the American dream. The overall vision is guided by the aesthetic
  achievements of undoc+ artists; the publication-by undoc+ writers who,
  like the curator of this project, have been or are currently
  undocumented. The names of all participants have been purposefully
  concealed for their protection"-- Provided by publisher.
Identifiers: LCCN 2025021166 | ISBN 9780998044552 paperback
Subjects: LCSH: Noncitizens in art--Exhibitions | Arts and society--United
  States--History--21st century--Exhibitions | LCGFT: Catalogs |
  Exhibition catalogs
Classification: LCC NX652.A52 I58 2025 | DDC
  704/.086910973--dc23/eng/20250614
LC record available at https://lccn.loc.gov/2025021166

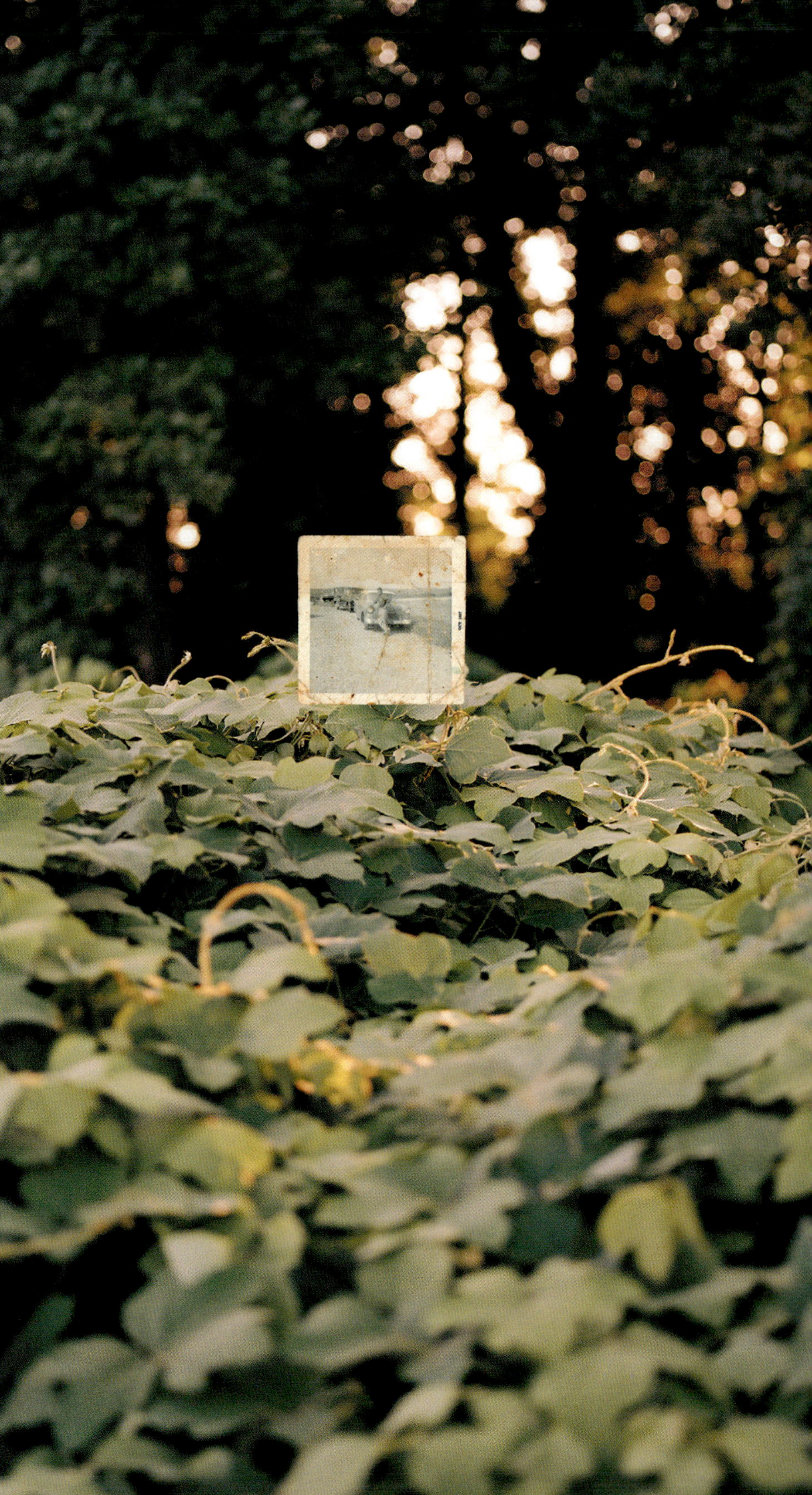

Contents

Foreword DIRECTOR

(b.1991, San Francisco
Coapan, Cholula, Puebla,
México)

*Tiricia de lo que nunca fue, de lo que
nunca murio* (detail), 2025
Mixed media: cazuela, guajolote,
machete, synthetic textile, and LED light
Circumference: 150 cm
Courtesy of the artist

Offering a glimpse into the materiality and imagery created by artists on the undoc+ spectrum, this publication introduces us to a poetics of fragments and opacity, which echoes the liminal state of the creators of these pieces. Many of the artworks on these pages evoke journeys of migration and displacement, community, solidarity, longing, and belonging. These are works that at once show and conceal, that invite the viewers to complete the picture by imagining what is not shown. Ultimately, they prompt us to reflect on the randomness that allows those born in certain nations to fully own their sense of humanity and citizenship, while individuals born elsewhere are forced into a condition of precarity, danger, exploitation, and invisibility. This is art that honors the painful reality of displacement, but also the resilience and creativity that define humanity. *(In)visibility* is a project that celebrates the work of artists dedicated to creating beauty and poetry regardless and despite of the challenges of their journeys.

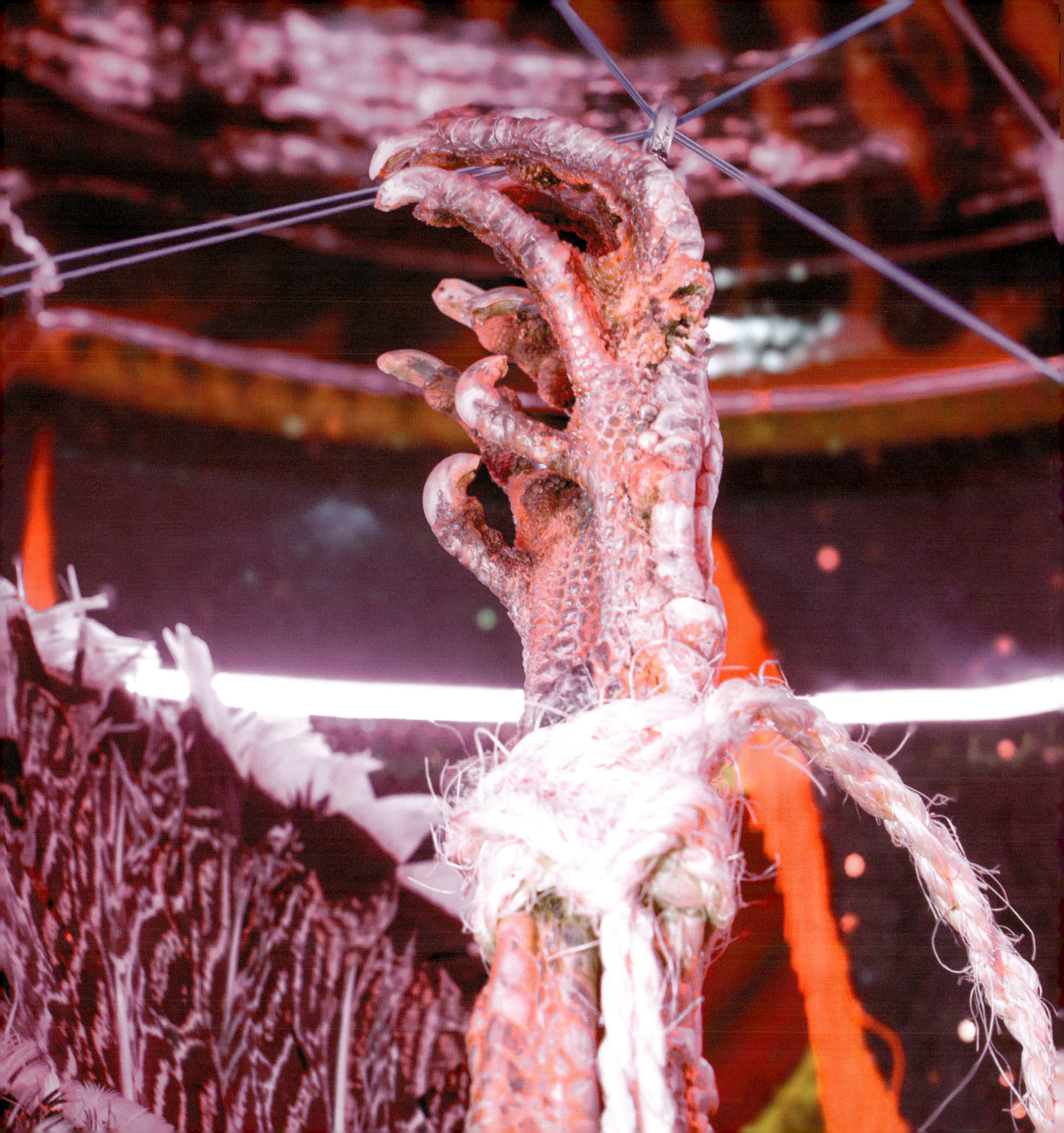

(b.1991, San Francisco
Coapan, Cholula, Puebla,
México)

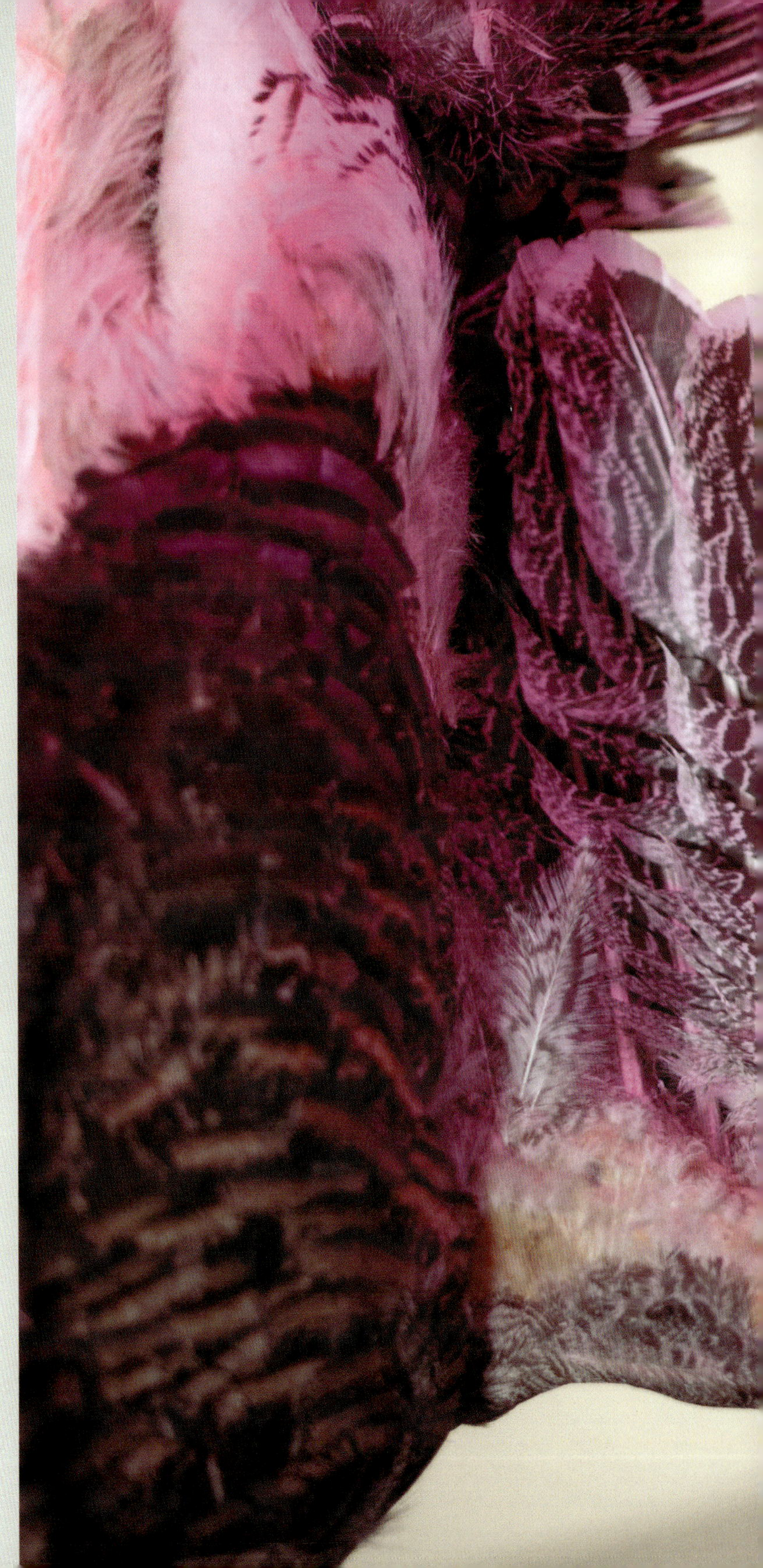

*Tiricia de lo que nunca fue, de lo que
nunca murio* (detail), 2025
Mixed media: cazuela, guajolote,
machete, synthetic textile, and LED light
Circumference: 150 cm
Courtesy of the artist

It has been inspiring and thought-provoking to be part of this project. We started the conversation with the curator and the artists with the idea of planning an exhibition that would bring all these artworks together in an evocative and poetic display. While that unfortunately had to be canceled due to funding challenges, we are honored to be able to contribute to the making of this volume. Our gratitude goes to the curator and author who dedicated many years to the research grounding this important and nuanced undertaking. We are grateful to the artists who shared their images and stories. We would also like to thank the many colleagues who helped with this project, the editor who skillfully managed the production of this book, and the designer who translated a vision into this beautiful volume.

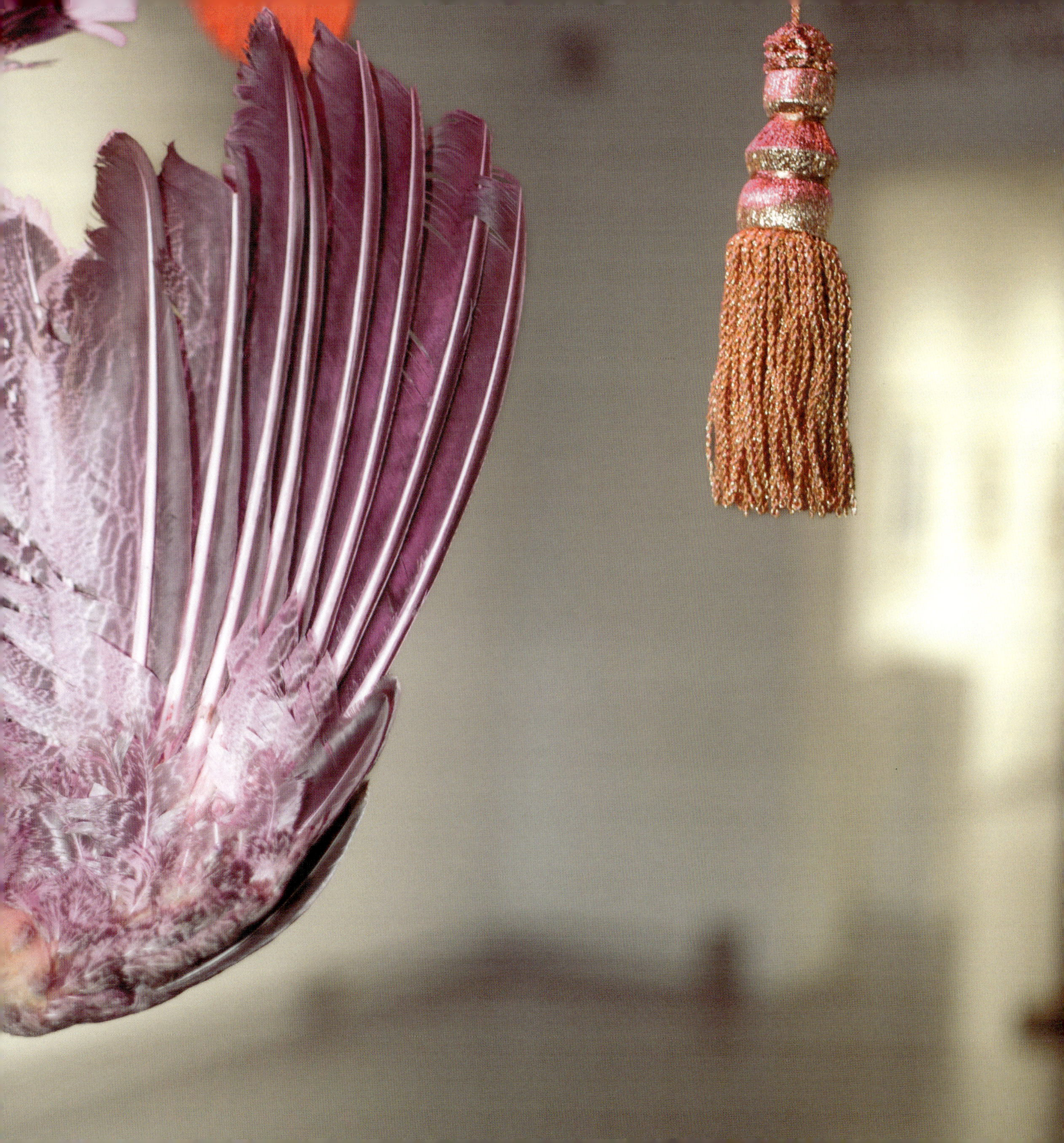

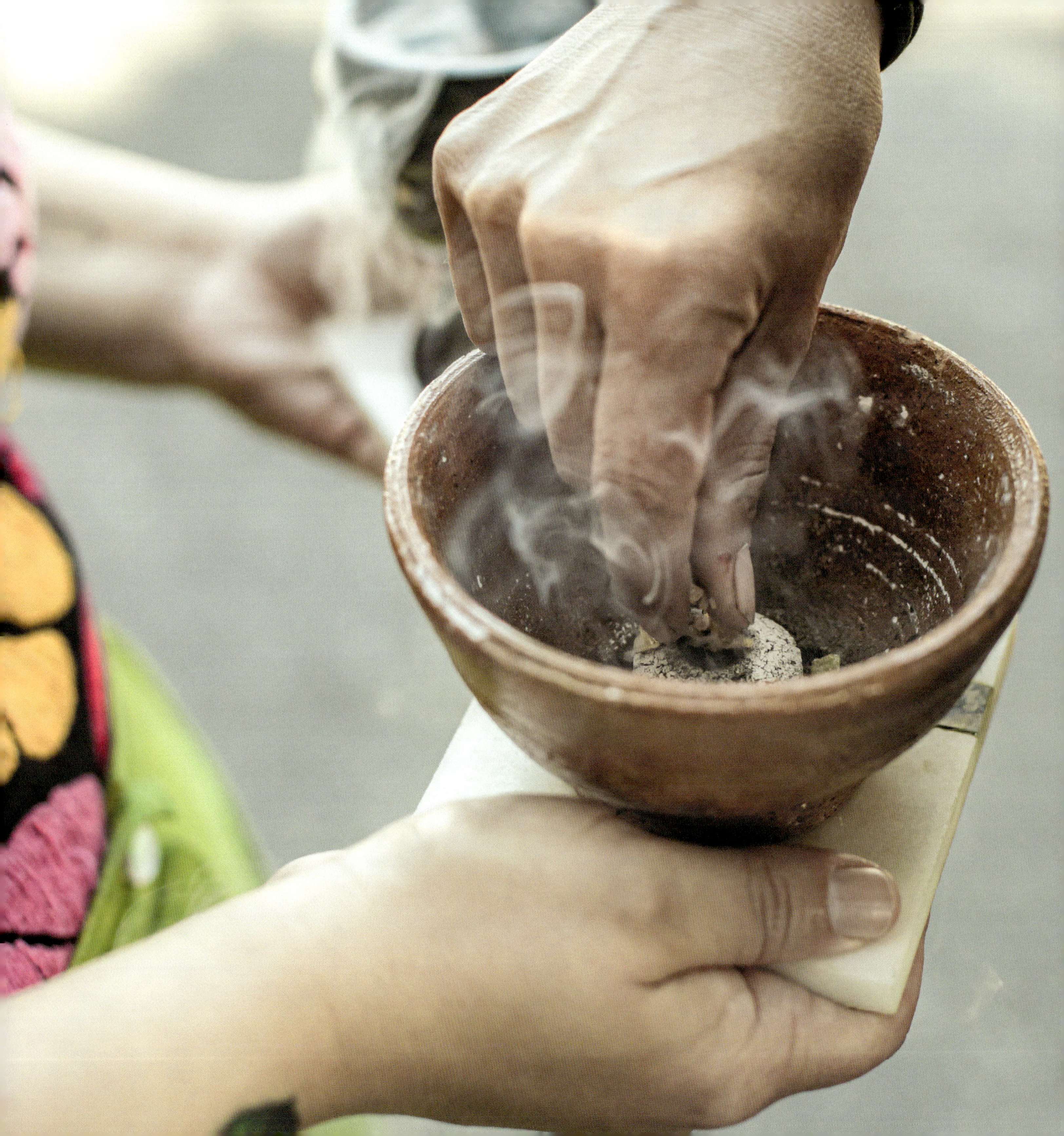

Acknowledgments CURATOR

26D ███████
(b.1985, Quetzaltengo,
Guatemala)

Gemidos de la Tierra (Wailings
of the Land/Soil), 2024
Archival footage of political art action
106 × 152 cm
Photograph by ███████
Courtesy of the artist, ████,
and ████████ Gallery

First and foremost, I would like to thank the many artists without whom this project would not have been possible.

My gratitude extends to each individual who has created a safe space and carved out time to make decisions in community across time zones; and has extended loving care to me and to one another during the development of this publication. To all my comadres and compadres in the arts —Tlazohcamati! One of my guiding principles in conceiving this project was to think of the museum as a sanctuary for the undoc+ community. I have encountered a plethora of expert allies who have made this project joyous, and it has been an absolute pleasure and honor to create knowledge alongside them. A list of names is customary in acknowledgments, yet it must be omitted in this instance. I would love nothing more than to name the dozens of undocumented, refugee, or exilee experts to whom I am grateful, yet doing so might cause them legal harm. I could list the undocumented diaspora allies who have graciously contributed to this venture, but it would be unjust toward those whose names have been withheld. Each of them stands in solidarity with my community and for that I am beyond thankful.

Untitled, 2017
Mixed media on found object
117 × 117 cm
Courtesy of the ████████ Estate

Instead of a list of names,
I offer my sincerest gratitude.

—CURATOR

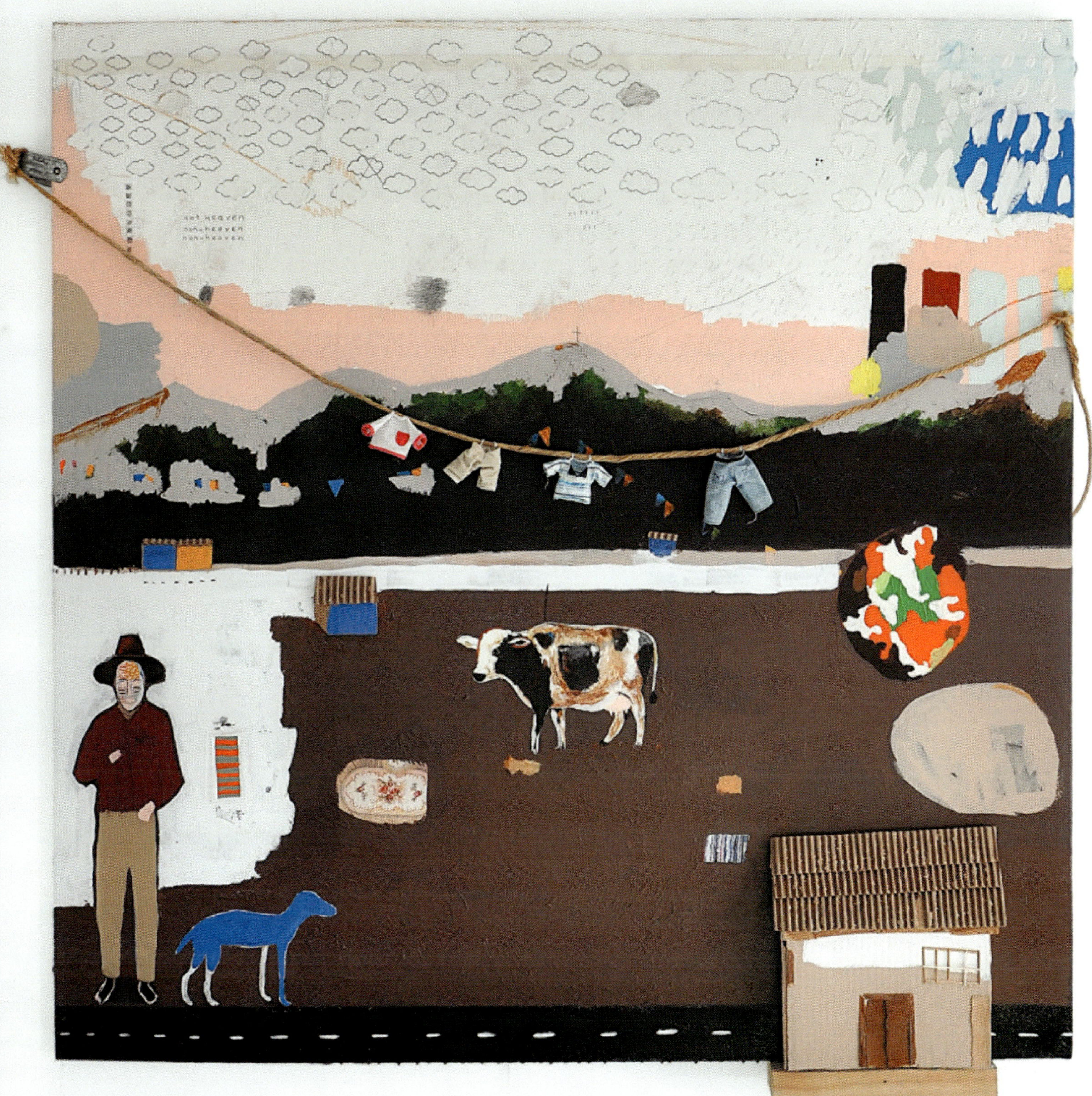

not Heaven
non-heaven
non-heaven

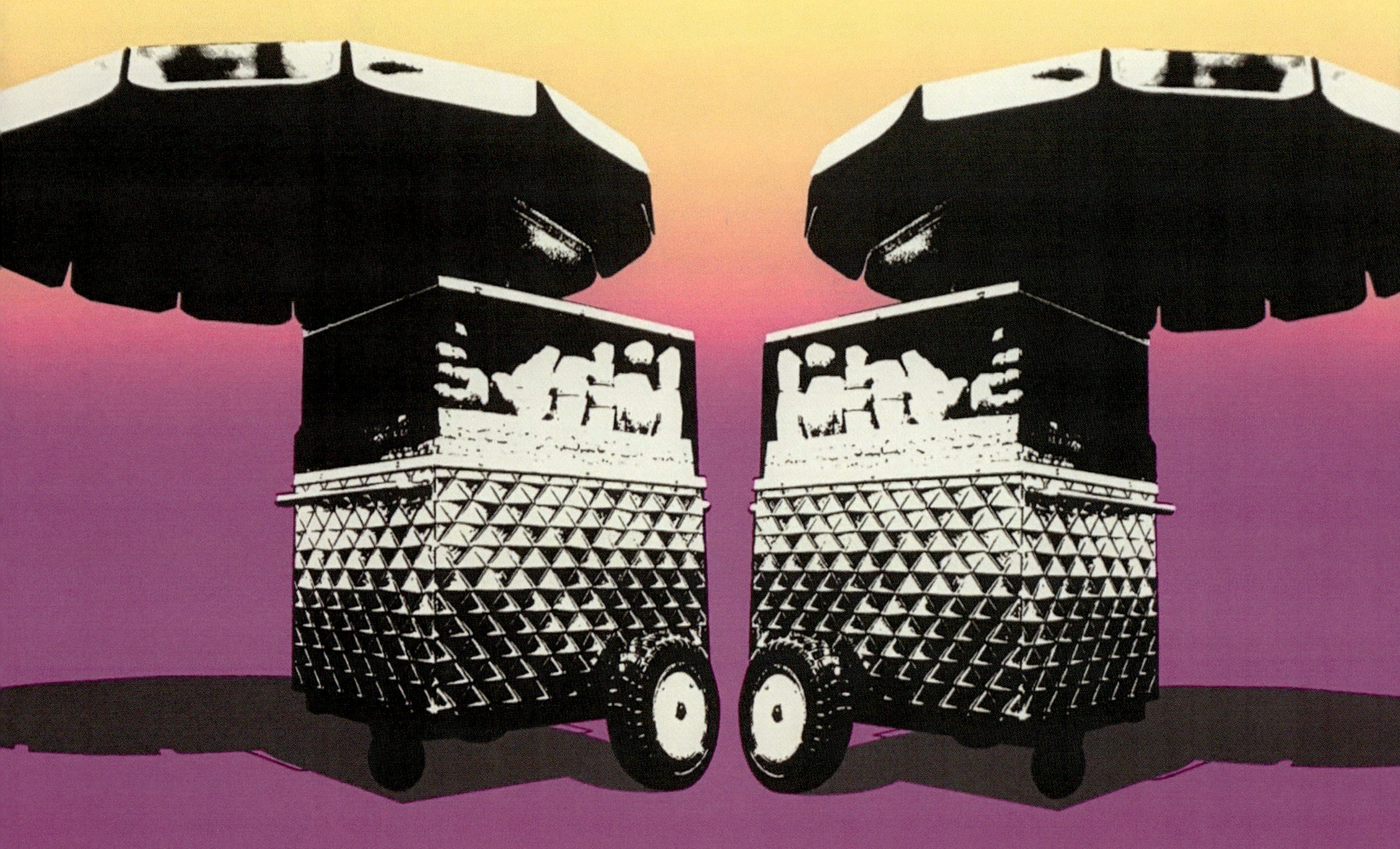

Solidarity through Opacity CURATOR

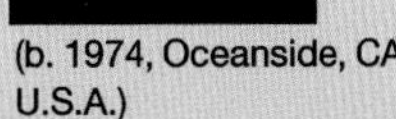

(b. 1974, Oceanside, CA, U.S.A.)

Fruteros, 2021
Serigraph on Coventry rag
45.72 × 60.96 cm
Courtesy of the artist and
██████ Gallery

"Nada somos sí solos caminamos, todo seremos si nuestros pasos caminan junto a otros pasos dignos."[1]

Édouard Glissant thought of the division between self and other as obsolete, demanding instead an opacity, which he conceived of as emancipatory from irreversible choices.[3] We call upon this emancipatory opacity by concealing the artists' names in this volume as a poetic gesture to protect the individuals most vulnerable and legally powerless against the U.S. government. This action is not intended as a symbolic erasure, a desire to silence people, or render them invisible or anonymous; instead, it is a sign of consideration and a protective embrace to generate distance from the current presidency and the country's political climate. This was not the single choice of any one individual. The artists and the curator of *(in)visibility* communally decided to stand in solidarity to shield those most in danger in this project. Although many in this community favor outspoken defiance, by standing together, we choose to unite with the millions of undocumented immigrants, refugees, and exilees currently living in this nation. In our communities, a single phone call can result in deportation, family separation, apprehension, or permanent removal. Together, we acknowledge our right not to translate ourselves,[4] and refuse to accept the probability of the irreversible choices constantly made by the government of this country, whose countless individuals cannot comprehend that it is also our home.

"How beautiful this is. I wonder what sort of solidarities and alliances we might form on the basis of such mutual respect, one in which we acknowledge our right not to translate ourselves."[2]

Aesthetics of
Undocumentedness CURATOR

"Yet, amongst ourselves,
we know."[1]

Introduction

Safety and protection as the longing memory of a young child (FIG.1); the gently spoken names of a community perishing through deterrence (FIG. 2). Such experiences and actions underly the *(in)visibility* project and the artworks it presents: an artisanal tablecloth that can cross the border while the family that produced it cannot (FIG. 3); an embroidered replica of a legal document (FIG. 4); ancestral cacti blooming with countless immigrant footprints (FIG. 5)—all created by artists in the undoc+ spectrum,[2] undocumented diaspora, refugees, and exiles who unite in bearing witness to undocumentedness beyond a set of legal approximations. This book visually explores undocumented immigrants' journeys, hyperdocumentation, in/visibility and assimilation, labor, remembrance, re-indigenizing, imperfect solidarities, and healing.

1 ███████████████
(b. 1990, Veracruz, México)

Homeland Insecurity, 2023
Mixed media on found object
250 × 130 × 250 cm
Courtesy of the artist

Homeland Insecurity creates a space that grants the viewer access to the artist's childhood memories. The environment is anchored by a pink fuzzy rug on which a bed made of crates takes center stage. On the bed are two stuffed animals. To the right, a nightstand holds a lamp. To the bed's left is a set of drawers with a television on top, a framed image, and a few porcelain figurines. At the foot of the bed lies child-size luggage.

The wallpaper of this little girl's room subverts its sweetness: it is made of hundreds of Deferred Action for Childhood Arrivals (DACA) I-821D forms over which the artist has added pink birds and yellow butterflies. The dresser, the nightstand, the framed image, and the video projecting from the television are also full of I-821D forms. The work speaks to the bureaucratic uncertainty accompanying individuals who qualify for the DACA program and the constant re-traumatization they endure as they continuously re-apply for the program. *Homeland Insecurity* reflects the feeling of being unsettled and harassed by the state that permeates even the most private spaces of immigrants' homes.

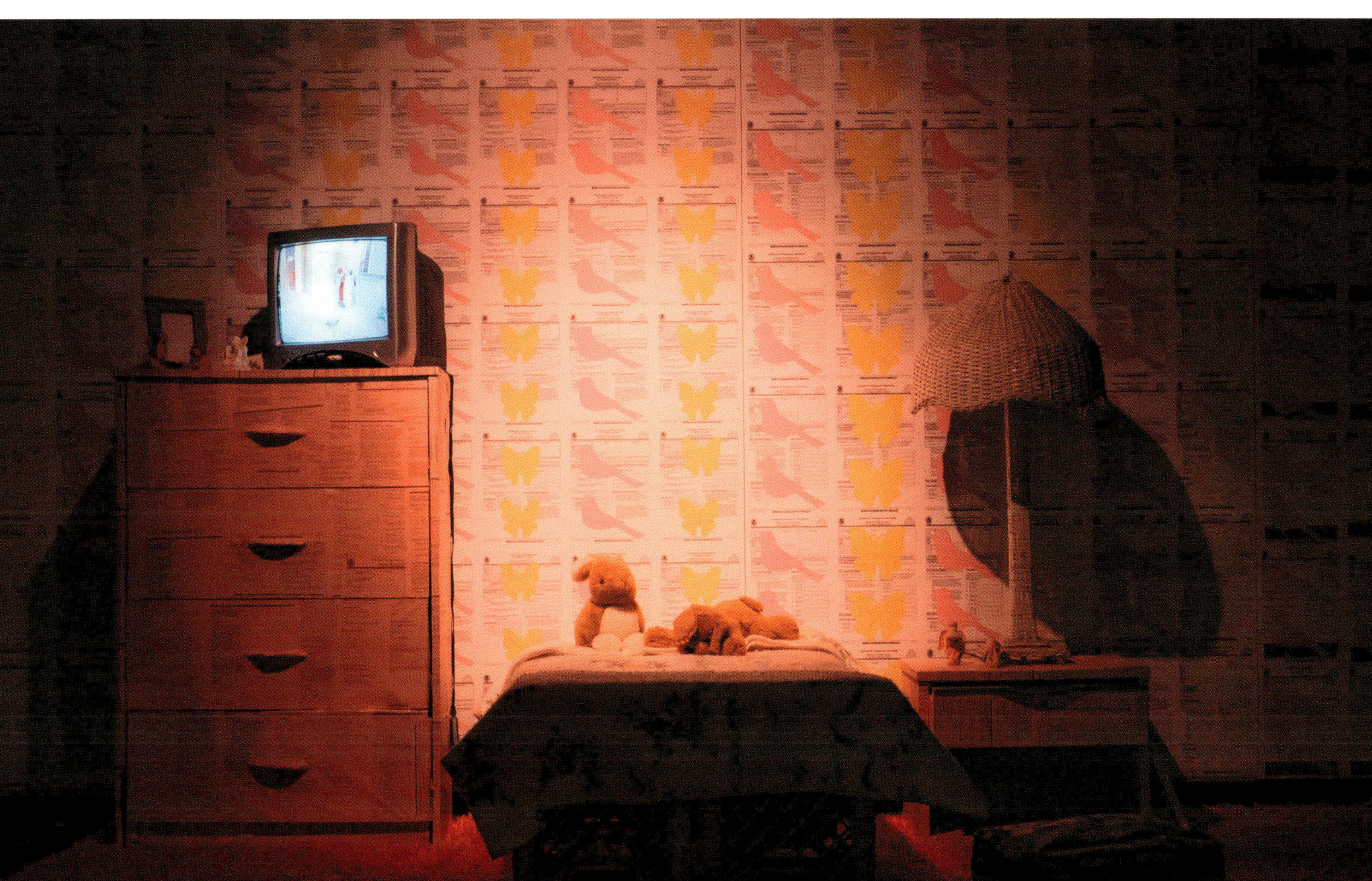

18

2 (A–F)

████████████████

(b. 1965, México City, México)

Ceremonia en la Tierra Sagrada
(Ceremony on sacred land), 2023
Video: 12 minutes 15 seconds
Courtesy of the artist

Ceremonia en la Tierra Sagrada is a 12-minute and 15-second single-channel video that documents the artist's political art action of transposing the Migrant Death Map list of undocumented immigrant deaths onto hand-made corn-husk paper. Each name is enunciated before being typed. The names come from a document produced in partnership between the Pima County Office of the Medical Examiner and Humane Borders, recording undocumented immigrant deaths in the Sonora Desert.

Today, Pima County is home to the Tohono O'odham Nation, where thousands of undocumented immigrants perish every day on sacred Indigenous territory. The political art action took place on the Tohono O'odham Nation's sacred grounds amid saguaro cacti (ha:sañ in the Tohono O'odham language)—sacred plants for the Tohono O'odham people who consider them respected community members possessing a different type of humanity. Saguaro cacti are protected by the Native Plant Protection Act and the Arizona Native Plant Law; stealing a saguaro can result in a 25-year prison sentence or a fine of $150,000. This work calls attention to Immigration and Customs Enforcement's infringement on sacred Indigenous sites.

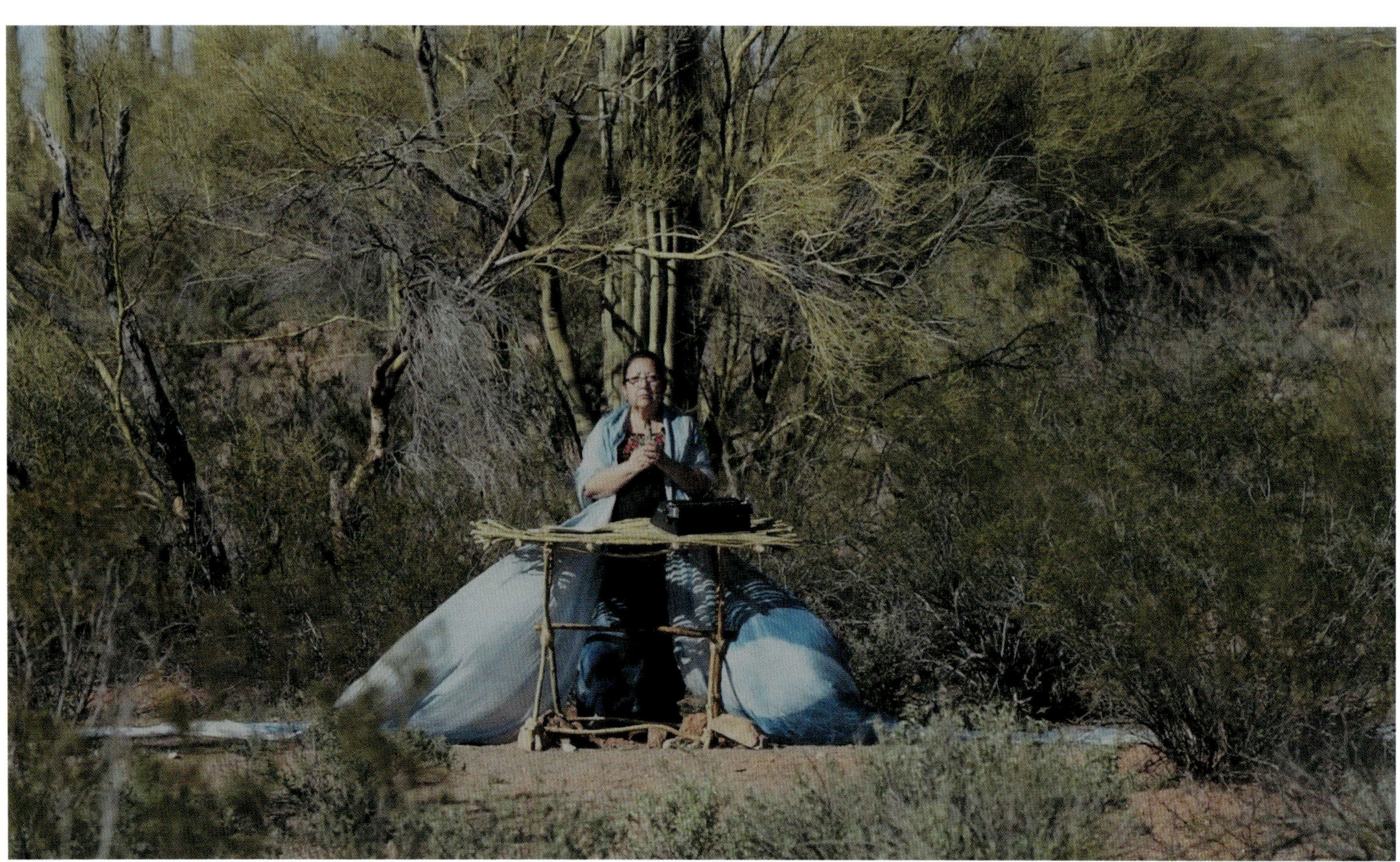

2A

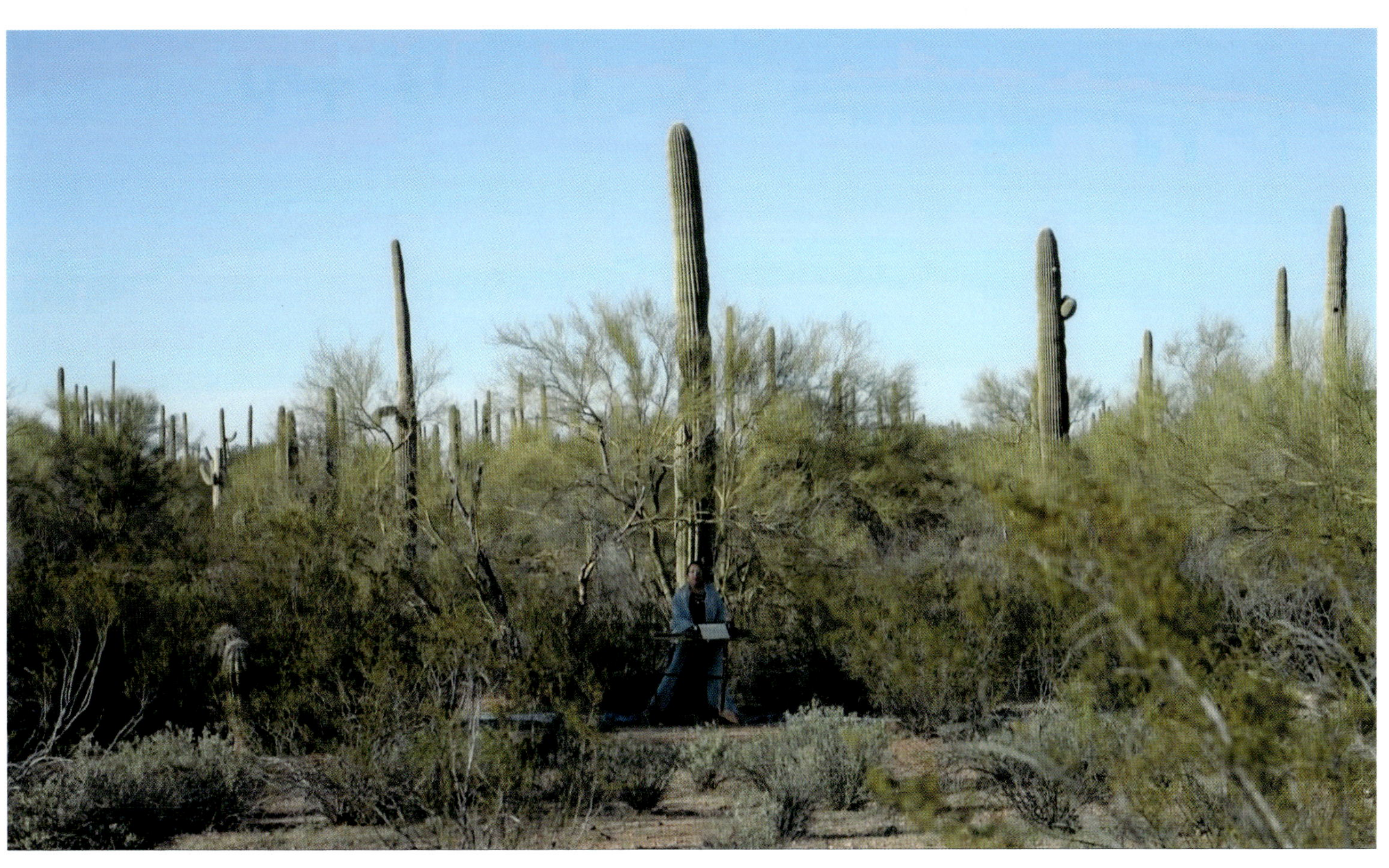

2B

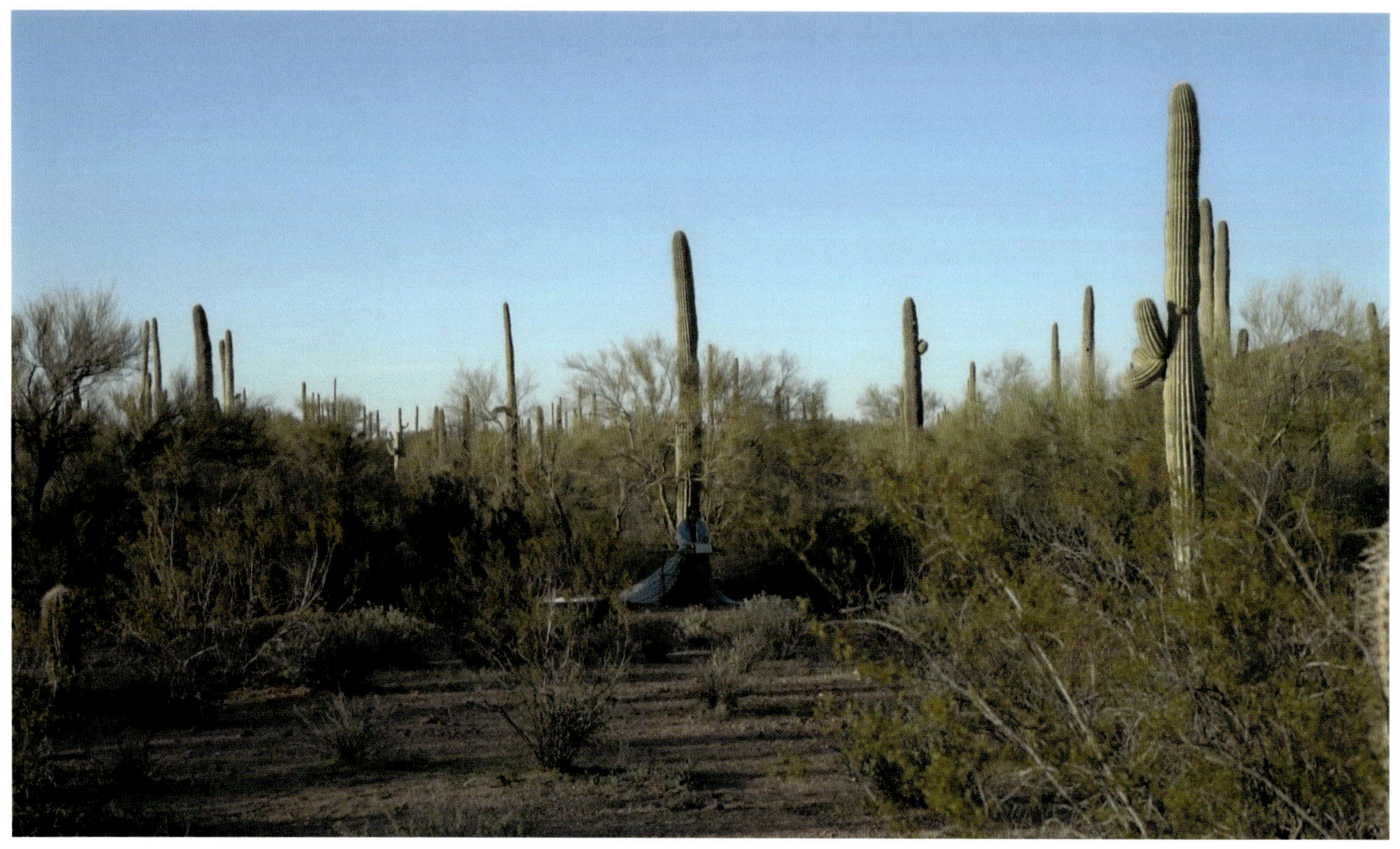

2C

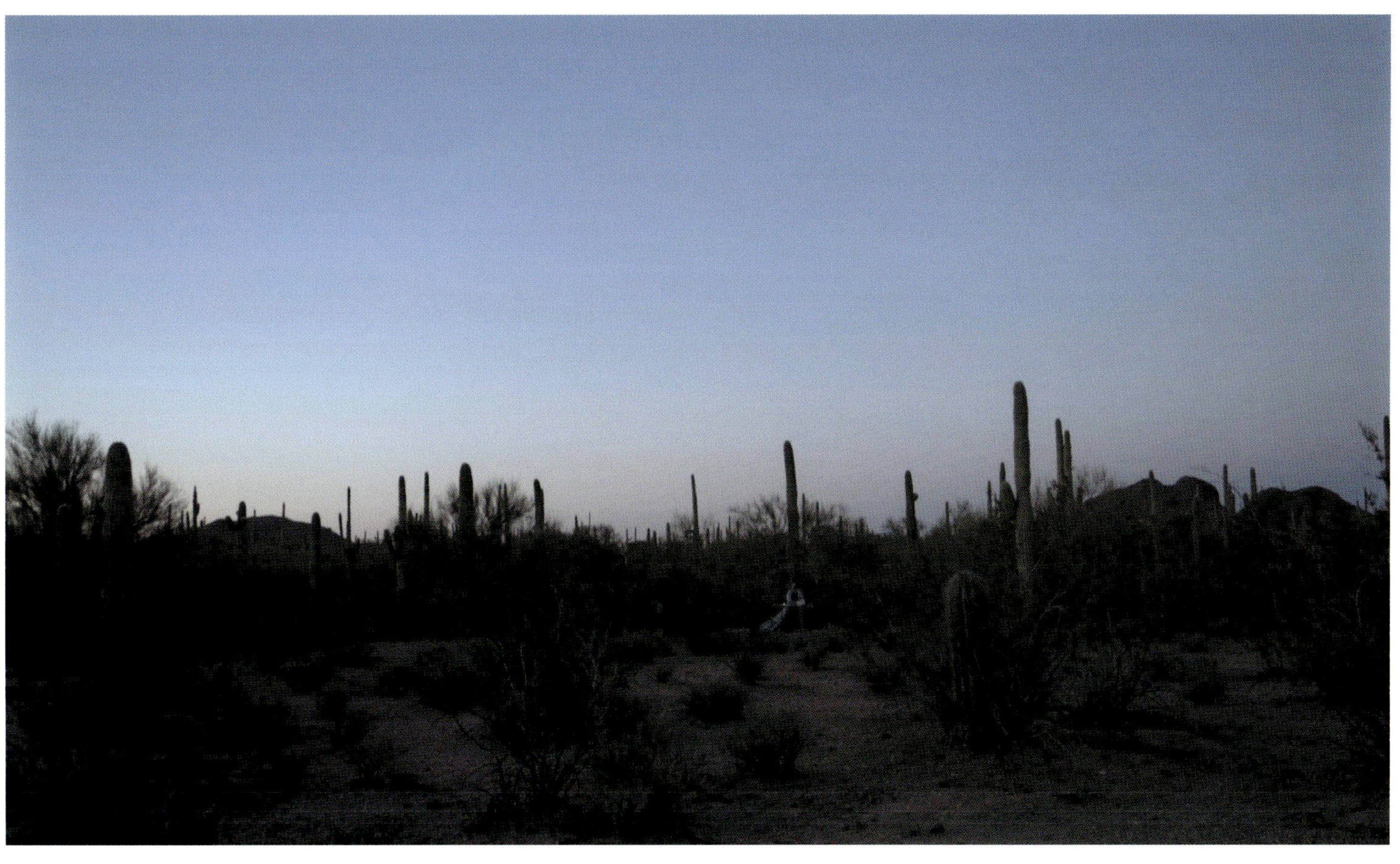

2D

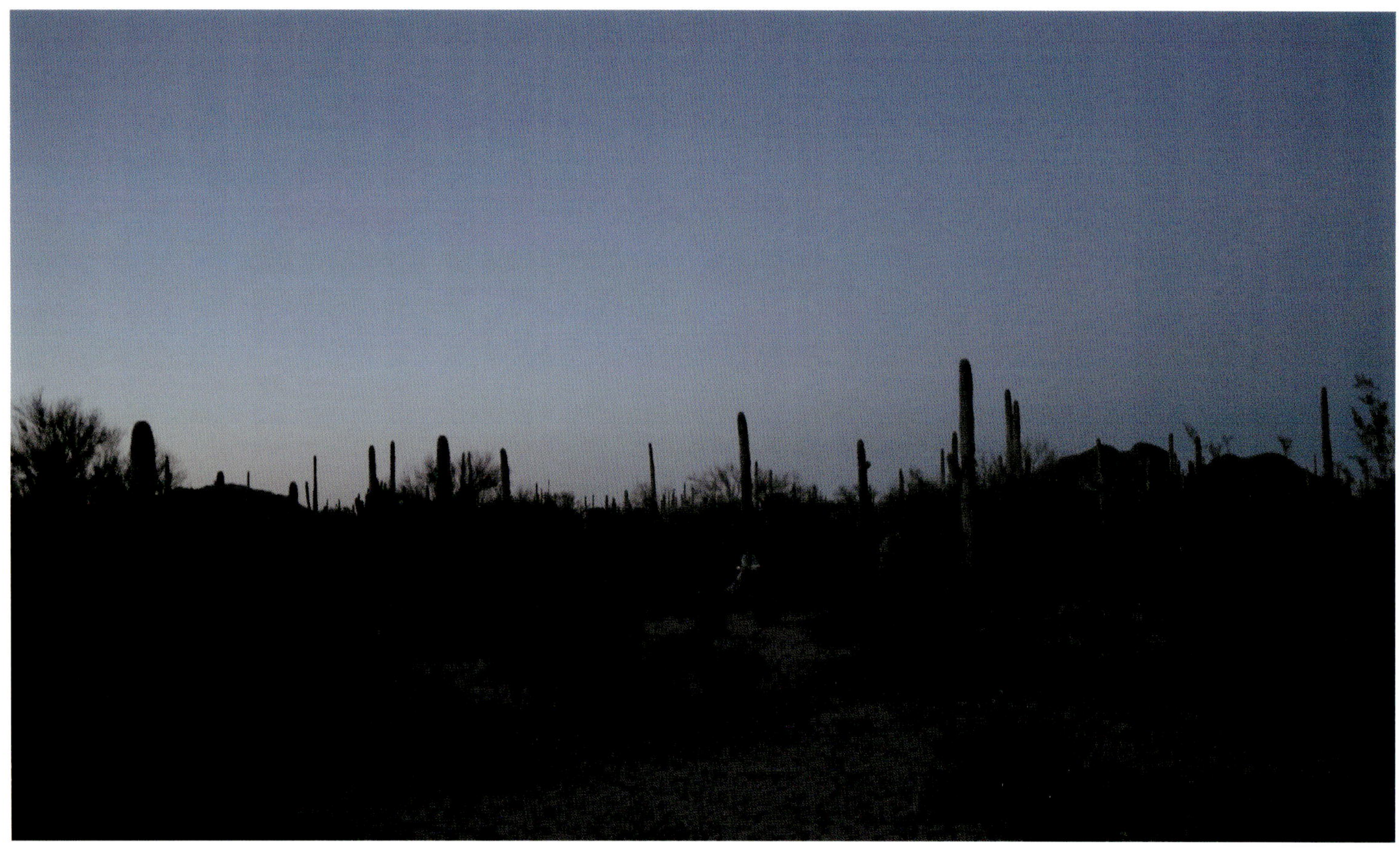

2E

2F

3 ██████████████
(b. 1981, Atotonilco El Grande,
Hidalgo, México)

*Mantel que cruzó la frontera, de ida y
vuelta, y mi hermana no* (Tablecloth that
crossed the border back and forth, but
my sister didn't), 2020
Video on embroidered tablecloth
Video: 9 minutes 18 seconds
Artwork: 340 × 183 cm
Courtesy of the artist

Mantel que cruzó la frontera, de ida y vuelta, y mi hermana no is a
hand-embroidered tablecloth made by the artist and his immediate
family, upon which a series of family portraits and videos are projected. The colorful and figurative patterns are emblematic of Otomí
ancestry. The Indigenous Otomí people predate Spanish conquest
and, to this day, inhabit México's states of Hidalgo, Puebla, Guanajuato, Querétaro, Tlaxcala, Michoacán, and México City.

The work highlights failed transnational migration. Unlike some
family members, this tablecloth crossed the border multiple times in
both directions. The images projected onto it are photographs of the
artist's immediate kin at quotidian gatherings, and videos in which
they are cooking, dancing, and making masks. While the Méxi-
co-U.S. border restrictions thwart simple human connections and
pastimes, objects have free passage back and forth.

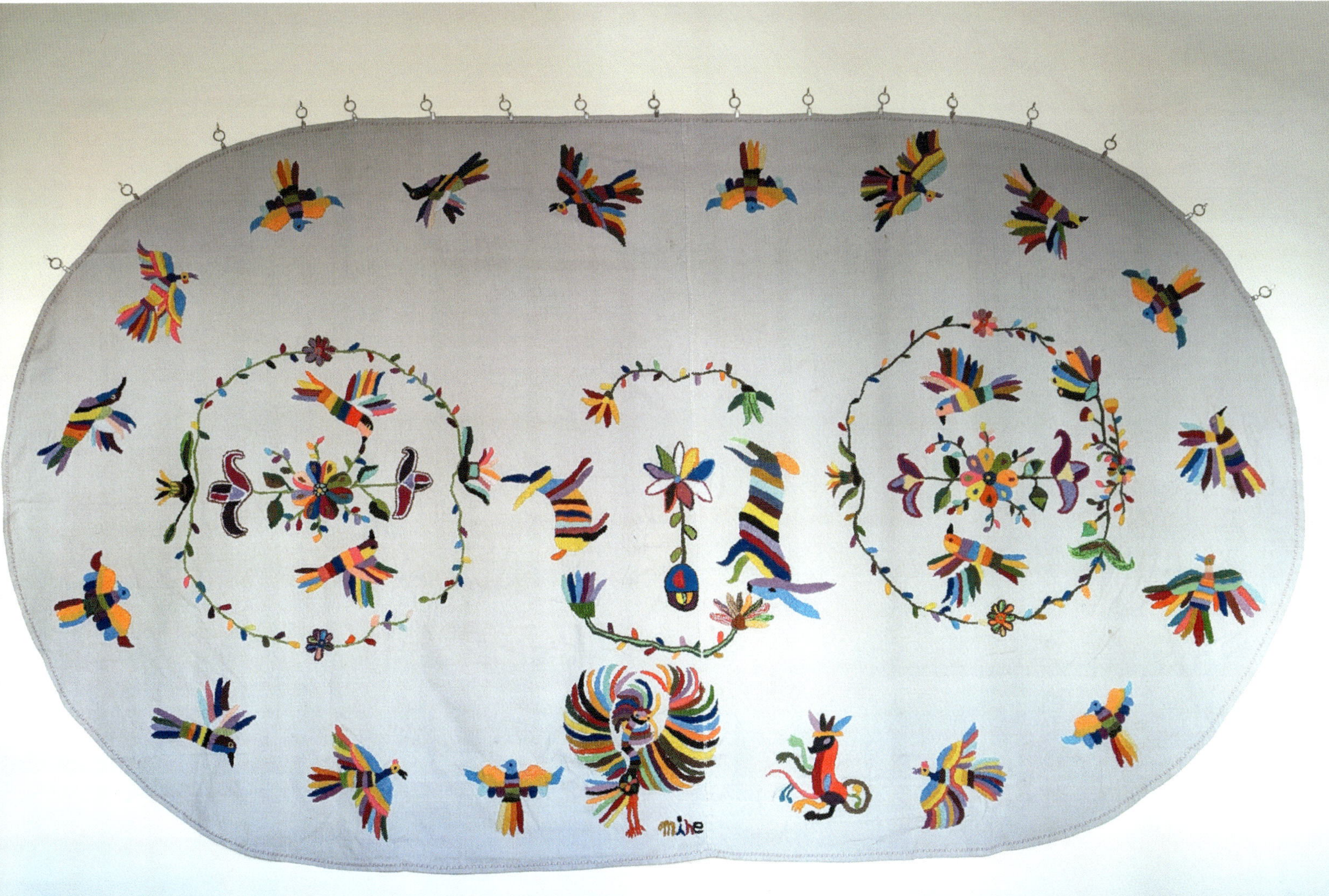

4 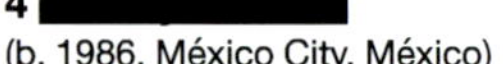
(b. 1986, México City, México)

Social Security from *the (Un)documented Series*, 2024
Embroidery thread on Lokta paper
6.35 × 9.5 cm
Courtesy of the artist

Social Security from the (Un)documented Series. Using thread on craft paper, the artist has rendered to scale the border of a Social Security card. A few lines of thread denote the break in the bottom frame where the letters U.S.A. appear. Two simplified Corinthian columns flank the sides of the card and hold up the arch that crowns the document, with the words "Social Security" silhouetted against it. All these elements are embroidered in blue thread, with "Social Security" traced in white and "U.S.A." in gold.

The artist has omitted the identifying information at the center of the card: the Social Security number, the name and signature of the document's holder, the Social Security emblem, and the date of issue. Today, there are over 50 versions of this document, all valid. In 2022, the language on the card was updated from "alien" to "noncitizen" (a detail also missing here). Through this work, the artist calls into question the bureaucratic underpinnings of the document and challenges the system that restricts resources to more than 11,000,000 undocumented immigrants who reside in the U.S. and contribute to Social Security every year.

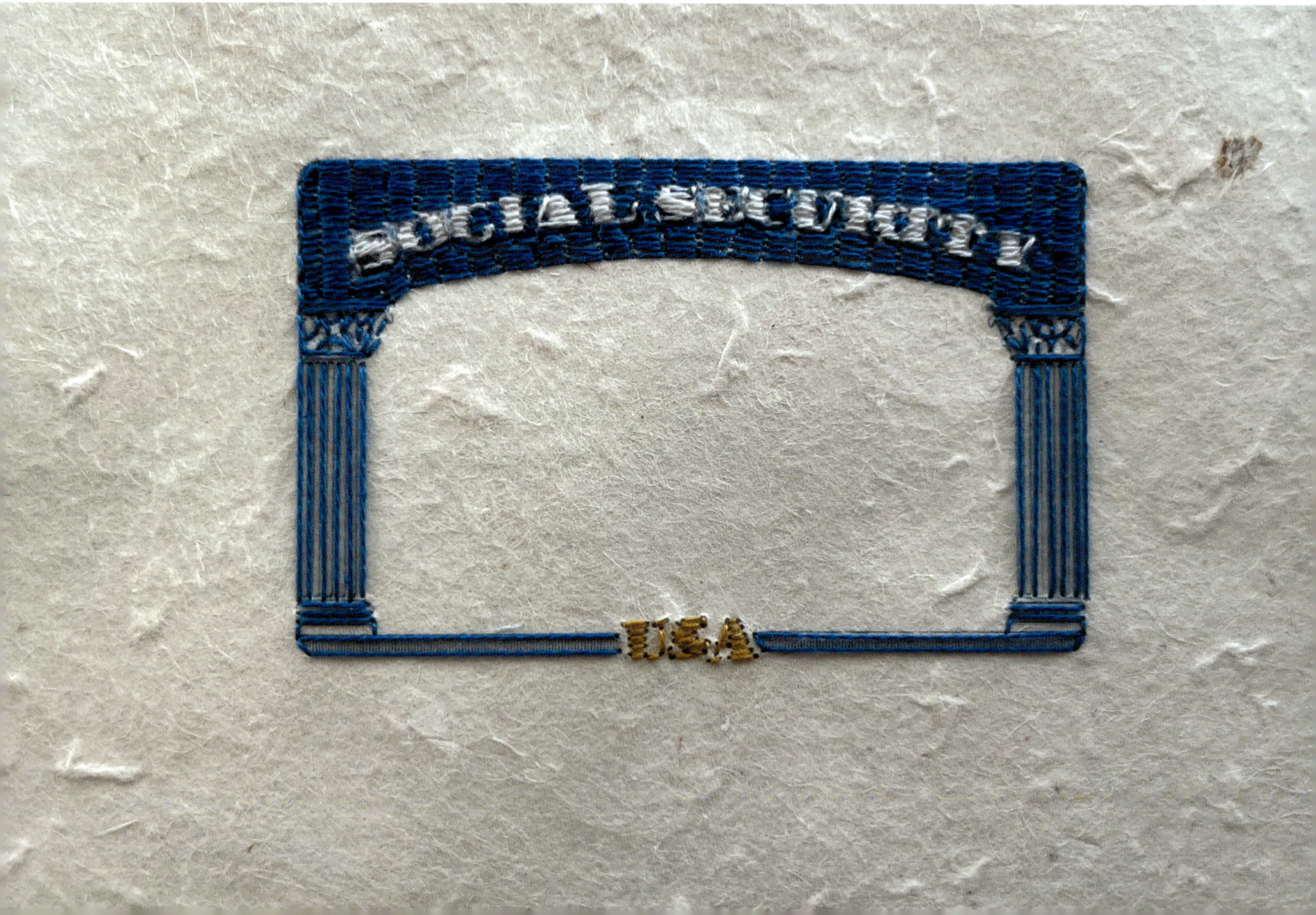

5 ▮▮▮▮▮▮▮▮▮▮
(b. 1984, México City, México)

Aquí Estamos (We are here), 2015–25
Mixed media (plaster, wood,
wire, concrete)
150 × 150 × 200 cm
Courtesy of the artist

Aquí Estamos is a desert garden made of cacti—each one blossoming with countless immigrant feet. The treatment of the materials and the size of the sculpture allude to Olmec heads, the Chalchiuhticlue Monolith, and tzompantlis, such as the one at Templo Mayor. A tzompantli is a skull rack that has been documented at various sites across multiple Mesoamerican civilizations, including Zapotec (at La Cañada de Cuicatlán), Toltec (in Tula), Maya (at Chichén Itzá), and Mexica (in Tenochtitlán). Although many presume that tzompantli is a symbol of war, according to Mexica cosmology, volunteering for a sacrifice ensured that one's lineage would have direct access to Mictlán (the underworld in Mexica cosmology).

The hundreds of immigrant footprints in this desert garden (implicitly situated on the land of the Tohono O'odham Nation in Arizona) evoke the individuals from the undoc+ community who have died crossing the border in the Sonoran Desert. Prevention through deterrence is a set of legal policies that focuses on concentrating immigration enforcement at crucial border access points. It ends up forcing undocumented immigrants to travel through the desert, whose steep terrain, lack of water, and temperatures reaching 120 degrees Fahrenheit contribute to the daily increasing death toll.

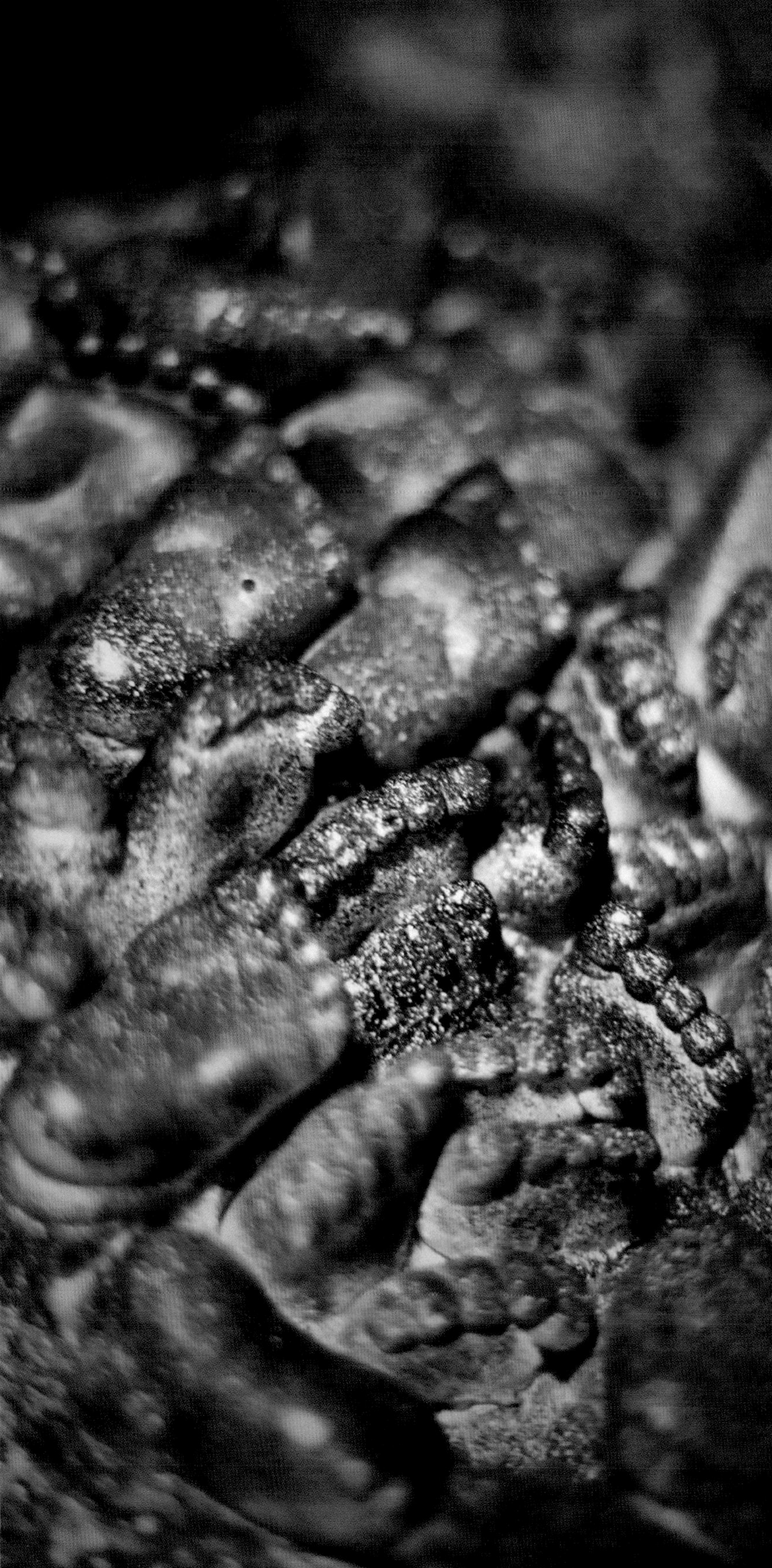

This project is not intended as a survey, nor does it represent every concern of undocumented, exiled, and refugee artists. Rather, it is an example of an imperfect solidarity. Epistemologically borrowing from Aruna d' Souza's invitation to understand the world beyond the binaries of self and other, we seek to imagine a form of political solidarity defined by opacity as a means of embracing the fundamental interconnectedness of human life.[3]

Édouard Glissant conceived opacity as a form of emancipation from unequivocal courses and irreversible choices.[4] In his words, "thought of self and thought of others become obsolete in their duality. Every other is a citizen…"[5] This book highlights the aesthetic achievements of individuals on the undoc+ spectrum and those in the undocumented diaspora who visually speak to the pleasures and cares of a community joined bureaucratically by the continuous burdens and faults of a broken nation that exploits them for labor and utilizes them as political scapegoats, while cyclically threatening them with mass deportations and exclusion from a place they call home. The artists' names have been concealed as a poetic gesture to protect those who are most vulnerable and legally powerless against the U.S. government. The intent in not symbolic erasure, silence, invisibility, or anonymity, but consideration and protection from the current political climate.[6]

In the U.S., undocumentedness is often presumed to stand in direct opposition to citizenship. Elizabeth Cohen outlines a series of differentiated citizenships in her discussion of political membership at different levels beyond full-citizen and non-citizen. She calls attention to individuals who lack full rights within citizenship, such as immigrants, children, the disabled, and queer individuals; they emerge in her study as examples of what she terms "semi-citizens."[7] These people, Cohen explains, lack access to a complete set of citizen rights; therefore, citizenship as a concept needs to be thought of as a gradient, not an absolute. Furthermore, the boundaries of citizenship overlap with other identifiers, such as race, territory, language, nationality, and religion.[8] Aviva Chomsky writes that it seems natural that people should be divided by citizenship and placed into different categories with differential rights. We assume that the world is naturally divided into countries and that people are supposed to stay in the country in which they were born, unless they can get special permission to enter another.[9] This type of flawed logic allows many to disregard the livelihoods of millions of people currently residing away from their homelands. Undocumentedness, meanwhile, is delineated by a series of legal constructs created by capitalist nation-states. Creating a state of legal vulnerability for large sections of the population allows countries all around the world to continue their colonial exploits and benefit from migrant labor, while disregarding sustainability for immigrants and failing to provide them with the most basic human rights.

Journey

"There is nothing natural about this state of affairs. Countries, sovereignty, citizenship, and laws are all social constructions: abstractions invented by humans."[10]

No two undocumented journeys are the same. There is no easy way to define undocumentedness and no single definition that stands true globally. In the words of José Antonio Vargas, "If there are an estimated 45 million immigrants living in America, then there are 45 million ways of being an immigrant in America. Like all groups, we are not a monolith."[11] Of those 45 million, 11 million currently residing in the U.S. are unauthorized, per Department of Homeland Security.[12] Each person has a unique migration journey: some cross a river, many traverse a desert; some arrive by walking, others are brought in cars, planes, or boats. Some hid to arrive safely; many lost their lives in the process.[13] Some decided to migrate as adults in pursuit of the fallacy of the American Dream. Others were brought here as teenagers, children, infants, babies, or in utero. A certain number made the perilous journey as unaccompanied children, following in their parents' footsteps (often without their parents' awareness) to reunite with them. Many journeys are too violent for words; many others have ended in deaths in transit—voices silenced, stories untold.[14]

Border patrol was established in 1924 as part of the Immigration Bureau in the Department of Labor. But it was permitted to guard the territory only within 25 miles of the land border until 1952.[15] The launch of Operation Gatekeeper in 1994, months after the signing of NAFTA (North American Free Trade Agreement), ushered in the militarization of the border.[16] In its first year alone, more undocumented immigrants died while crossing it than in the entire 70-years border patrol history until that time.[17]

Laws, border patrol, and surveillance tactics are parts of the hierarchical economy that provides protection for citizens and demands that undocumented immigrants be kept at bay. In the ideation of the nation's imaginary, a cisgender heterosexual male adult immigrant departs his impoverished homeland in search of a better life, migrates once, and assimilates to the host nation. The reality is that there are also transnational queer immigrant fem children who migrate dozens of times before settling in this nation to inhabit a state of perpetual unsettling, and many others. The artists in this section problematize the complexity of immigrant journeys with deep respect, as many share a closeness to the subjects they depict.

Imagining Your Last Breath (FIG. 6) is a series of photographs of the sky at the precise locations where immigrants have perished in Arizona's Sonoran Desert. The photographs demand that the viewer visualize the last breath of an immigrant, while bearing witness to the beauty of this area—part of the Tohono O'odham nation, used by immigration enforcement since the 1990s as one of the key sites for enacting deterrence policies. *Aquí Estamos* (FIG. 5) also echoes desert crossings by creating a garden desertscape in which cacti bloom with hundreds of immigrant footprints, visually alluding to a tzompantli, a Mexica skull rack.

Artifacts from Important Meals (FIG. 7) was made by an artist who sought to highlight immigrant communities' unique relationships to the land, which surpass the boundaries of the settler colonialist concept of legal citizenship. This work asserts connections that go beyond contemporary borders.[18] It also alludes to communal barbacoa celebrations held by immigrant campesinos. Traditionally, barbacoa (barbequed meat) is wrapped in maguey and slow-cooked in a pit dug into the ground—a method largely inaccessible to undocumented immigrant communities in the U.S. *Mantel que cruzó la frontera, de ida y vuelta, y mi hermana no* (FIG. 3) speaks directly to the neoliberal border policies that bestow transnational freedom on material goods, while impeding humans from sharing the same benefits. The work is a hand-embroidered tablecloth made by the artist and his immediate family, upon which a series of family portraits and videos are projected. In contrast to the works above, focused on past undocumented journeys, *Untitled* (FIG. 8) envisions future joys of undocumented immigrants who will be able to savor festivities in their communities. *Tenku Ania* (FIG. 9) explores the artist's sense of belonging to the land, while granting viewers direct access to their memoryscape, conveyed through pictures from their childhood.

Beyond the glimpse into the last breath of an undocumented immigrant whose life has ended in the desert, *Reverencia: Arizona Migrant Death Mapping* (FIG. 10) directly borrows the tools of Immigration and Customs Enforcement by transposing a set of names onto habotai silk. With this work, the artist makes use of the undocumented immigrant death list in Arizona, created through a partnership between the Pima County Office of the Medical Examiner and Humane Borders (an organization whose primary mission is to save people from death by dehydration and exposure, while working to create a more just and humane border). *Reverencia: Arizona Migrant Death Mapping* aesthetically conveys the precarity encountered by thousands of undocumented immigrants who move through the Arizonan desert. By using the list of immigrants' deaths, the artist draws attention to the increasing number of these tragedies. The information rendered on silk includes the exact location where a body was found (geographic coordinates in latitude and longitude), their name, gender, date of discovery, and, when available, cause of death. Today, Pima County is home to the Tohono O'odham Nation, where undocumented immigrants

6A ▮▮▮▮▮▮▮▮▮▮
(b. 1965, México City, México)

Imagining Your Last Breath: Ahogo en Ironwood Forest (Drowned in Ironwood Forest), 2022–23
Archival pigment, digital images on natural fiber paper
Sizes vary
Courtesy of the artist

Imagining Your Last Breath is a series of 26 photographs on natural fiber paper that show the sights at the last breath taken by undocumented immigrants who died while crossing the Sonoran Desert. The images are often opaque, hazy, or blurry. They render visible the last moment of beauty seen by a person who is no longer among us to tell their story.

The artist used the list of undocumented immigrant deaths, drawn up by the Pima County Office of the Medical Examiner and Humane Borders organization. This document contained 4308 names (with more added daily) and geographical coordinates for where the remains were found. The artist visited several of the locations and took each photograph at the exact site where an undocumented immigrant's remains were recovered. What distinguishes this series (others have taken photographs of similar subjects on the same sites) is the focus on placing the viewer in the very spot where an immigrant breathed their last and showing that desolate location from their perspective at that moment.

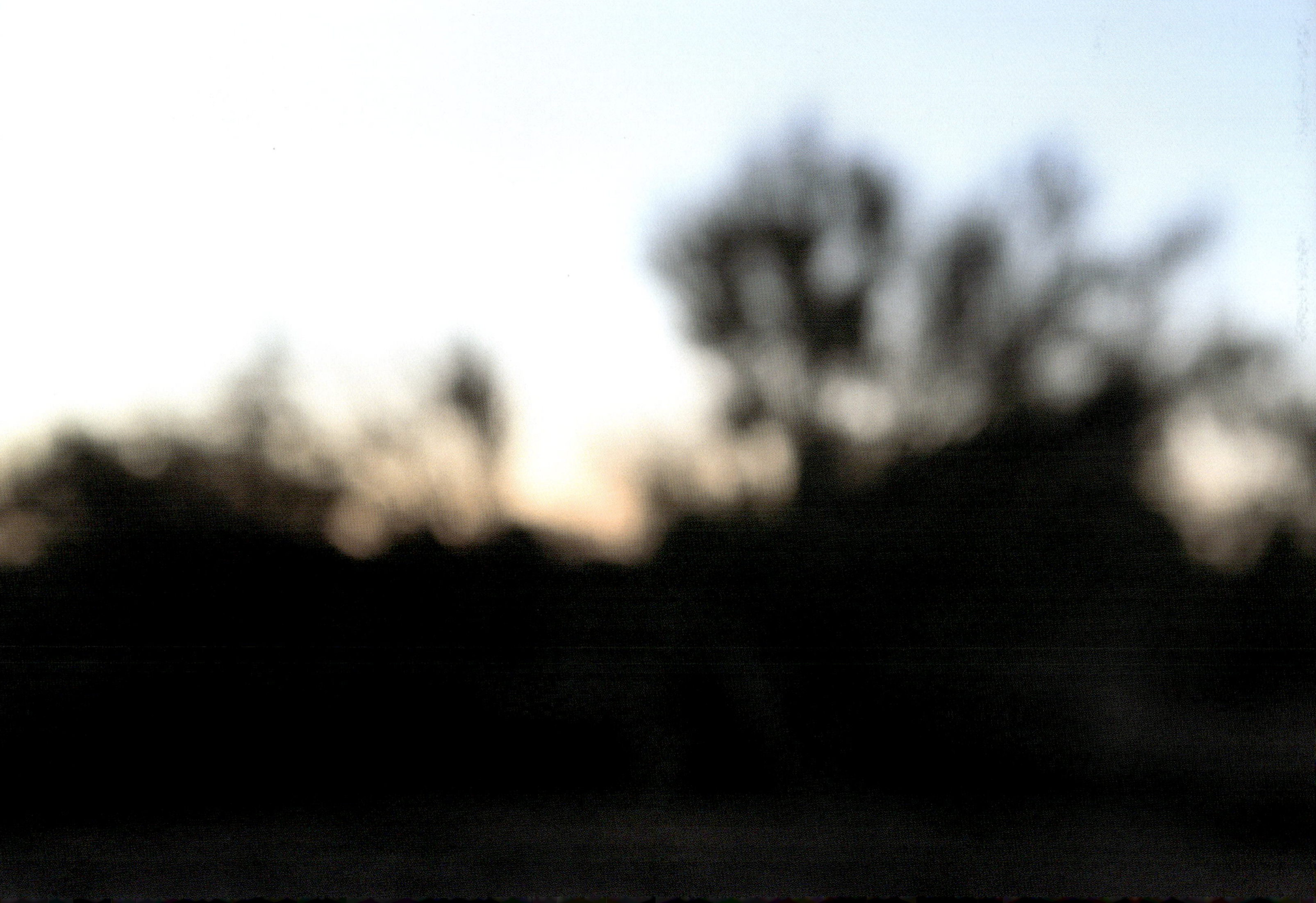

6B ███████████████
(b. 1965, México City, México)

Imagining Your Last Breath:
Al partir (To depart), 2022–23
Archival pigment, digital images
on natural fiber paper
Sizes vary
Courtesy of the artist

6C ███████████████
(b. 1965, México City, México)

Imagining Your Last Breath:
Arivaca, 2022–23
Archival pigment, digital images on
natural fiber paper
Sizes vary
Courtesy of the artist

6D 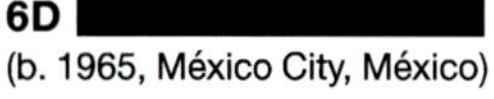
(b. 1965, México City, México)

Imagining Your Last Breath:
Cholla, 2022–23
Archival pigment, digital images
on natural fiber paper
Sizes vary
Courtesy of the artist

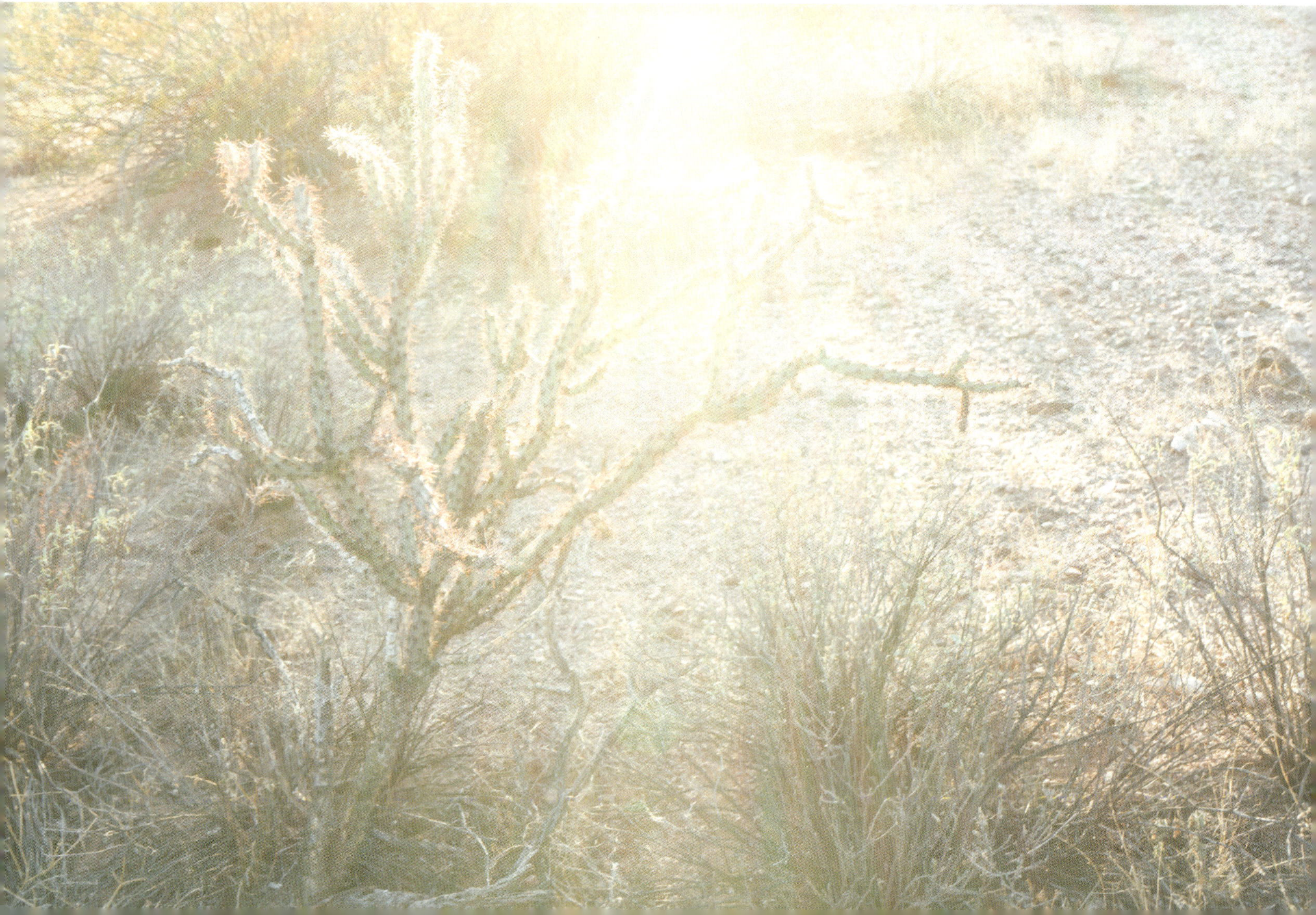

6E ▮▮▮▮▮▮▮▮▮▮▮▮
(b. 1965, México City, México)

Imagining Your Last Breath:
Susurro (Whisper), 2022–23
Archival pigment, digital images
on natural fiber paper
Sizes vary
Courtesy of the artist

6F ███████████████
(b. 1965, México City, México)

Imagining Your Last Breath:
El Campo Cienega (Cienega field),
2022–23
Archival pigment, digital images
on natural fiber paper
Sizes vary
Courtesy of the artist

6G ██████████
(b. 1965, México City, México)

Imagining Your Last Breath:
El Pesar (Weighing), 2022–23
Archival pigment, digital images
on natural fiber paper
Sizes vary
Courtesy of the artist

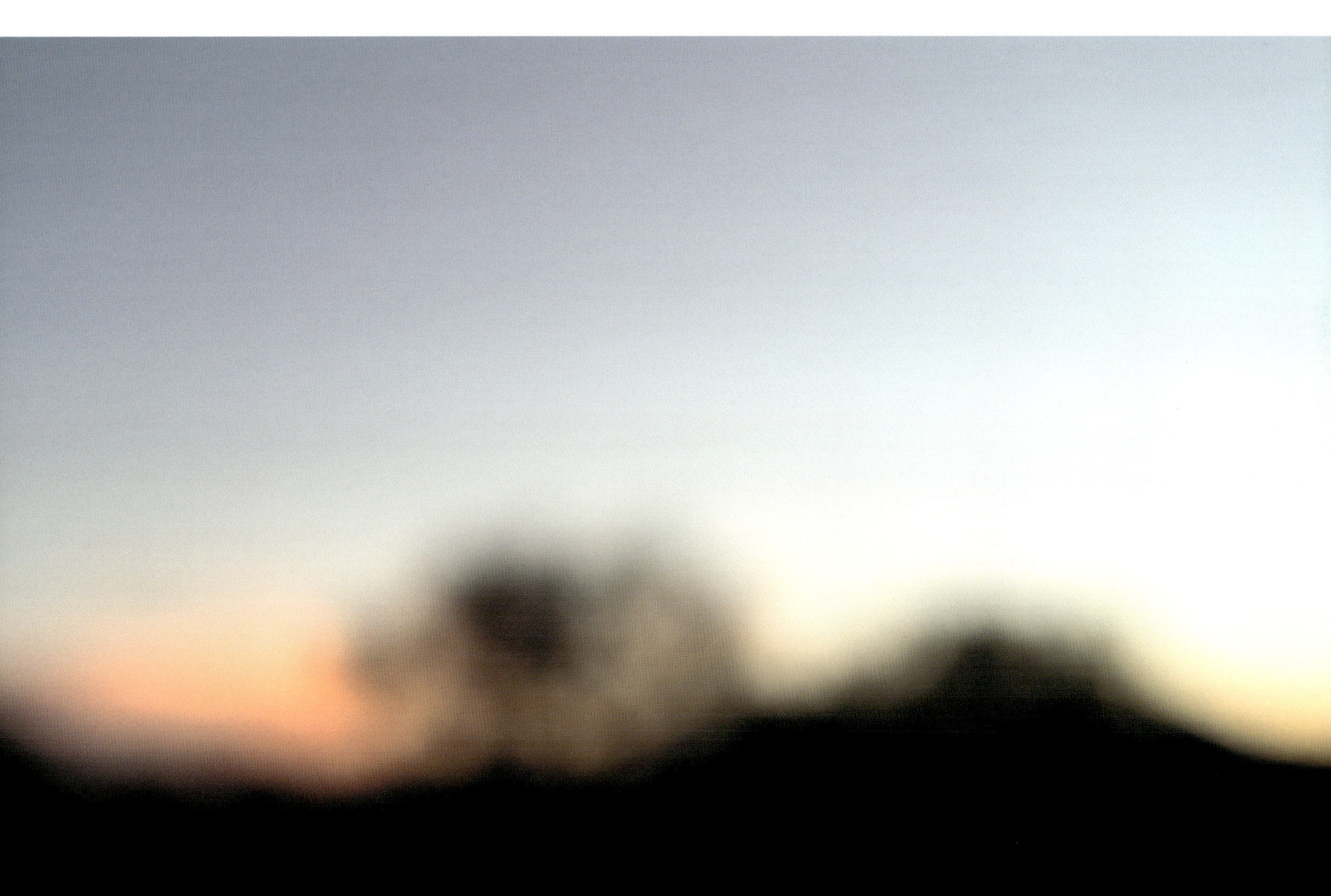

6H ▮▮▮▮▮▮▮▮▮
(b. 1965, México City, México)

*Imagining Your Last Breath: Ramas
Rotas* (Broken branches), 2022–23
Archival pigment, digital images on
natural fiber paper
Sizes vary
Courtesy of the artist

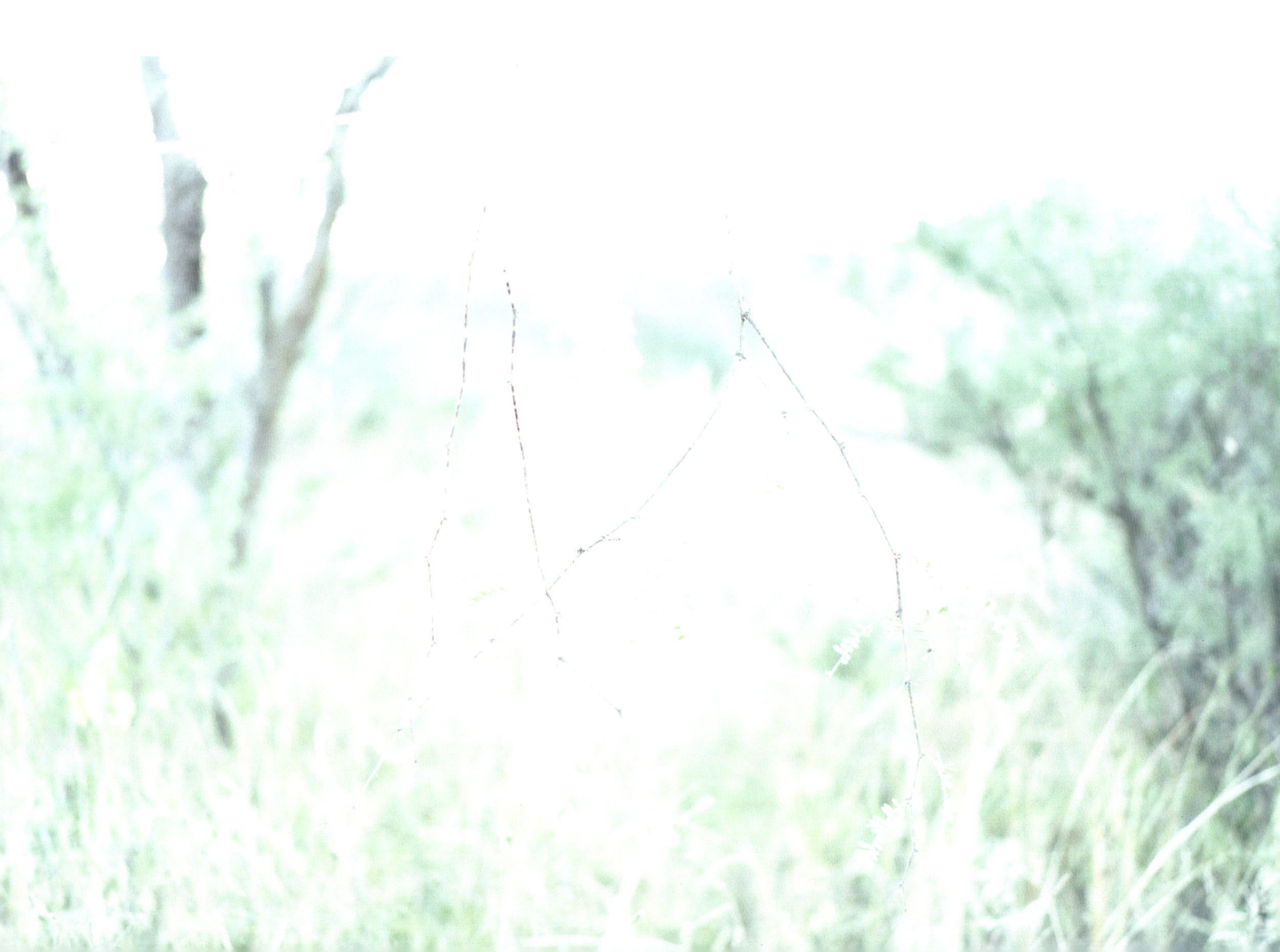

6I 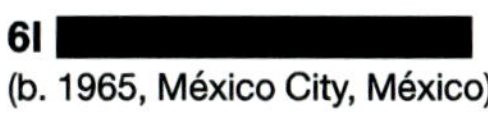
(b. 1965, México City, México)

Imagining Your Last Breath:
Fuego Fatuo (Wildfire), 2022–23
Archival pigment, digital images
on natural fiber paper
Sizes vary
Courtesy of the artist

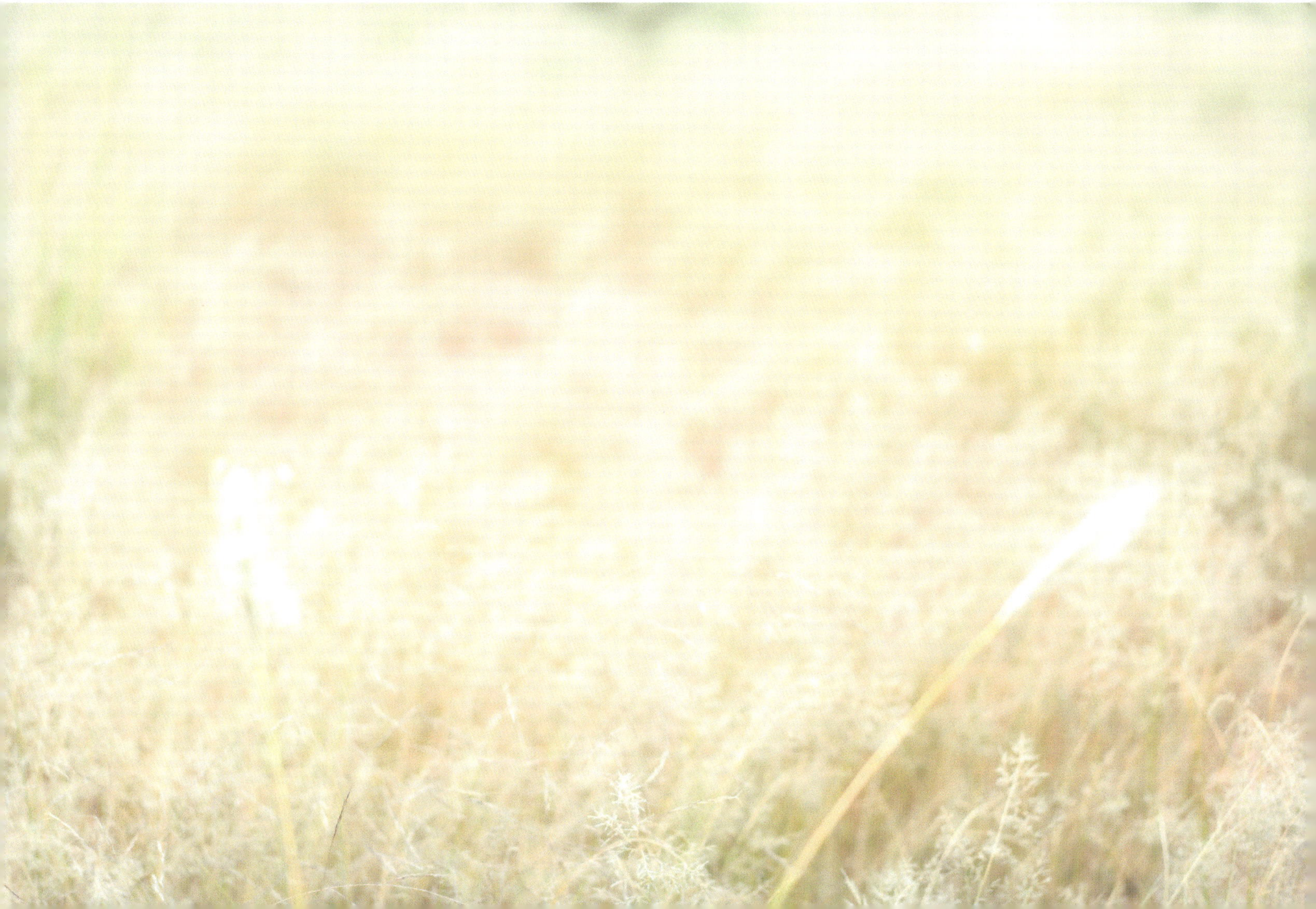

6J ███████████
(b. 1965, México City, México)

*Imagining Your Last Breath:
Maguey*, 2022–23
Archival pigment, digital
images on natural fiber paper
Sizes vary
Courtesy of the artist

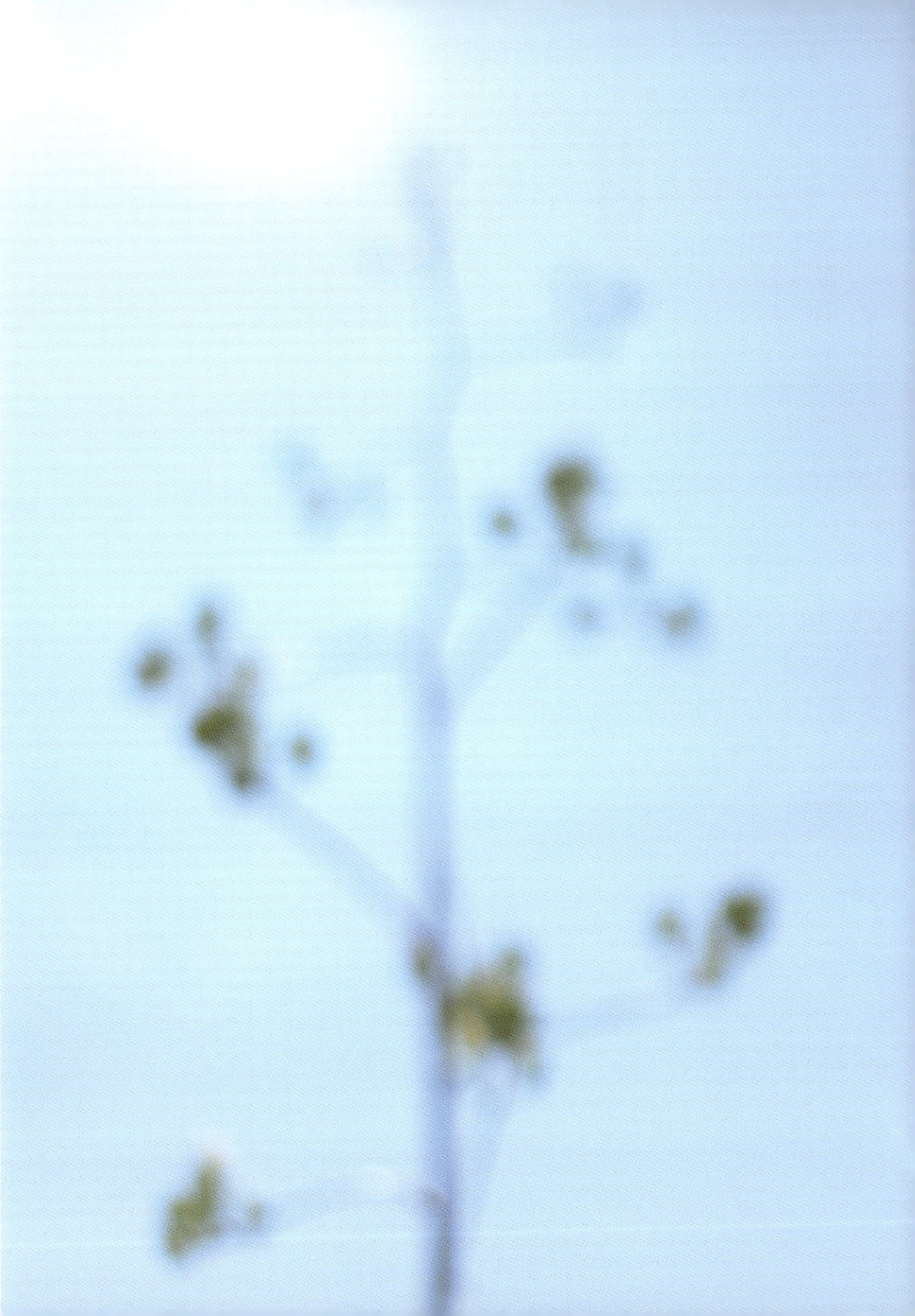

6K ▮▮▮▮▮▮▮▮▮▮
(b. 1965, México City, México)

Imagining Your Last Breath:
Melancoía (Melancholia), 2022–23
Archival pigment, digital images
on natural fiber paper
Sizes vary
Courtesy of the artist

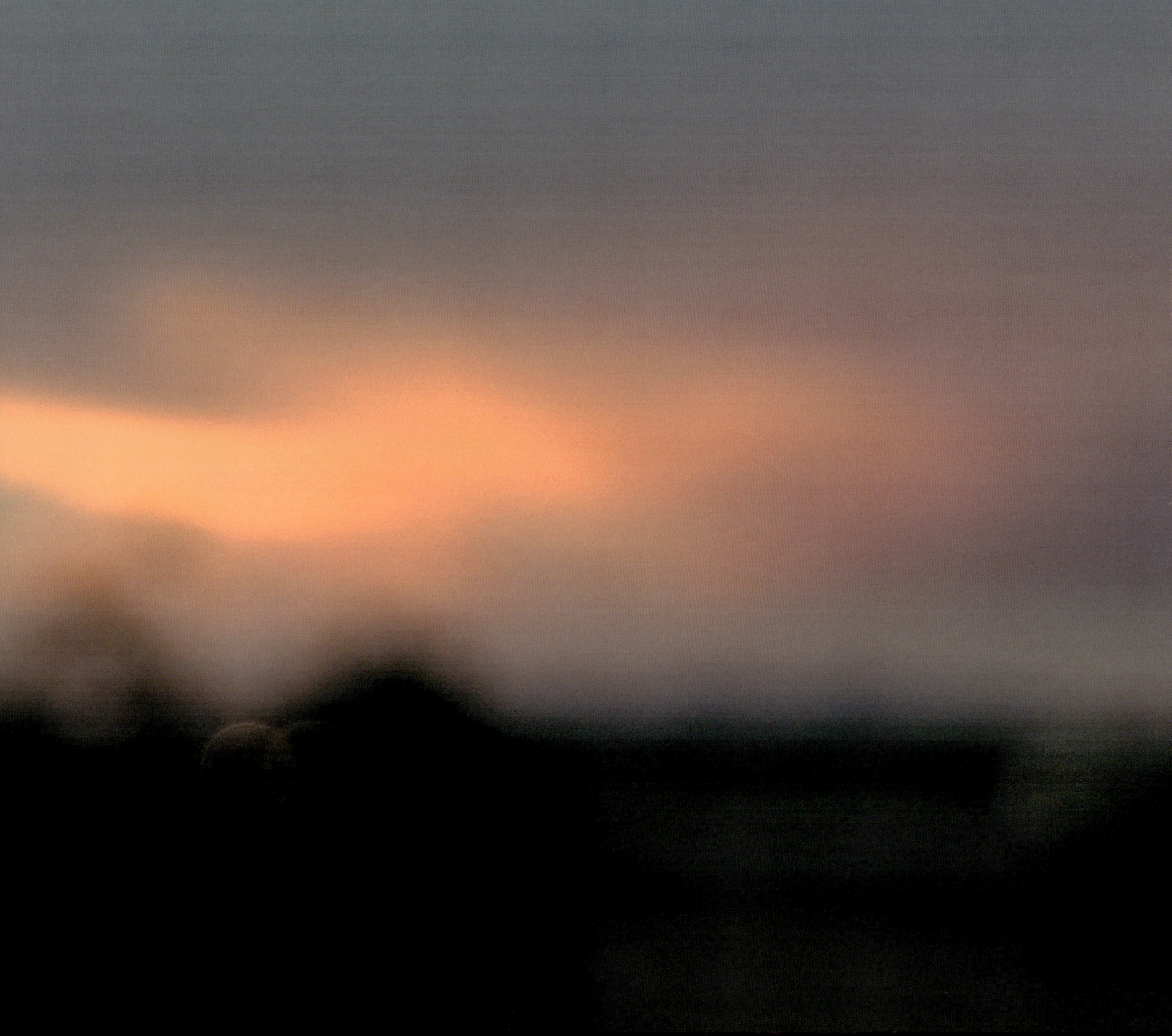

6L ███████████████
(b. 1965, México City, México)

Imagining Your Last Breath:
Murmullos (Murmurs), 2022–23
Archival pigment, digital images
on natural fiber paper
Sizes vary
Courtesy of the artist

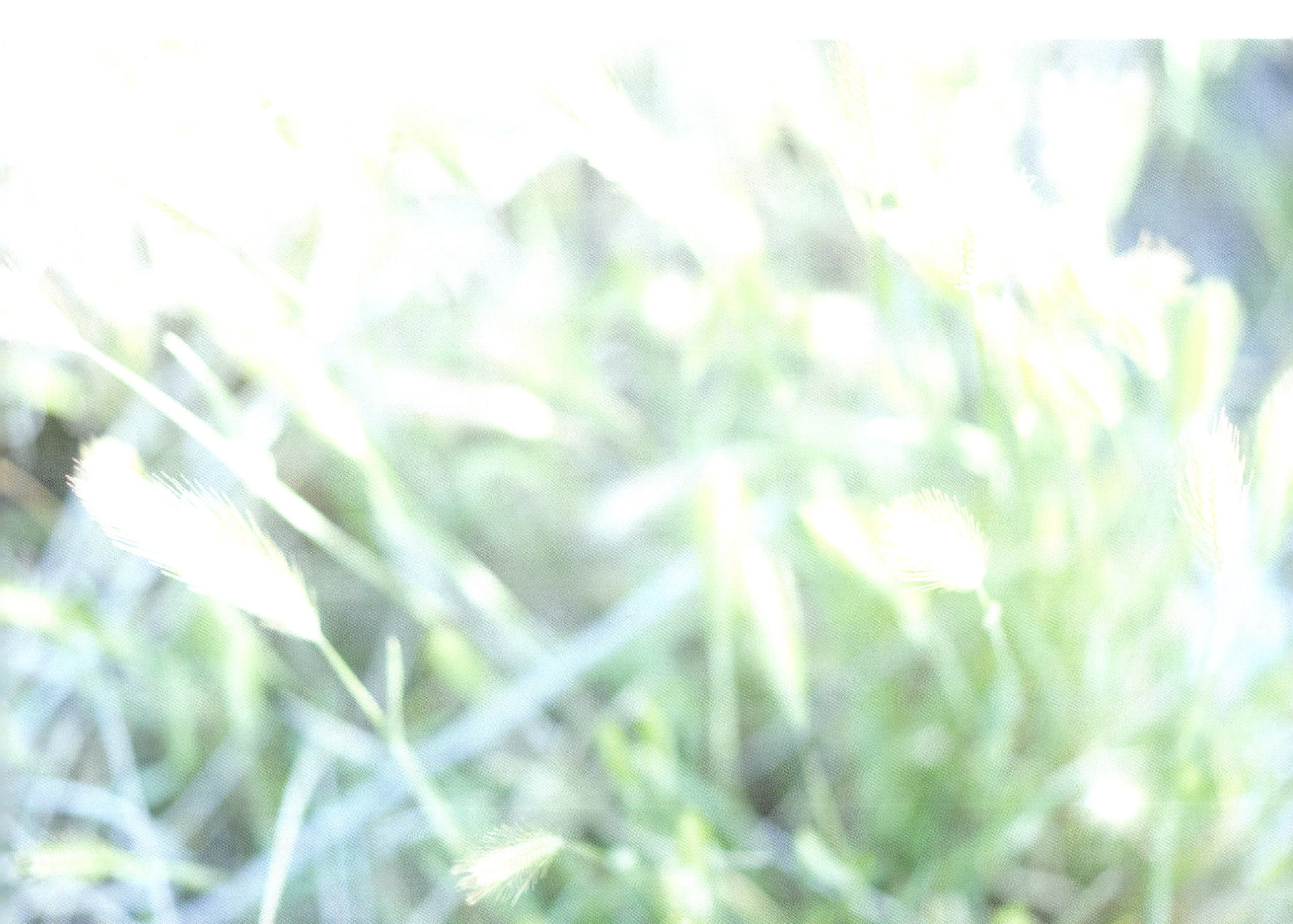

7 ██████████ *Artifacts from Important Meals*,
(b. 1981, Atotonilco El Grande, 2022–23
Hidalgo, México) Beads on lamb skulls
36 × 58 × 33 cm
Courtesy of the artist

Artifacts from Important Meals consists of three beaded lamb skulls. The beading alludes to Wixárika visual arts. The Wixárika people live in the Mexican states of Nayarit, Jalisco, Zacatecas, and Durango, and in the U.S. states of Arizona, California, New Mexico, and Texas. Non-Nahua-speaking Spanish settlers deemed them "Huichol" (Spanish mispronunciation of Wixarika) during contact, and this moniker has yet to die out.

The lamb heads are the remains from a communal barbacoa celebration that the artist held alongside undoc+ immigrant campesinos (agricultural workers). Before colonial contact, the Tlaxcalteca people would use maguey leaves to slow-cook armadillos or rabbits in pits dug in the ground. Spaniards brought sheep to the Americas, and lamb barbacoa evolved from colonial contact with ancestral Mexica practices. This work also alludes to migrating culinary traditions and the need to make more resources available to immigrants, whose old cooking methods require access to land, maguey plants, and time in community. All of these are largely inaccessible to undocumented immigrants who often do not own their homes and lack free time from their labor-intensive jobs.

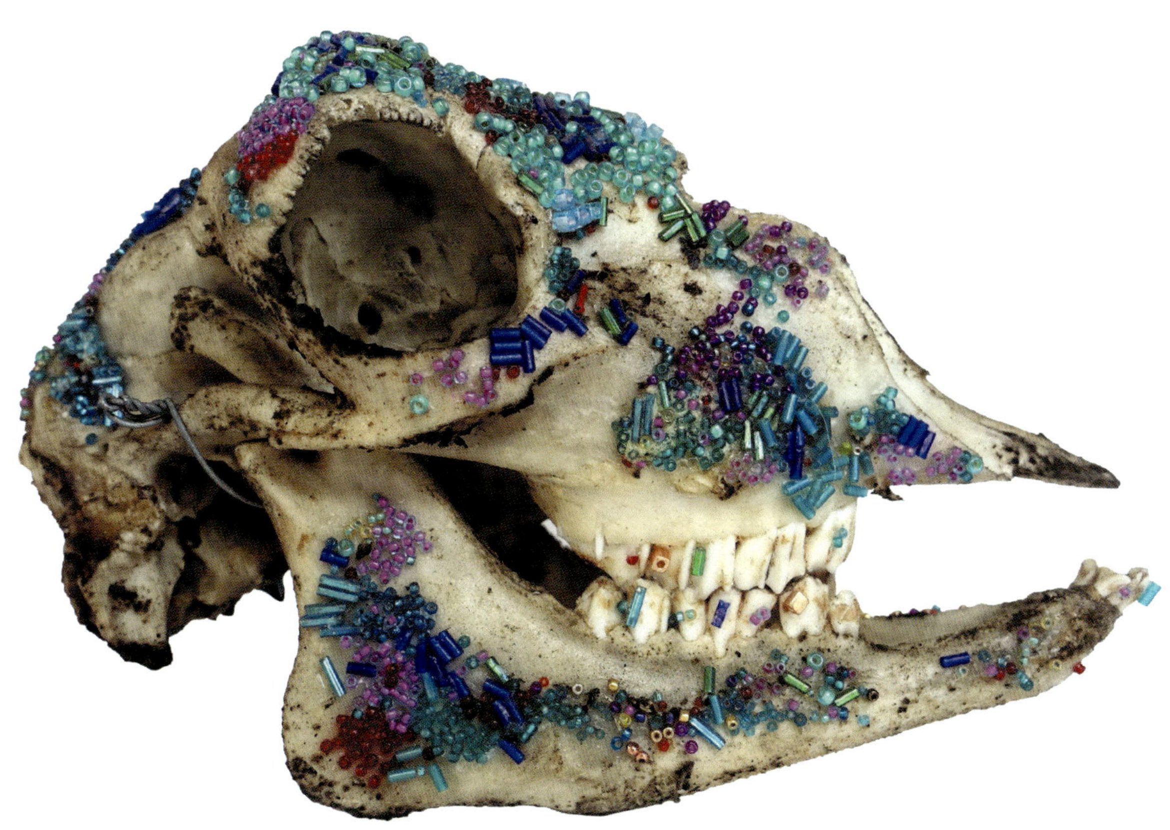

8 ███████████
(b. 1989, San Francisco
Coapan, Cholula, Puebla,
México; d. 2017)

Untitled, 2017
Mixed media on found object
61 × 76 cm
Courtesy of the ████ Estate

Untitled depicts undoc+ futurity, an imagined archetypal realm where undocumented immigrants can exist freely and rejoice in the comfort of their community. The figure at left, on top of a horse, has the lightest skin of anyone in the painting and carries what appears to be a U.S. flag in the colors of the flag of México (green, white, and red).

Although often associated with bad omens, here a maquiz-coatl (double-headed serpent) is portrayed near the center of the painting to symbolize duality and rebirth. This is but one possibility for an immigrant heterotopia in which individuals dare to exist beyond the labor they provide to their host country. The painting shows day laborers, cleaning ladies, and street vendors at leisure, swimming with their families and enjoying a communal meal. This imagined realm in Nepantla (space in between) exists where México and the U.S. collide (beyond the violence of the border) in the joy of the transnational communities that dare to belong equally in both countries.

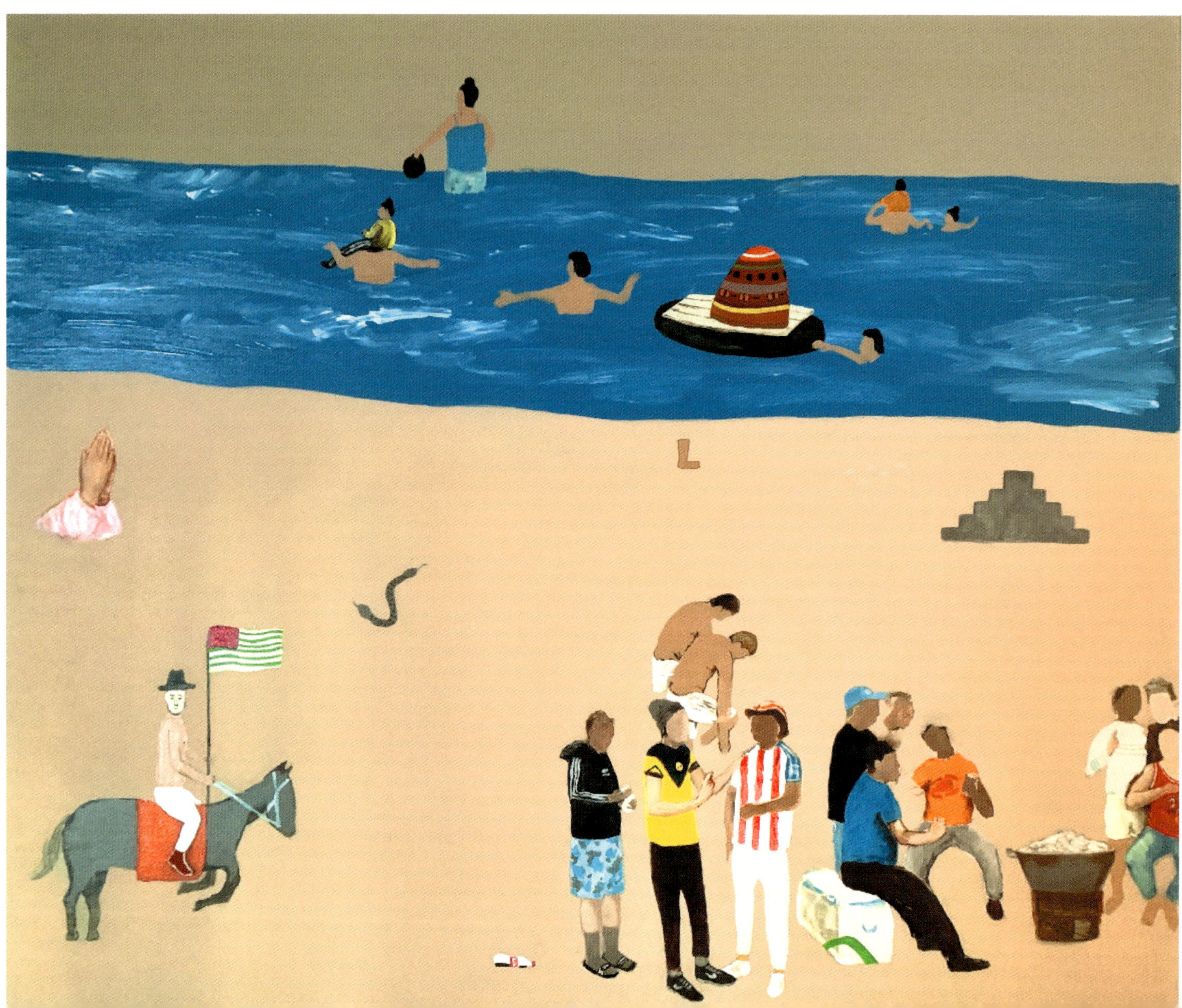

9 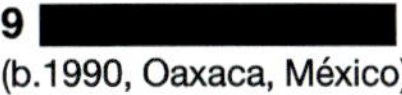
(b.1990, Oaxaca, México)

Tenku Ania, 2024
Photography on found object
40 × 45 cm
Courtesy of the artist

Tenku Ania is a reference to the private dream world of each Yaqui individual. Neighbors to the Tohono O'odham Nation, the Yaqui people live on their ancestral lands in the Yaqui River Valley in Sonora, México. This work—a piece of tree bark with wildflowers—holds the artist's family archive (Oaxaqueñe): three photos of family gatherings, one of them torn apart. With *Tenku Ania*, the artist highlights stories of Indigenous technologies and knowledge systems, fusing Oaxaqueñe and Yaqui epistemologies.

This juxtaposition speaks to a broader narrative about who is included and excluded from the national identity and the Indigenous relationship to land and all it produces. Land Back, a global movement that seeks to return stolen lands to Indigenous stewards, responds to the violent destruction of the environment by colonial settlers. *Tenku Ania* serves as a reminder of the complex circumstances of land stewards who, through immigration, are removed from their ancestral homes yet remain committed to Indigenous knowledge.

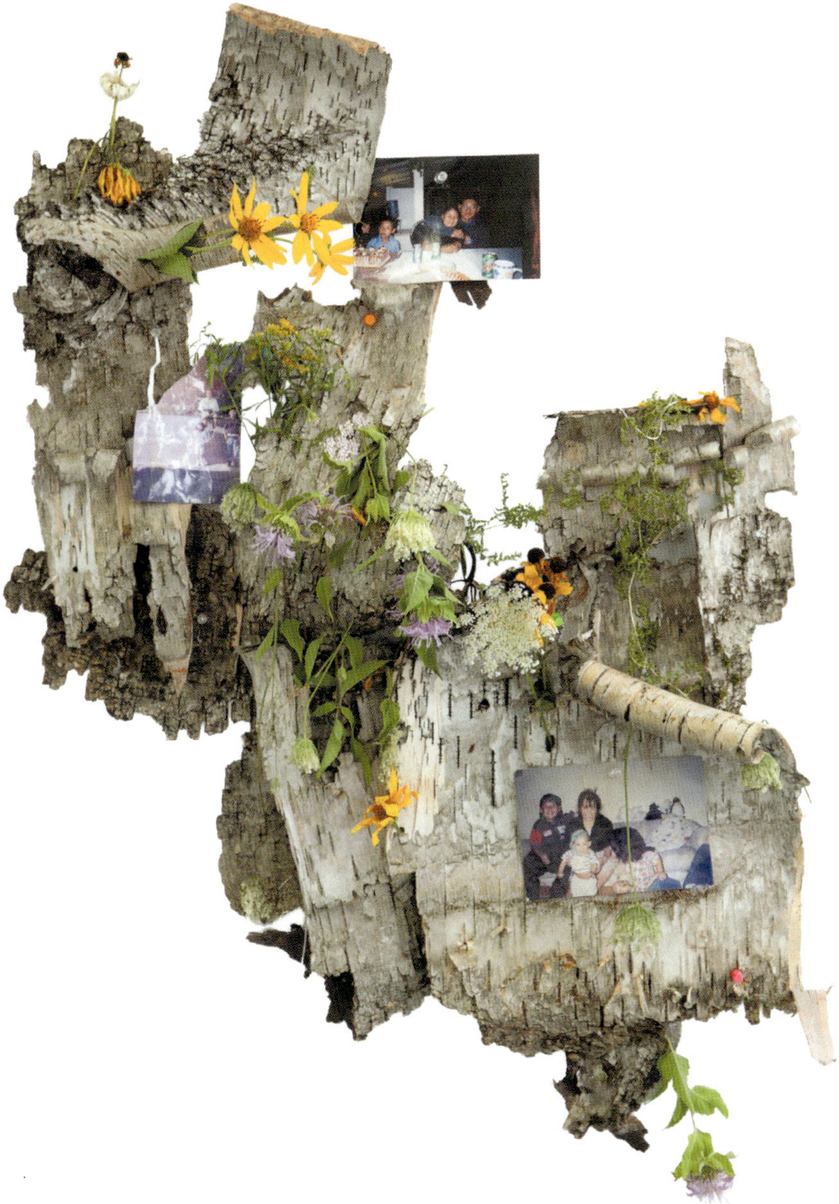

10A 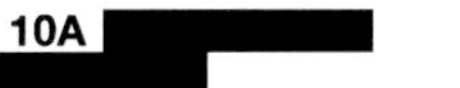

(b. 1965, México City, México)

Reverencia: mapeo de muertes migrantes en Arizona (Reverence: Arizona Migrant Death Mapping), 2023
Archival pigment on habotai silk
508 x 71 cm (each of 10)
Courtesy of the artist

Reverencia: Arizona Migrant Death Mapping was produced from the list of undocumented immigrant deaths generated in partnership between the Pima County Office of the Medical Examiner and Humane Borders. For this work, the artist has transposed the legal document onto 10 habotai silk scrolls. The information rendered visually includes the exact location where a body was found (geographic coordinates in latitude and longitude), the name (when available), the gender of the deceased, the date of discovery, and, if available, the cause of death. With this work, the artist pays reverence to the lives of all the undocumented immigrants who have perished in the deadly landscape overseen by the U.S. Immigration and Customs Enforcement.

```
...ntified","female","","2010-06-30","Private","N 32.75901...
300ft./100m)","6","Sasabe","Drowning","DROWNING","1","Fully fleshed","< 1 day",...
"10-01297","DABOXTHA-DANIEL, ALFREDO","male","28","2010-07-01","Tohono Oodham Nation"...
300ft./100m)","7","San Miguel","Exposure","PROBABLE HYPERTHERMIA","1","Fully fleshed"...
"10-01308","QUINTANA-VALENZUELA, NICOLAS","male","28","2010-07-02","US Forest Service"...
300ft./100m)","5","Nogales","Exposure","PROBABLE HYPERTHERMIA","4","Skeletoni...
Cruz",31.611566,-111.112383,489341,3497387
"10-01309","BORRERO PAULINO, FATIMA","female","41","2010-07-02","Tohono Oodham Nation"...
300ft./100m)","7","San Miguel","Exposure","PROBABLE HYPERTHERMIA AND DEHYDRATION","1","Fully fleshed"...
"10-01310","LOPEZ CARRILLO, ANGELA MARIXA","female","31","2010-07-02","Tohono Oodham Nation"...
300ft./100m)","7","San Miguel","Exposure","DEHYDRATION AND HYPERTHERMIA","1","Fully fleshed"...
"10-01311","LOPEZ CARRILLO, HUGO ARNALDO","male","21","2010-07-02","Tohono Oodham Nation"...
300ft./100m)","7","San Miguel","Exposure","DEHYDRATION AND HYPERTHERMIA","1","Fully fleshed"...
"10-01312","LOPEZ SALINAS, ORLANDO ANTONIO","male","35","2010-07-02","Tohono Oodham Nation"...
300ft./100m)","7","San Miguel","Exposure","DEHYDRATION AND HYPERTHERMIA","1","Fully fleshed"...
"10-01320","LUNA APACECHEA, YIMI","male","27","2010-07-04","Tohono Oodham Nation"...
Miguel","Skeletal Remains","UNDETERMINED - SKELETAL REMAINS","6","Complete skeletoni...
","Arizona","Pima",32.000883,-111.73575,430505,3540769
"10-01321","Matias Martin, Basilio","male","46","2010-07-04","Tohono Oodham Nation"...
distances, and landmarks (precise to within 1mi/2km)","7","San Miguel","Exposure","PROBABLE HYPERTHERMIA"...
","Arizona","Pima",31.964191,-112.269988,379993,3537170
"10-01324","SORIANO GONZALEZ, GREGORIO","male","39","2010-07-05","Tohono Oodham Nation"...
within 10mi/15km)","7","San Miguel","Exposure","PROBABLE HYPERTHERMIA","1","Fully fleshed"...
"10-01327","AKY ALVAREZ, PATRICIO","male","19","2010-07-05","Tohono Oodham Nation"...
and landmarks (precise to within 1mi/2km)","7","San Miguel","Undetermined","UNDETERMINED","1","Fully fleshed"...
day","Arizona","Pima",32.169353,-111.484587,454313,3559310
"10-01332","REYES CARDENAS, JONATHAN","male","27","2010-07-03","Tohono Oodham Nation"...
300ft./100m)","7","San Miguel","Skeletal Remains","UNDETERMINED - SKELETAL REMAINS","7","Complete skeletoni...
","Arizona","Pima",32.202633,-111.91605,413664,3563264
"10-01337","Baquiax Yat, Rodrigo","male","22","2010-07-06","Tohono Oodham Nation"...
300ft./100m)","7","San Miguel","Undetermined","UNDETERMINED","4","Skeletoni...
"10-01338","ORTIZ CORTES, AURELIO","male","31","2010-07-06","Tohono Oodham Nation"...
300ft./100m)","7","San Miguel","Undetermined","UNDETERMINED","4","Skeletoni...
"10-01353","LIMA GARCIA, MARCELINO","male","46","2010-07-08","Tohono Oodham Nation"...
300ft./100m)","7","San Miguel","Exposure","PROBABLE HYPERTHERMIA","3","Decomposed w/ focal skeletoni...
","Arizona","Pima",31.770866,-111.7045,433292,3515254
"10-01354","ANTONIO RAMIREZ, PEDRO","male","31","2010-07-08","Tohono Oodham Nation"...
distances, and landmarks (precise to within 1mi/2km)","7","San Miguel","Exposure","PROBABLE HYPERTHERMIA"...
","Arizona","Pima",31.774616,-111.85196,419331,3515769
"10-01358","FRANCO RAMOS, SERGIO","male","44","2010-07-08","Tohono Oodham Nation"...
300ft./100m)","7","San Miguel","Exposure","PROBABLE HYPERTHERMIA","2","Decomposed"...
"10-01363","RAMIREZ DOMINGUEZ, JOSE ISIDRO","male","19","2010-07-09","Tohono Oodham Nation"...
300ft./100m)","8","Cowlick","Skeletal Remains","UNDETERMINED (SKELETAL REMAINS)","7","Skeletoni...
","Arizona","Pima",32.0365,-112.3124,376082,3545234
"10-01366","LORENZO-GARCIA, MARIA JULIETA","female","23","2010-07-09","Tohono Oodham Nation"...
300ft./100m)","7","San Miguel","Exposure","COMPLICATIONS OF HYPERTHERMIA","1","Fully fleshed"...
"10-01369","MARTINEZ MARTA, IRENE","female","38","2010-07-09","Tohono Oodham Nation"...
300ft./100m)","8","Cowlick","Exposure","PROBABLE HYPERTHERMIA","3","Decomposed w/ focal skeletoni...
"10-01375","CRUZ HERNANDEZ, SALVADOR DE JESUS","male","43","2010-07-11","Tohono Oodham Nation"...
ca. 300ft./100m)","7","San Miguel","Skeletal Remains","UNDETERMINED (SKELETAL REMAINS)"...
","Arizona","Pima",31.793366,-112.43375,364266,3518427
"10-01376","VARGAS PARRA, FIDEL","male","17","2010-07-11","Tohono Oodham Nation"...
300ft./100m)","7","San Miguel","Exposure","PROBABLE HYPERTHERMIA","2","Decomposed"...
"10-01377","HERNANDEZ TZIC, EULOGIO LEONSO","male","37","2010-07-11","Tohono Oodham Nation"...
300ft./100m)","7","San Miguel","Exposure","PROBABLE HYPERTHERMIA","2","Decomposed"...
"10-01378","PONCIO AJPACAJA, JOSE ALFREDO","male","24","2010-07-11","Tohono Oodham Nation"...
300ft./100m)","7","San Miguel","Exposure","PROBABLE HYPERTHERMIA","1","Fully fleshed"...
"10-01379","Unidentified","male","","2010-07-11","Private","N 31 57.982 W 111 ...
300ft./100m)","6","Sasabe","Skeletal Remains","UNDETERMINED (SKELETAL REMAINS)","7"...
","Arizona","Pima",31.966366,-111.28855,472736,3536743
...,"City of Tucson","4620 NORTH MESQUITE ...
```

perish every day on sacred Indigenous territory; this artist brings attention to this complexity through her aesthetic practice. "The land was Mexican once, was Indian always, and is and will be again."[19] *Ceremonia en Esta Tierra Sagrada* (FIG. 2) also honors the thousands of migrant lives lost. These works explore issues of home and belonging, identity, displacement, erasure, and the tragedy of human loss in this terrain.[20] In the artist's words,

> In all its beauty, the Arizona desert has become a place that holds unimaginable despair and sorrow. The luminous landscape is one many migrants cross in desperate need of a new home, opportunity, and a better, safe life. Men, women, and children will take this path when all others are exhausted. They risk everything in pursuit of the American Dream. This journey, heartbreakingly, will often lead to death. Through evocative, non-representational works, I imagine and suggest the moments right before the migrants perish. In this work, I consider and reflect on the lives lost that ultimately reside within the desert soil.[21]

Reverencia: Arizona Migrant Death Mapping (FIG. 10 A, B) and *Imagining Your Last Breath* (FIG. 6 A-L) speak to the deadly topography through which migrants pass; invite us to recognize the humanity of people losing their lives in the desert; and reckon with the beauty of this perilous environment.

Hyperdocumentedness

"American common sense tells us that being undocumented is a euphemism for being illegal, illegitimate, and inhuman."[22]

Aurora Chang's analysis grounds this section. Chang's findings, based on autoethnography, explain that hyperdocumentedness is the perpetual effort to accrue documentation, in her case, in the form of awards, accolades, and, eventually, academic degrees to compensate for undocumentedness. Chang introspectively questions the pursuit of documentation, in her case academic, as a means of attaining legitimacy.[23] All the artists in this segment visually challenge this form of legitimacy and complicate the bureaucratic need for documentation by using legal documents as visual anchors and material artifacts in their artworks. Social Security cards, DACA (Deferred Action for Childhood Arrivals) application forms, correspondence directed to and received from the United States Citizenship and Immigration Services (USCIS), a decade-long accumulation of bureaucratic paperwork that includes fake and real permanent resident cards,[24] and university-issued student identifications collide to visually convey hyperdocumentedness.

The *Social Security Card (Un)documented* (FIG. 4, P. 26) series is the meticulously embroidered representation of multiple Social Security cards on craft paper. Each replicates in thread a Social Security document or form SSA-3000, though omitting the number, name, and signature of the individual affiliated with a given card and thus abstracting the bureaucratic underpinnings of the document. This gesture alludes to the resources tied to having a Social Security number and card—that are unavailable to undocumented immigrants who can financially contribute to this system but not benefit from it. The artwork also calls into question the document itself and the structure erected around Social Security in the U.S. *Reoccurrence One-Liner* (FIG. 11) uses screen print to render an I-797 form, a legal document issued by USCIS to communicate with applicants about their immigration process, and places it in front of a $20 bill and a series of empty invoices from the School of Art Institute of Chicago (SAIC)[25] to signal the financial burden of naturalization proceedings, which affects every immigrant regardless of their journey into the country. *10-Year-Old Book* (FIG. 12) is a collection of a decade's worth of legal documents and found objects turned into a collage-based sculpture.

Homeland Insecurity (FIG. 1, P. 17) speaks to the artist's history of growing up in a foreign country she calls home and her dacamented experience in the U.S. through an installation that reinterprets her childhood bedroom while challenging hyperdocumentedness. In the artist's words, "I do not remember anything about my life in my home country of México."[26] The work visually recalls the colossal amount of paperwork she completed every two years as part of her DACA application process.[27] As she explores her childhood memories, she expresses her longing for serenity amid uncertainty. The installation includes a child-size mattress placed on top of four plastic crates; a pink comforter with flowers covering the mattress; two plush bunnies near the wall; and wallpaper made of countless USCIS I-821 forms (used to request DACA) decorated with pink birds and yellow butterflies. To the left of the bed, a small television sits on top of a four-drawers dresser, alongside two angel figurines and an empty picture frame. The dresser has also been covered in 1-821 forms, while the television displays superimposed images of the same form and the artist's baby pictures. To the right of the bed is a nightstand (also covered by I-821 forms) on top of which stands a wick lamp and more celestial figurines. The nightstand drawer has been left open, with toys peering from inside. Near the foot of the bed, a flower-patterned, child-size luggage rests atop a fuzzy pink rug. The installation is purposefully lit with a single light, obscuring the edges of the space as if to grant the viewer a peek at but not a full access to the artist's childhood memory.

Each of these artists visually intervenes in, aesthetically replicates, or artistically deconstructs the tools of a bureaucratic system that ends up uniting an immigrant community in a defiant stance against hyperdocumentedness. As one of the artists in this volume states, "Xeroxes are the stuff of bureaucracy. I had to do a ridiculous amount of paperwork to get a work permit and, eventually, a green card."[28] By using legal documents as a medium and material, artists subvert this system and its mechanisms that serve to delineate and segregate resources from immigrants, while simultaneously uniting them in their often decade-long legal processes.

11 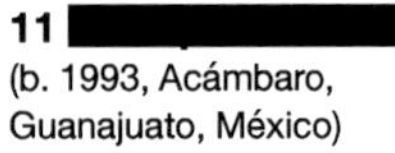
(b. 1993, Acámbaro,
Guanajuato, México)

Reoccurrence One-Liner, 2017
One color screen print
26.6 × 21.59 cm
Courtesy of the artist

Reoccurrence One-Liner is a single-color screen print depicting invoices, money, and immigration documents. At its center is an I-797 Notice of Action issued by the United States Citizenship and Immigration Services (USCIS) on August 29, 2012, informing the recipient that their Deferred Action for Childhood Arrivals (DACA) approval is valid from 10/12/2012 to 10/11/2014. The form is discretionary and does not qualify the person for a work permit (which is issued separately); it does require that the applicant inform USCIS of any change of address during the stated time frame. Beneath the form are sections of a $20 bill and invoices from the School of the Art Institute of Chicago. With this work, the artist points to the ways bureaucratic processes and paperwork collide as they define his access to resources, be it education, labor, or sustainability.

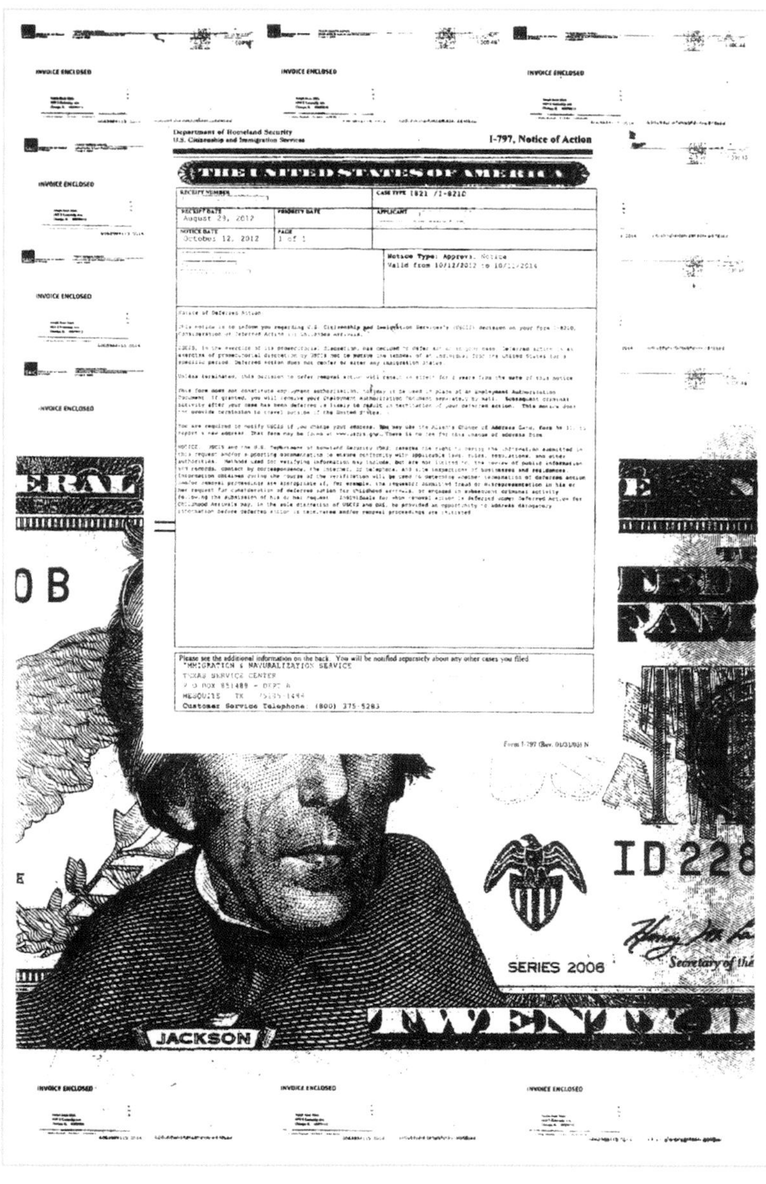

12 ████████████

(b. 1981, Atotonilco El Grande, Hidalgo, México)

10-Year-Old Book, 2007–17
Collage on found object
43 × 91 × 104 cm
Courtesy of the artist

10-Year-Old Book is a cacophony of materials that signal the artist's hyperdocumentation. The notebook is laced with collaged images juxtaposing Mesoamerican archeological sites with contemporary runway fashion models. Aside from these images, real and fake documents appear on many pages, including a resident alien card and a Social Security SSA-3000 form.

Over the years, the artist accumulated multiple micas chuecas (fake identification cards) to work as an undocumented immigrant. *10-year-old book* questions excessive documentation and the system that produces documents to legitimize access to rights and resources; and challenges the idea of belonging within the delineated borders of a nation grounded in colonialism and capitalism.

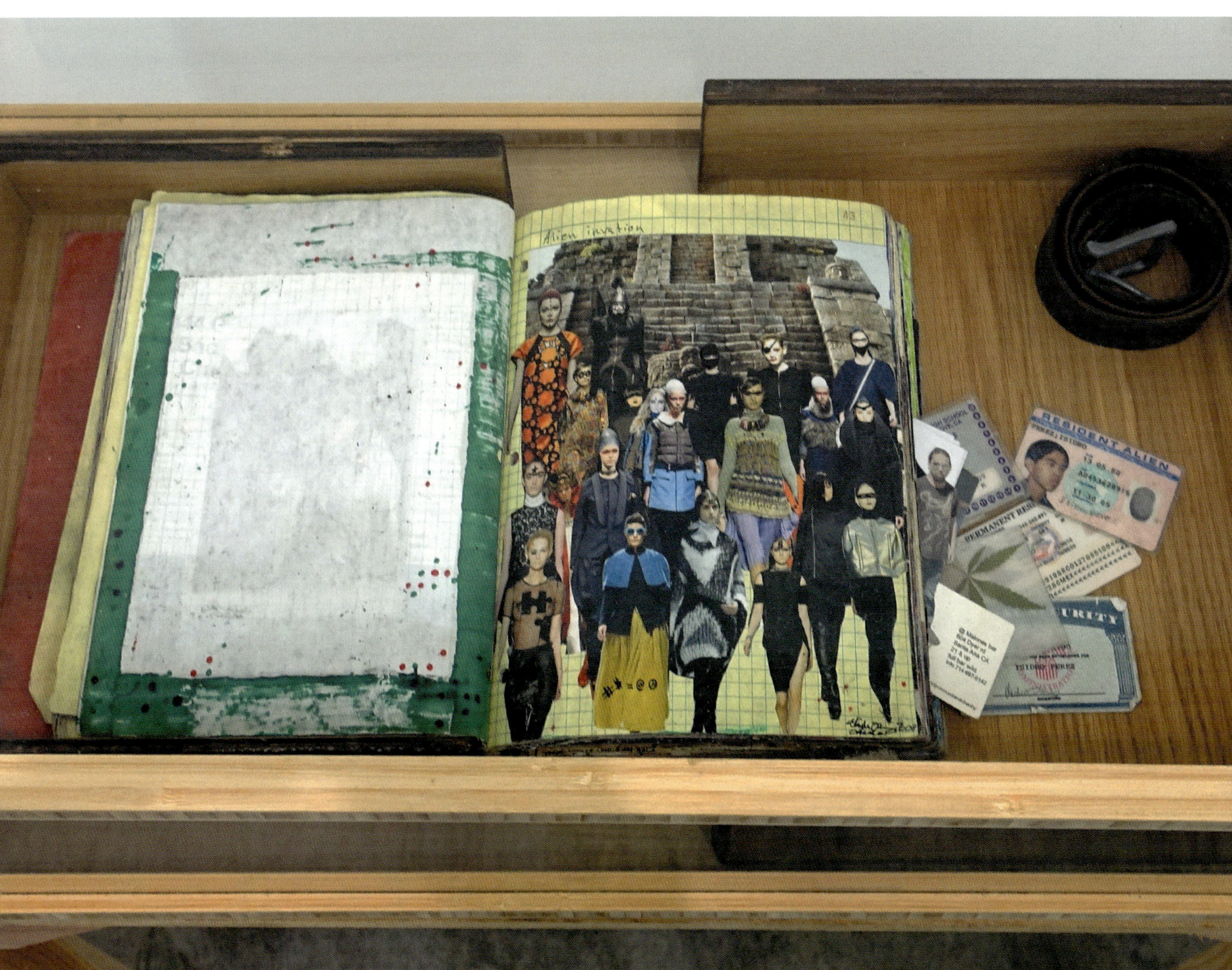

In/visibility

"I could hear Amá's words rattle in my head. 'Never tell anyone.' She didn't need to remind me. I knew."[29]

Whereas every member of the undoc+ community is an immigrant, not every immigrant is part of the undoc+ spectrum. "Never tell anyone," instructed young ▮▮▮▮▮▮▮▮▮ Amá. Like millions of undoc+ individuals in the U.S., his Amá, who faced deportation proceedings and was constantly triggered by Immigration and Customs Enforcement (ICE), delivered safety guidance and intimate parental care in the form of trauma bonding with her child. The struggles and gained wisdom of undoc+ elders are passed on to younger undoc+ generations through menacing looks, whispers, and the ever-present policing of performative cues intended to facilitate hiding in plain sight. For to be a member of the undoc+ spectrum while living in a society that fears and hates undocumentedness translates into having to perpetually disidentify portions of oneself so as to be palatable to the host country's citizenry. In the words of ▮▮▮▮▮▮▮▮▮▮▮, "We were young but could already turn off the parts of ourselves that hurt, like a light switch."[30] Undocumented children internalize this psychologically damaging game driven by cruelty as they grow up; and learn how to police every bit of their lives for the sake of mainstream society.

The artists in this section problematize the demands for in/visibility placed upon undocumented immigrants. *Detention Center Performance* (FIG. 13) takes place at Dobbs Ferry Detention Center, "The Children's Village" in upstate New York where the artist taught art and performance workshops to detained teenage immigrants from Central America. The video illustrates a 24-hour teen life cycle at the center. Each participant wears a paper mask to conceal their identity. *The State of Being Numb* (FIG. 14) uses abstract figural forms digitally rendered to look like gold-colored metal. The use of avatars allows this artist to explore themes of in/visibility, belonging, becoming, and collective existence. *Mirage* (FIG. 15) is a visual interplay of pictorial linguistics, as the title of the work peers from behind a fence that denies the viewer full visual access. This artist, too, challenges in/visibility, both visual and linguistic, as he negotiates accessibility to and for the viewer. *Casa De La Abuela/Grandma's House* (FIG. 16) plays with textile, acrylic, and thread on Amate bark paper as it depicts two children through their outlined silhouettes, rather than facial features. The artist thus shields undoc+ children from menacing looks, hostile whispers, and censorship. *Mi Alien Number is* (FIG. 17) presents a video collage that combines multiple audio-visual references drawn from political speeches, news interviews, films, and songs to call into question the in/visibility demands placed on the "alien" population.

Assimilation was defined one hundred years ago by Park and Burgess as the process of interpenetration and fusion by which people acquire the sentiments and attitudes of another group.[31] Park and Burgess proposed that by sharing their experience and history, members of the new group gain the potential to be incorporated into the larger group's everyday cultural life.[32] In the U.S. today, immigrants are thought to embark on an unavoidable process of "assimilation," in which they increasingly begin to live with, speak, act, work, play, and think like Americans.[33] *Americanization* (FIG. 18) is deeply grounded in the violence inflicted upon Asian American and Pacific Islander (AAPI) immigrant communities as a result of the association of "American" identity with whiteness, and English with a primary/desired mode of communication.[34] *Americanization* challenges assimilation by refusing the predominance of English and repudiating "American" beauty standards.

Untitled from the Series *Campesinos y Colores* (FIG. 19) takes a different approach to the complexity of assimilation by borrowing from photographic Depression Era depictions. Deep within these three works on paper are hints of Dorothea Lange's *The Assignment I'll Never Forget: Migrant Mother*. Adopting the visual vocabulary of the Depression-Era's Farm Security Administration's photojournalists and the colors of the U.S. flag, the artist contests assimilation, immigrant in/visibility, and Americanness. In the words of ██████████ █████, "When I came undocumented to the U.S., I

13 ███████████
(b. 1976, San Salvador,
El Salvador)

Detention Center Performance, 2022
Single-channel video: 5 minutes
13 seconds
Courtesy of the artist and
███████, New York

Detention Center Performance takes place at Dobbs Ferry Detention Center—"The Children's Village" in upstate New York where the artist taught art and performance workshops to teenage immigrants from Central America. The video illustrates a 24-hour life cycle at the Village. Each participant wears a paper mask to conceal their identity. The 5-minute and 13-second video captures a performance by seven detainees guided by the artists, who instructs them to execute such daily tasks as eating, showering, brushing their teeth, and sleeping.

The Children's Village cares for children legally removed from their parents, many of whom are new immigrants to New York. The average length of stay at the center is 29 days. In 2021, the Village reported expenses totaling over $60,000,000 for immigration services alone. This is but one of 15 such centers in New York and 87 nationwide.

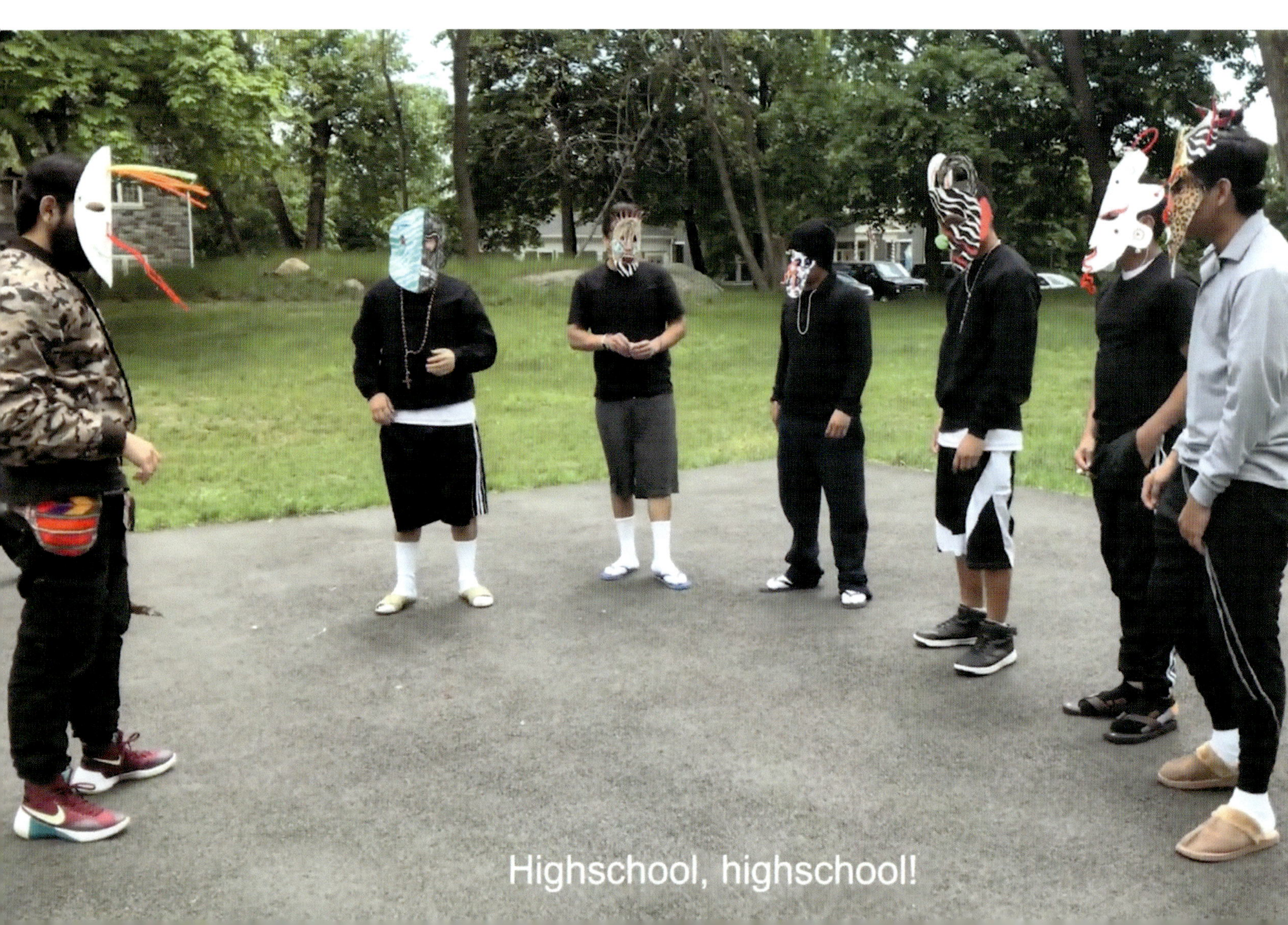

14 █████████
(b. 1999, San Salvador,
El Salvador)

State of Being Numb, 2022
Single-channel video
3 minutes 34 seconds
Courtesy of the artist

State of Being Numb is a 3-minute and 36-second single-channel video depicting anthropomorphized gold sculptural forms that speak to remembering, becoming, and being alive. In the video, the central figures find themselves in what appears to be a forest of emptiness where nothing but light and foliage exists. In part one of the video, multiple figures emerge from the light into an empty, vast, white abysm. Part two portrays a single figure hiding amid digital shrubs whose foliage appears to grow upside down. It is not until part three that we gather that each figure is not alone but exists under surveillance, represented by a grid-like structure that contains hundreds of figures, each individually packed in the same repetitive environment.

Being under constant surveillance or feeling like one is always being watched while simultaneously existing alone is part of an undocumented immigrant's reality. Continually remembering portions of one's past self and simultaneously living in a foreign country far from home can leave many numb and depleted. This works both visualizes and challenges these realities.

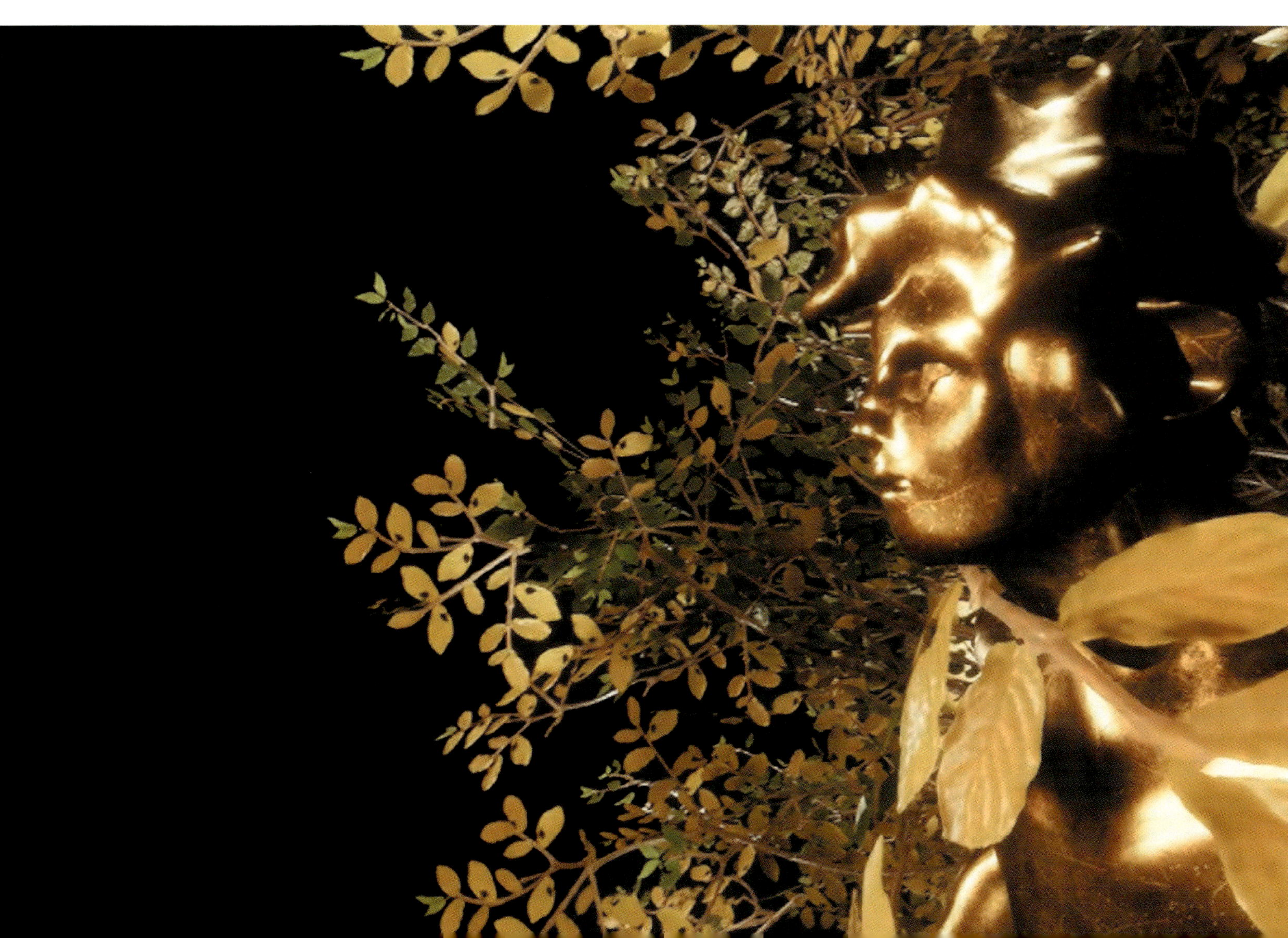

15 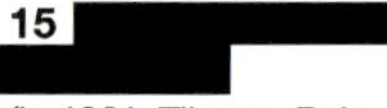

(b. 1961, Tijuana, Baja California, México)

Mirage, 2024
Mixed media
152.4 × 254 cm
Courtesy of the artist

Mirage is an interplay of vernacular aesthetics: the title of the work peers from behind the image of a border fence. The artist challenges in/visibility as he negotiates visual and linguistic accessibility to and for the beholder. The letters are made of mirrors, which create an illusion of the viewer being trapped by the border inside the desert landscape. The work explores the architectural, industrial, and monumental nature of geopolitical symbols; and alludes to the lure, risks, and fallacy of the American Dream.

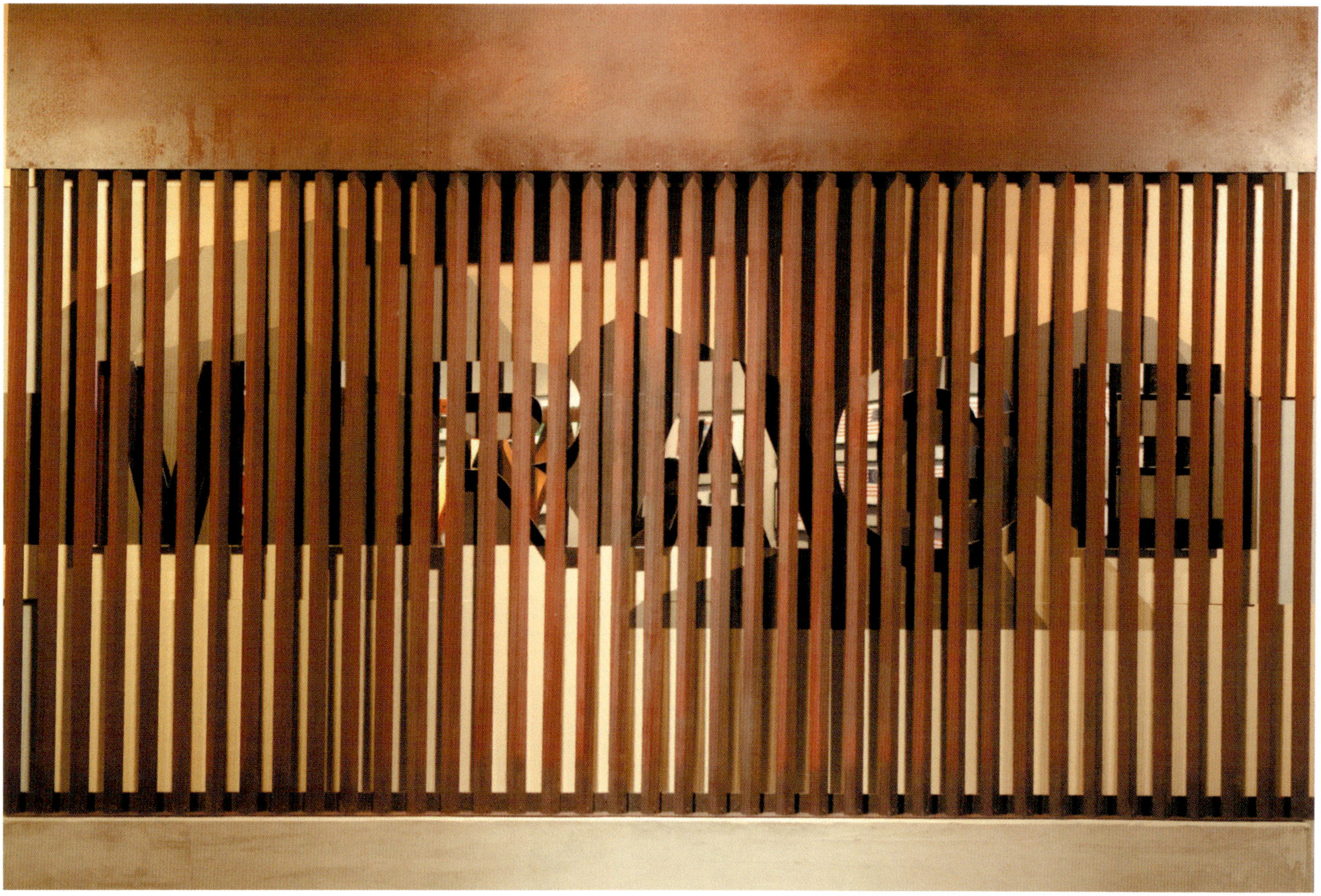

16 ███████
(b. 1993, Michoacán, México)

Casa De La Abuelita /
Grandma's House, 2024
Acrylic, textiles, and thread on Amate
paper made by Jose Daniel Santos
de la Puerta in Puebla, México
122 × 152cm
Courtesy of the artist and
███████████ Gallery

Casa De La Abuelita / Grandma's House is made of embroidery
thread and textile affixed to amate paper. The piece depicts two
children playing ball under a wisteria tree. The one on the left wears
a white bandana as a t-shirt and has an upside-down sheep on his
diaper. The one on the right wears a top with embroidered patterns
typical in the Meseta Purépecha y Zona Lacustre of Michoacan,
México and holds a blue ball. Both figures lack recognizable facial
features, alluding to their in/visibility. The wisteria tree is shedding
its foliage.

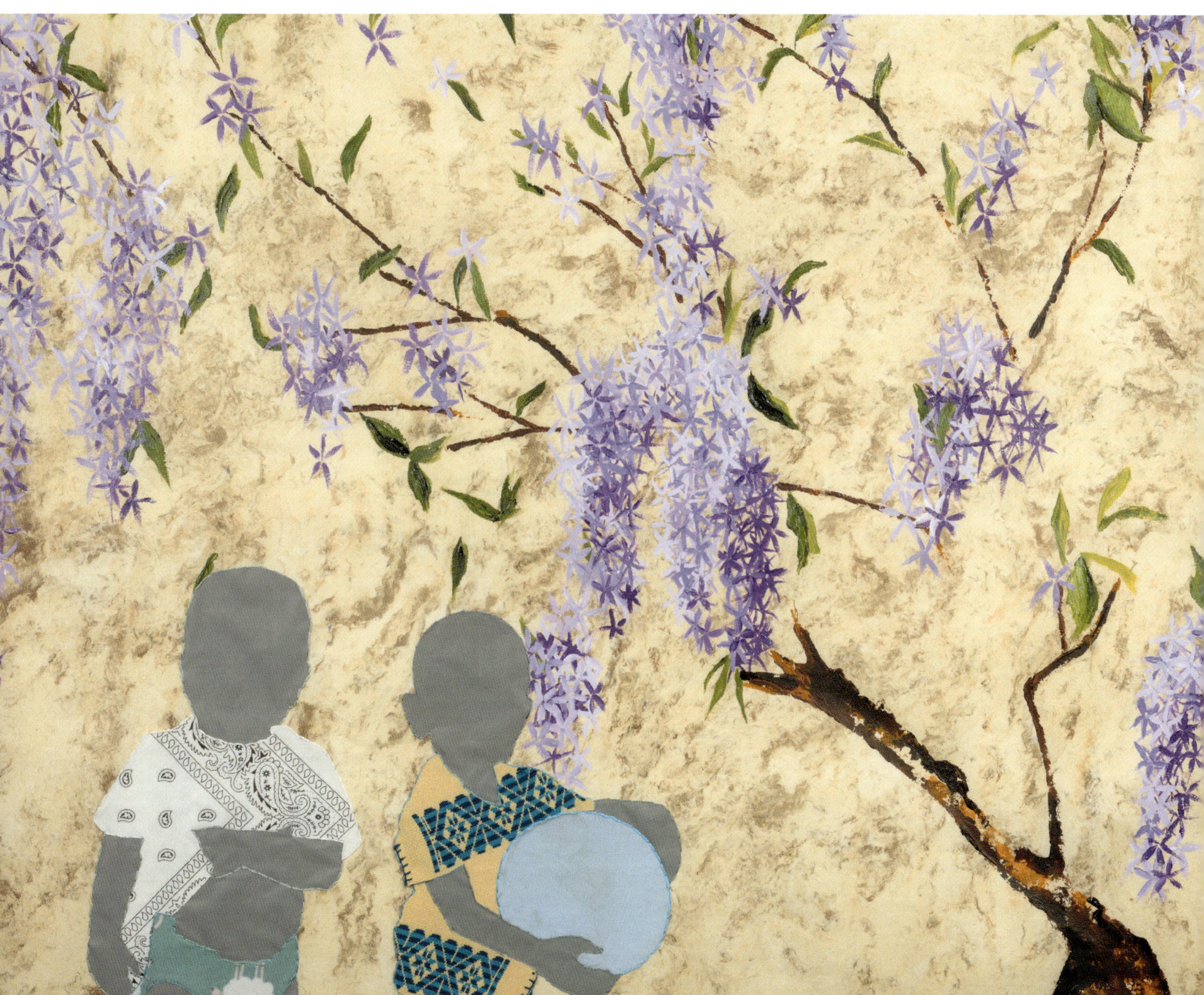

17 ███████
(b. 1995, México City, México)

Mi Alien Number Is, 2024
Single-channel video: 3 minutes
31 seconds
Courtesy of the artist

Mi Alien Number Is—a 3-minute and 31-second single-channel video—uses this medium for political rhetoric. It begins with a clip of a Republican Congressman speaking about undocumented individuals mocking the U.S. sovereignty; the video then transitions to a Spanish song whose lyrics translate as "even if it hurts, superman is illegal." The work is a satirical examination of the word "alien" and how it has been weaponized against the undocumented community. It first appeared in the U.S. legislature in 1937, though its origins date back to the 14th century and derive from Latin word for "other."

Beyond a digital collage of cartoons moving to techno beats, the video includes dancing aliens and excerpts from pseudo-experts speaking about extraterrestrial life. The work challenges misconceptions regarding deportation by juxtaposing sci-fi movie snippets with the tune of "Dame tu Cosita" by El Chombo.

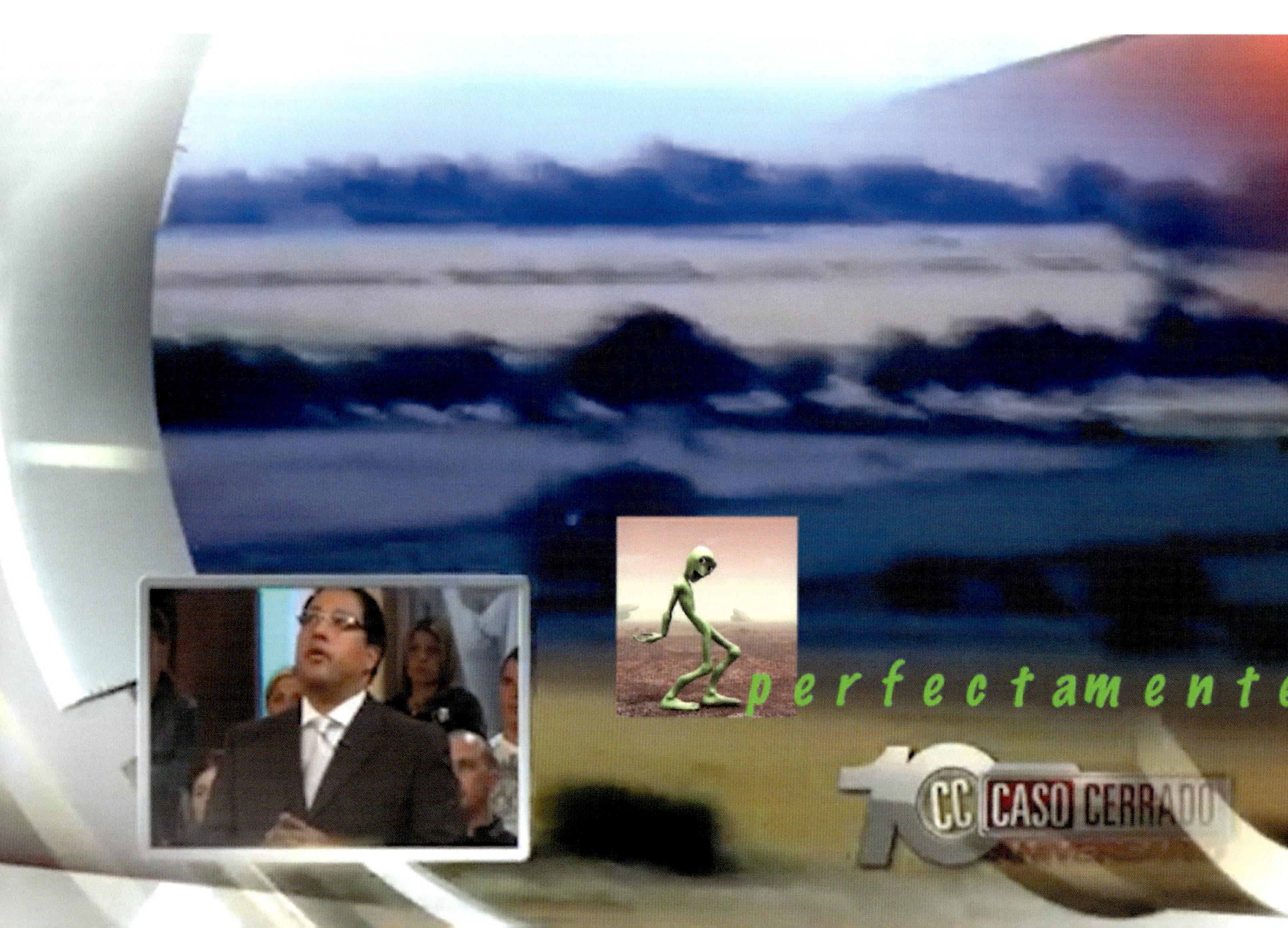

18 ████████████
(b. 1977, Rach Gia, Vietnam)

Americanization, 2022
Mixed media collage
121 x 243 cm
Courtesy of the artist and
████████████Gallery Los Angeles

Americanization foregrounds the artist's journey toward Americanness and her refusal to let English vernacular erase her mother tongue and have whiteness take priority as a cultural norm. A Southeast Asian refugee, she grew up in the U.S. with no dolls or television series reflecting her culture, and felt constrained by unforgiving societal norms, such as turning whiteness into the standard of beauty. Her hanging collage transposes traditional black and white Asian photographs onto full color magazine pages to challenge such expectations of assimilation and adherence to Western norms.

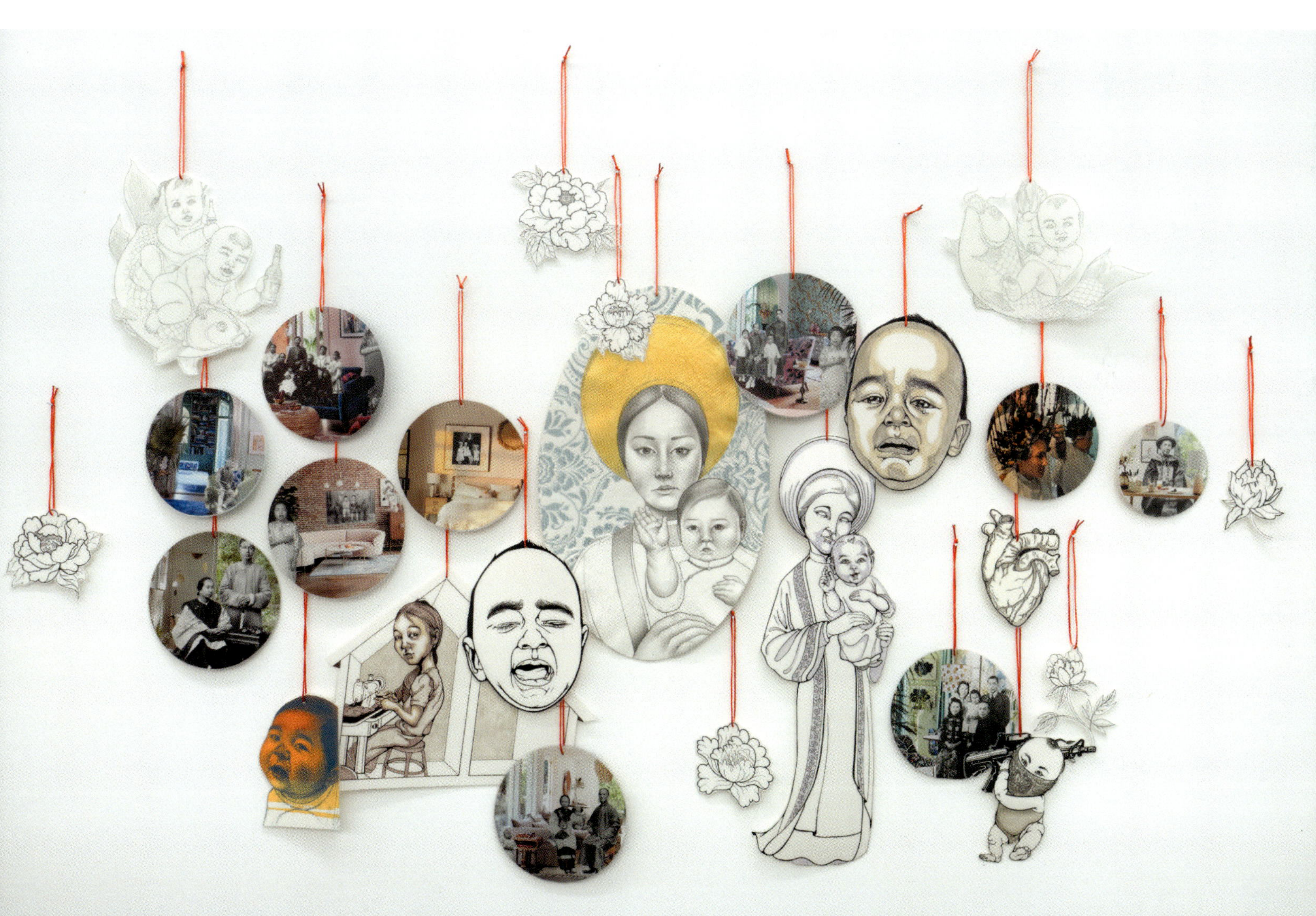

19A (RIGHT)

(b. 1961, México City, México)

Untitled, from *Campesinos y Colores* series, 2016
Mixed media, silk screen on Coventry rag
126 × 96.5 cm
Courtesy of the artist

Untitled, from the series Campesinos y Colores, defies assimilation by borrowing directly from Depression Era's Farm Security Administration photojournalism. Deep within these three works on paper are hints of Dorothea Lange's *The Assignment I'll Never Forget: Migrant Mother*. By making the backgrounds of the works the colors of the U.S. flag, the artist contests immigrant invisibility and perceptions of Americanness.

19B (PAGE 63, LEFT)

(b. 1961, México City, México)

Untitled, from *Campesinos y Colores* series, 2016
Mixed media, silk screen on Coventry rag
126 × 96.5 cm
Courtesy of the artist

19C (PAGE 63, RIGHT)

(b. 1961, México City, México)

Untitled, from *Campesinos y Colores* series, 2016
Mixed media, silk screen on Coventry rag
126 × 96.5 cm
Courtesy of the artist

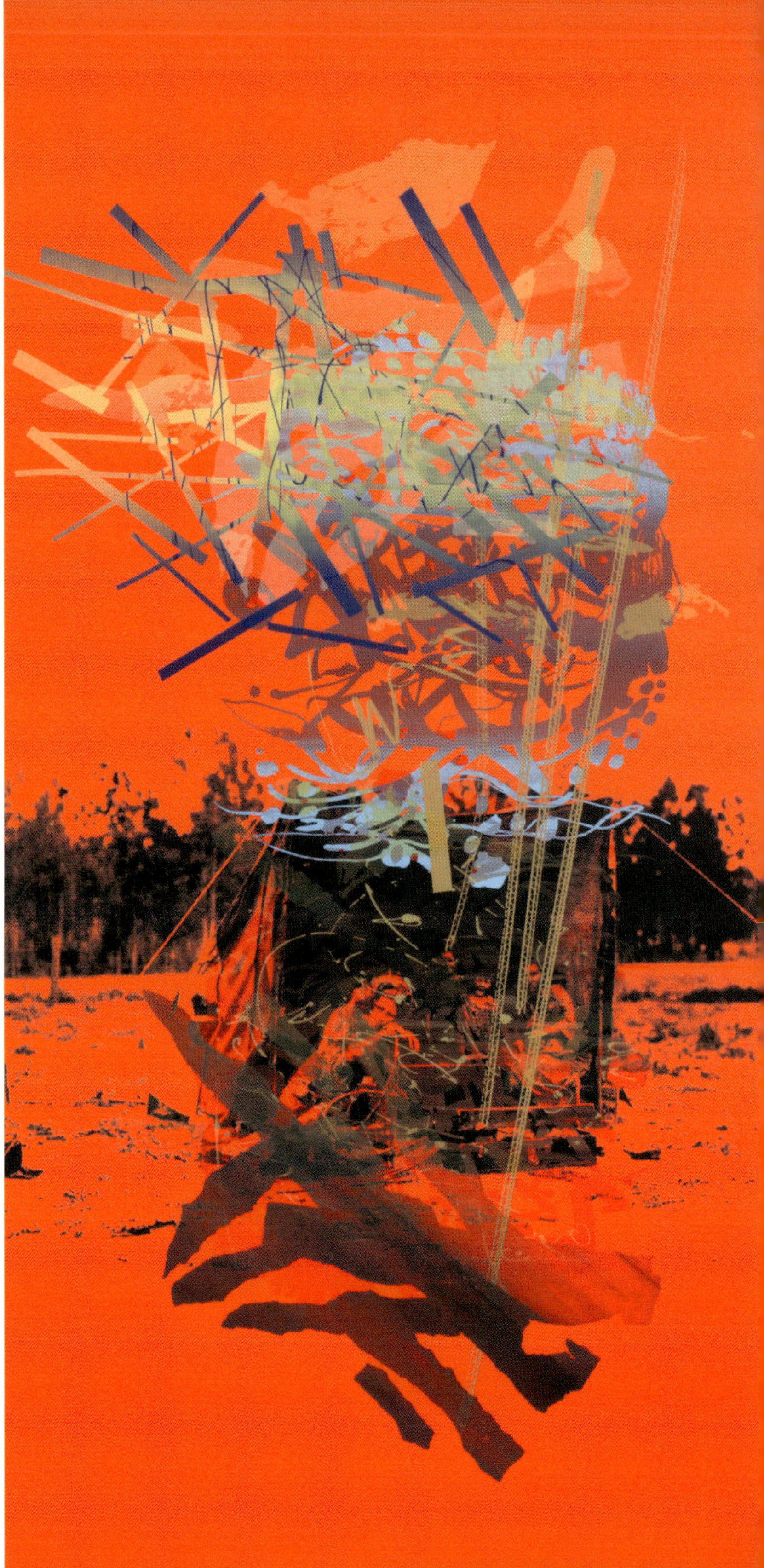

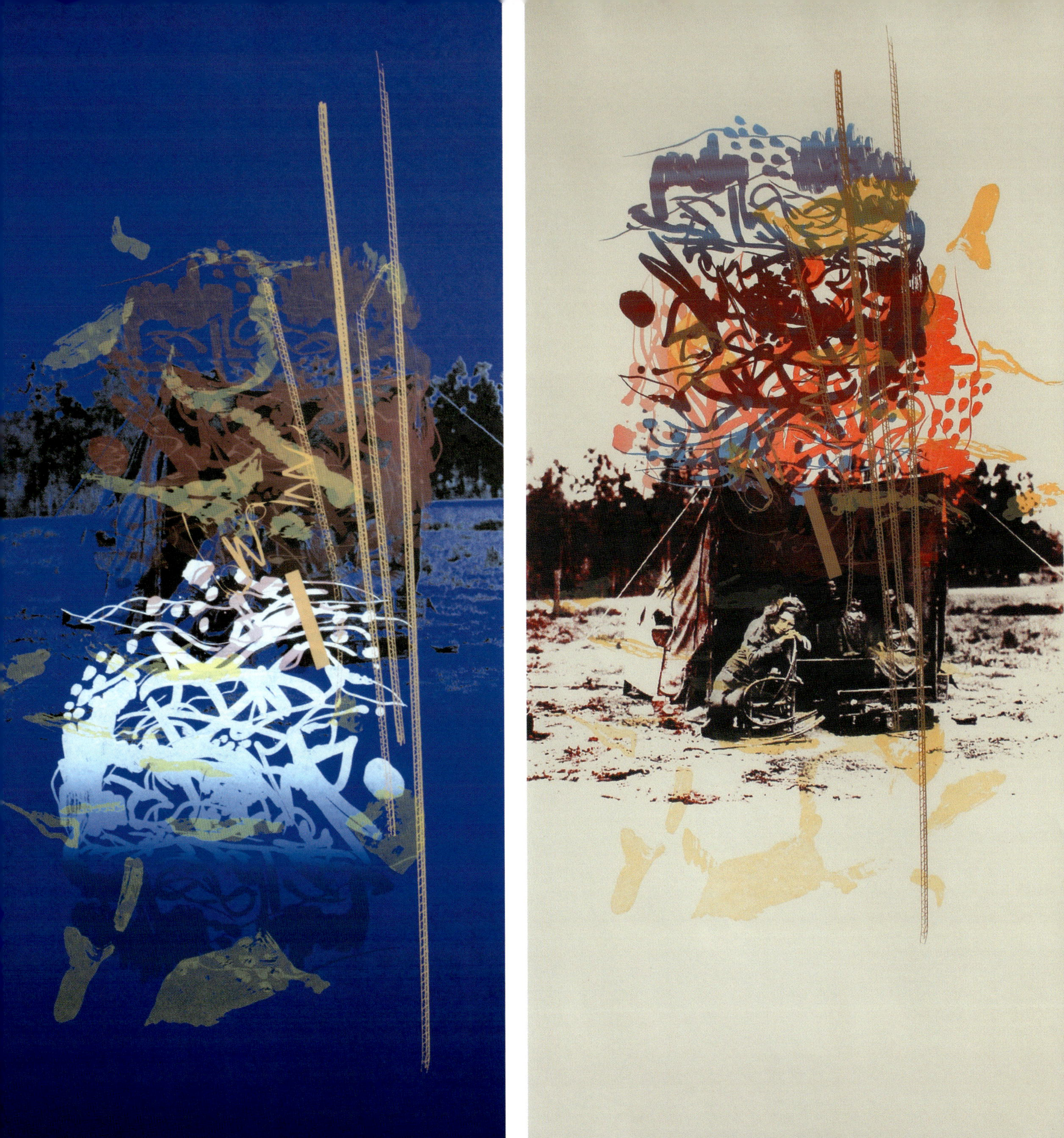

crossed into a threshold of invisibility. Every act of living became an act of trying to remain visible. I was negotiating a simultaneous absence and presence that was begun by the act of my displacement: I am trying to dissect the moment of my erasure. I tried to remain seen for those whom I desired to be seen by, and I wanted to be invisible to everyone else."[35]

Labor

"We were brown bodies made to labor… the workers are very brown, brown from their moms, browned from the sun."[36]

    Immigrants have an extremely complicated relationship to labor. "They are taking your jobs," is a popular media headline that constantly vilifies members of the undoc+ community.[37] Historically, however, the U.S. has cyclically given immigrants access to this nation for labor-related reasons. For example, the Bracero Program (1942–64) was a government-sponsored agreement between México and the U.S., giving men labor-based contracts to come to the U.S.[38] Today,

immigration policies have special permissions to account for immigrant labor. For instance, the DACA program (2012–21) granted individuals the right to work but not citizenship.[39] Whereas some individuals in the undoc+ spectrum do not have employment authorization, many do, including those who were formerly undocumented, naturalized residents, and those going through naturalization proceedings.[40] Largely, undoc+ individuals understand before departing their homeland that when they enter the U.S., they will become part of the labor economy and pay taxes despite the fact that they do not qualify for Social Security retirement plans, health benefits, and other essential resources available to the nation's citizenry.

    The artworks in this segment visualize the complicated relationship between undocumented immigrants and various forms of labor, including domestic work, gardening, construction, and street vending. According to the Women's Bureau in the U.S. Department of Labor, domestic workers tend to earn below-average wages, are excluded from many labor protections, often work without formalized employment arrangements, and face a high risk of gender-based violence and harassment.[41] *Untitled; My Mother's Labor, Dustpan; My Mother's Labor, Iron* (FIG. 20) and *Del Piso a la Pared* (FIG. 21) deal with female domestic labor. The latter installation, comprised of 15 used cleaning rags and mop heads, comments on how female immigrant domestic workers are made invisible in this nation. *Rosa Hernandez* (FIG. 22), a political art action by the same artist, embodies an immigrant domestic worker. By cleaning spaces like the México–U.S. border, or museums and galleries, she challenges the exploitation of immigrant females in the U.S. domestic labor industry.

20 ███████████
(b. 1973, Ibagué, Colombia)

My Mother's Labor, Dustpan and Brush, 2023
Ready-made dustpan and brush with dust, hair, trash, and other particles swept and sealed with non-fired clay, ink and pencil
23 x 33 x 8 cm
Courtesy of the artist

My Mother's Labor, Iron, 2023
Ready-made vintage iron sealed with non-fired clay, ink, and pencil
30 x 16.5 x 13 cm
Courtesy of the artist

My Mother's Labor, Dustpan and Brush and *My Mother's Labor, Iron* is a series of sculptures that pays tribute to the domestic labor performed by the artist's undocumented mother outside her home to support her family; it reflects her tireless dedication to her loved ones as well as her courage and perseverance. The artist alludes to his mother's unwavering commitment to caring for her kin by replicating the tools of her labor. The inclusion of Mayan glyphs represents the untold stories and the emotional toll of labor on the body, highlighting the sacrifices made by individuals on the undoc+ spectrum and fostering appreciation for their contributions to their host society.

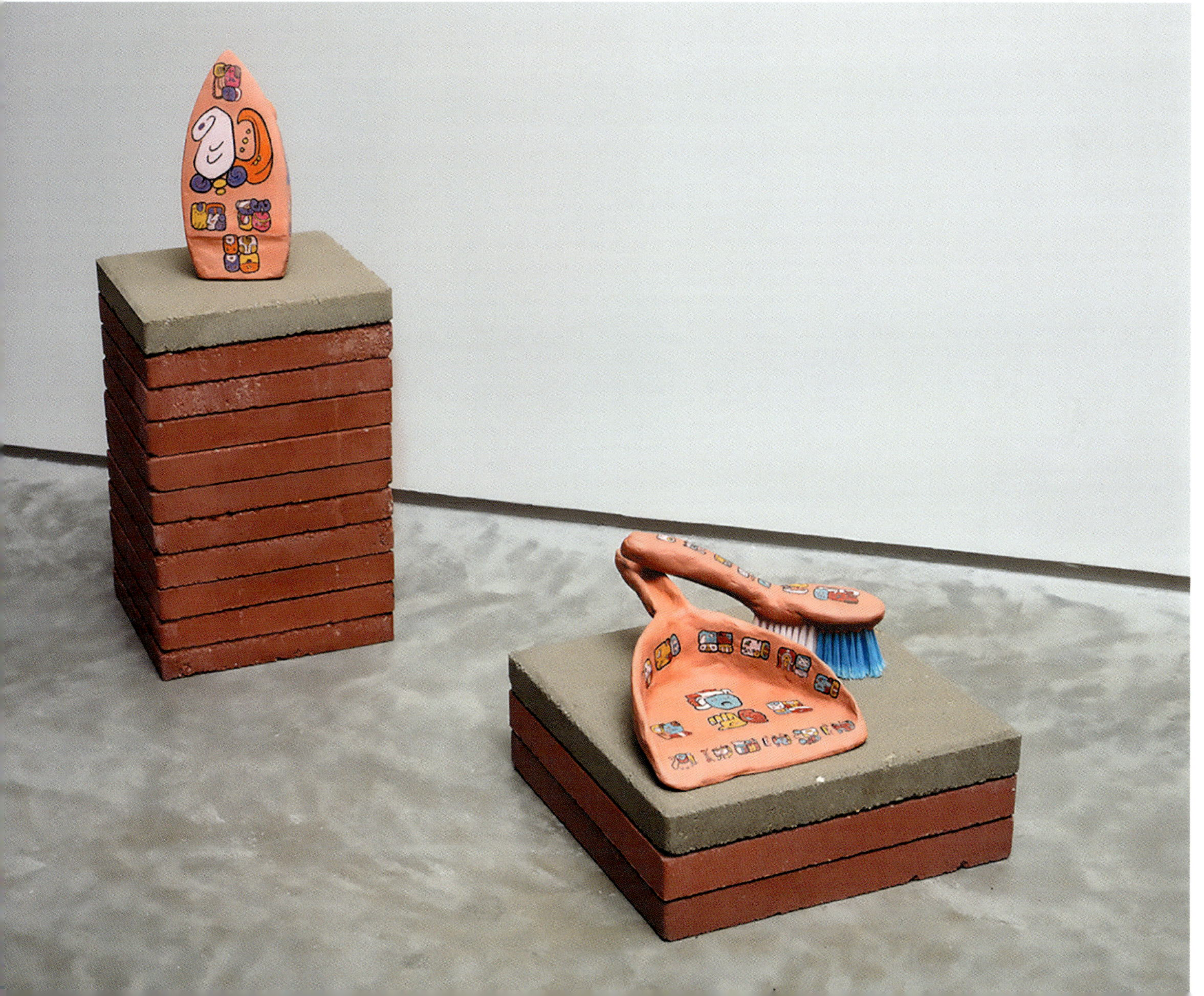

21 ████████
(b. 1966, Toluca, México)

Del Piso a la Pared
(From the floor to the wall), 2014
Mixed media
121 × 243 cm
Courtesy of the artist

Del Piso a la Pared (From the floor to the wall) is made of 15 used instruments of domestic labor: mop heads, sweeper covers, dirty rags. They have been used to perform household chores, as apparent from their wear and tear. With this installation, the artist is challenging the invisibility of domestic labor performed by countless undocumented immigrant Latina women, work that often goes unnoticed and underpaid. Latinas earn 51 cents per dollar on average in contrast to their white male counterparts. Over a 40-year working life, that is over a million dollars lost to pay inequity.

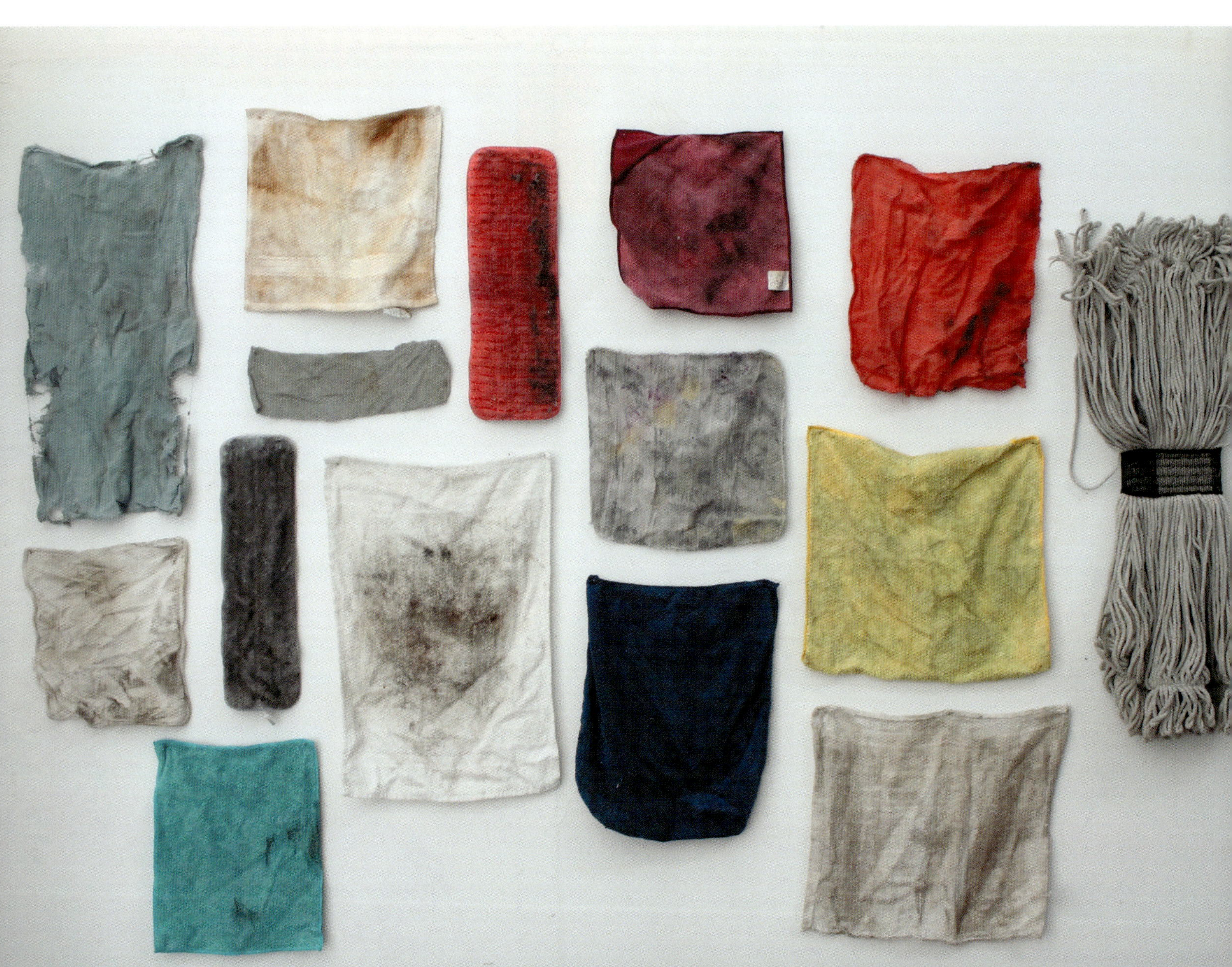

22 ████████
(b. 1966, Toluca, México)

Rosa Hernandez at Friendship Park,
San DiegoTijuana Border, 2013
Pigment print
46 × 61 cm
Courtesy of the artist

Rosa Hernandez at Friendship Park, San Diego Tijuana Border is a
photograph of the artist's alter ego sweeping Friendship Park on the
San Diego/Tijuana border. The lower left corner is anchored by a sign
that reads, "U.S. Property, No Trespassing"; in the background is a
lighthouse beyond a gray fence. The only individual in the image is
a cleaning lady in a salmon-colored uniform and a white apron who
sweeps the coastal park. This work visualizes domestic labor by
immigrant women north of the México–U.S. border.

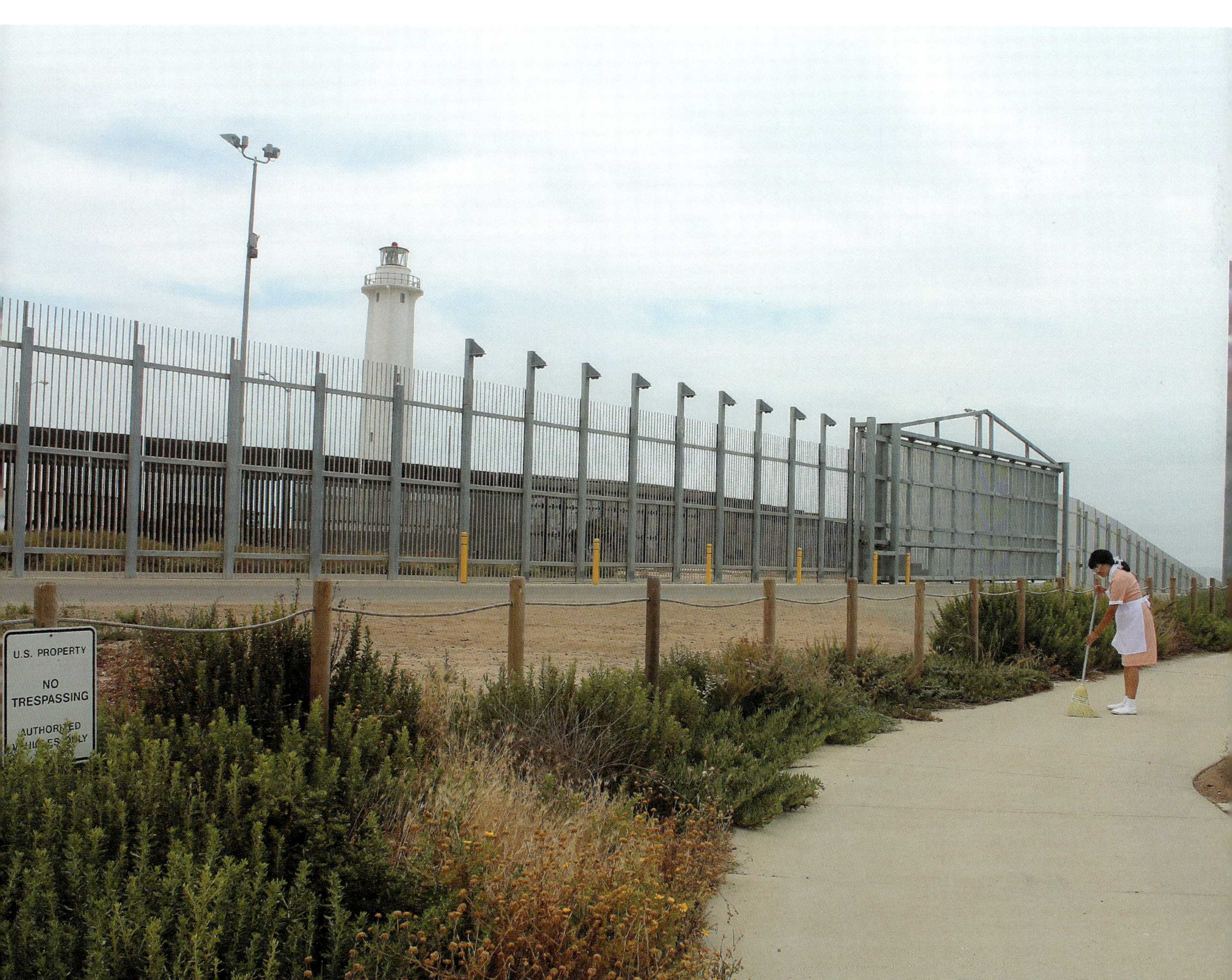

Con La Miel en la Boca (**FIG. 23**) refers to the collectivity of labor required for this nation to thrive. Here, working bees serve as an allegory of the undocumented immigrant communities in the U.S. responsible for food production. The video component of this multi-disciplinary artwork features first-hand testimonials of many undoc+ women who share their migration stories, which are juxtaposed with the images of beehives and adjacent sculptural forms that accompany this project. By highlighting the voices and lived experiences of undoc+ females, this artist creates a shared space for learning from the collectivity of their actions and simultaneously celebrates their journey beyond labor. *Prole* (**FIG. 24**) offers a glimpse into undoc+ day laborers' mentality as a group of men gather to play soccer and talk about their quotidian lives. *Rose Grower* (**FIG. 25**) depicts an individual surrounded by pink flowers that echo his red plaid shirt; the honor and beauty of his labor take center stage in his portrait. He proudly wears a tejana hat as he looks straight into the camera, his pants dusty from a long day of hard and honest work. The landscape surrounding him serves as a reminder of the beauty that undoc+ individuals bring with them during their migration journeys.

Remembrance

"Here, you and me, you and them, we together, we are in pain. We grieve. Grieving breaks us apart, indeed, and keeps us together."[42]

This section addresses the realities that carry the most heartbreak in the undoc+ community: the thousands of uncompleted journeys, the many individuals lost, and the death toll of the American Dream. "Undocumented immigrants are being disappeared into the silence… and they often just ship them to detention centers, never to be seen again."[43] *Gemidos de la Tierra* (**FIG. 26**) emphasizes these unspoken and unheard stories. This work started in 2022 as a series of wooden slabs on which the artist recorded the names of each immigrant who had died while in Immigration and Customs Enforcement's (ICE) custody. Each name was meticulously carved and filled with soil collected from the state where the individual passed away.

23 ███████
(b. 1976, Bogotá, Colombia)

Con Miel en La Boca
(With honey in the mouth), 2023
Two-channel video: 13 minutes
24 seconds
Courtesy of the artist

Con Miel en La Boca highlights the fact that honeybee labor is necessary to sustain our global ecosystem. Their synchronicities and pollination techniques exemplify purposeful collective action. Migratory pollination has become essential to agriculture. Human migration is also vital to it: undocumented immigrants exploited for their labor nurture the United States. The artist grew up with bee colonies, learned at a young age about their collective models of sustainability, and sought to highlight their importance to society at large. The work juxtaposes bee labor with the oral stories of immigrant women who travel north for employment.

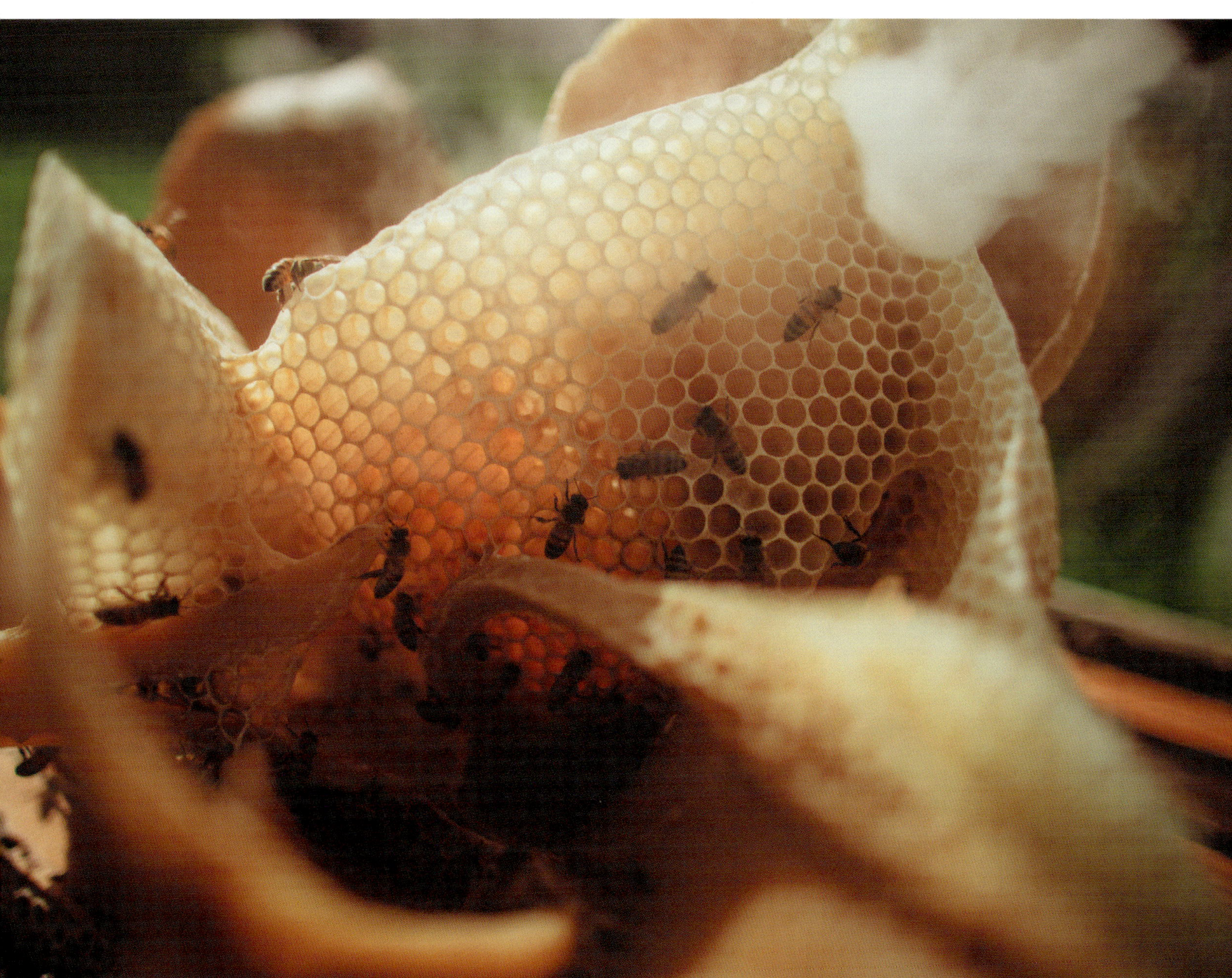

24 ▮▮▮▮▮▮▮▮▮▮▮▮
(b. 1982, Santiago, Chile)

Prole, 2025
Single-channel video
8 minutes 47 seconds
Courtesy of the artist

Prole is an 8-minute and 47-second single-channel video that follows a conversation about unionization by day laborers at an indoor soccer game. The video's title comes from the word "proletariat," which can be a derogatory term or a proud affirmation of class identity. The artist, a former day laborer, draws parallels between soccer, the politics of labor, and collective action to reflect on the spectacle of sports and the unseen labor. Apparent in the video are the assimilation and segregation politics that divide Latine communities, making it nearly impossible to form a cohesive union.

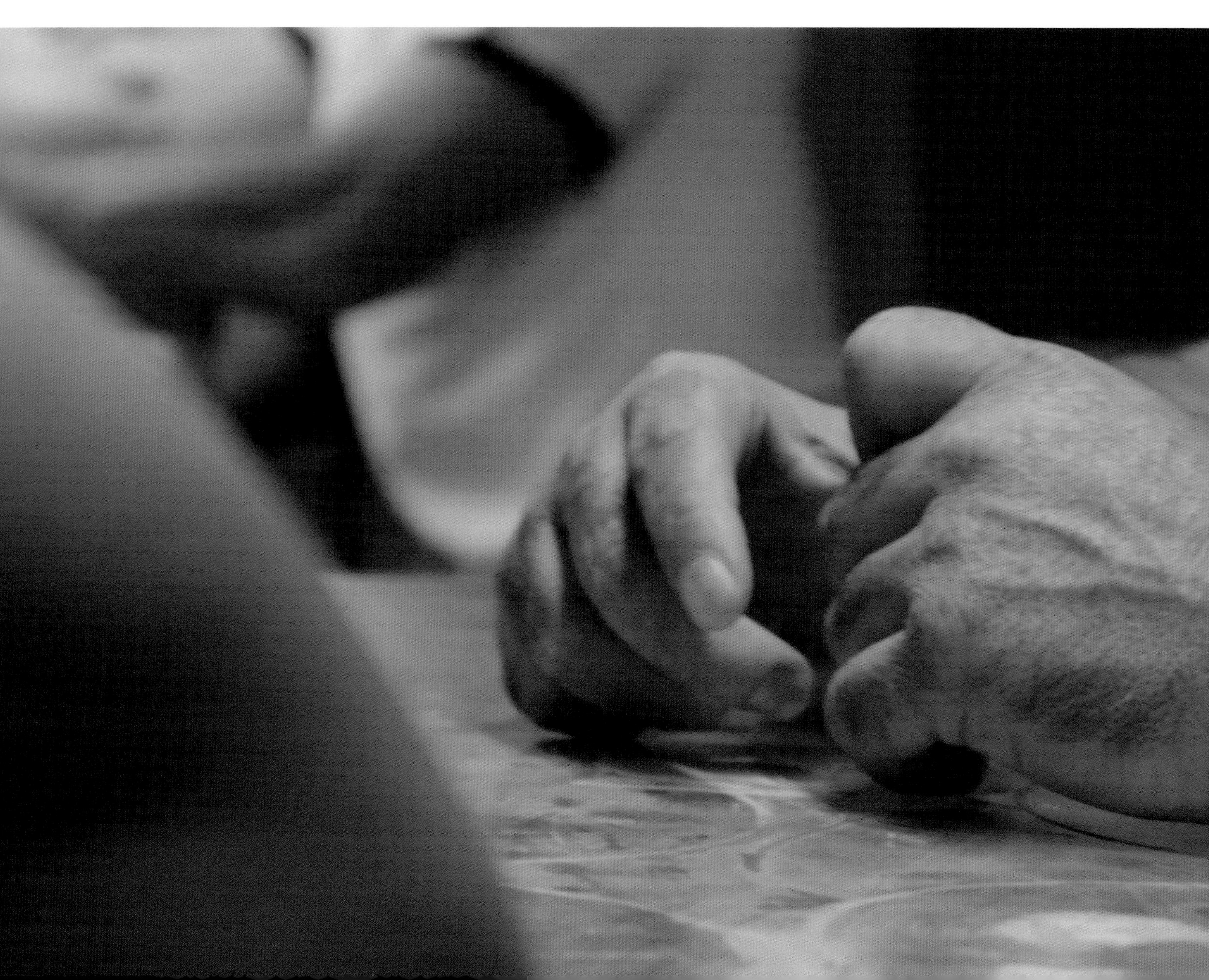

25 ████████████
(b. 1992, Leon, Guanajuato,
México)

Rose Grower, 2021
Archival ink-jet print
mounted on wood panel
101 × 81 cm
Courtesy of the artist

Rose Grower is a full-body portrait of an individual surrounded by pink flowers that echo his plaid red shirt. Although no tools of his trade are present in the image, one can surmise that he is responsible for the flowers growing behind him and the upkeep of the garden where the picture was taken—judging by the dust on his pants and his footwear. The man proudly wears a tejana as he looks straight into the camera. His facial expression shows both certainty and slight discomfort; his stance conveys that he is a regular person, not a posed model.

Although the photograph alludes to labor, it focuses on the individual beyond his profession. The landscape that surrounds him represents the beauty the undoc+ individuals bring with them as they find a new home in a country away from their place of origin, and the special care with which they beautify their sur-roundings—such as the red rose bushes, the lusciously pink Tuscarora crape myr-tle behind the man, or the white flowers in the background that require months of dedicated nurture.

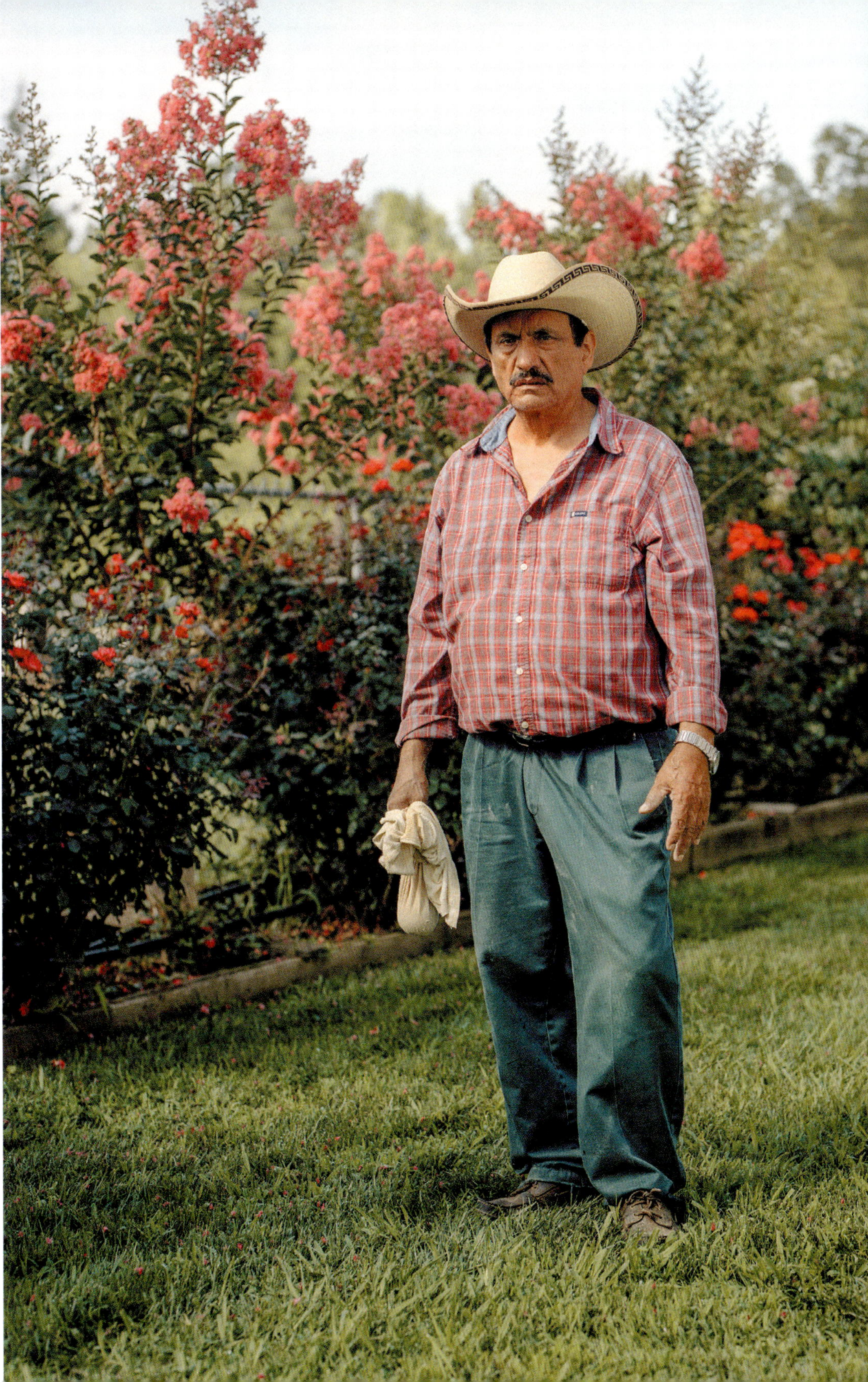

26A ████████████
(b.1985, Quetzaltengo,
Guatemala)

Gemidos de la Tierra
(Wailings of the land), 2020–24
Photograph of the political art action
by ████████
Slabs made of soil from the states
where each individual passed away,
masa (corn dough), salt, and rainwater
on wood and copper
244 × 121 cm (each of 12)
Courtesy of the artist, ████, and
████████ Gallery

Gemidos de la Tierra focuses on the unheard and unspoken stories of perished undocumented migrants. The work comprises a series of wooden slabs on which the artist has inscribed the names of those who had died while in Immigration and Customs Enforcement's (ICE) custody. Each name was meticulously carved and filled with soil collected from the state where the individual passed away. The artist confronted the Detainee Death Report and the Detainee Locator System—both released by the U.S. Department of Homeland Security—during her family's asylum-seeking process. For months, she scrutinized these lists, trying to ascertain the whereabouts of her missing family members after they crossed the border.

Gemidos de la Tierra photographic series, captured by Gina Clyne, archives the political art action: a funerary procession led by the artist to honor the immigrants who had died while in ICE custody. The action began with the artist carving names onto wooden slabs and culminated in a public reading of the ever-growing public death list produced by the Department of Homeland Security. The procession brought attention to the institutions that perpetuate systemic oppression of undocumented immigrants in Los Angeles, and to the organizations that work against it.

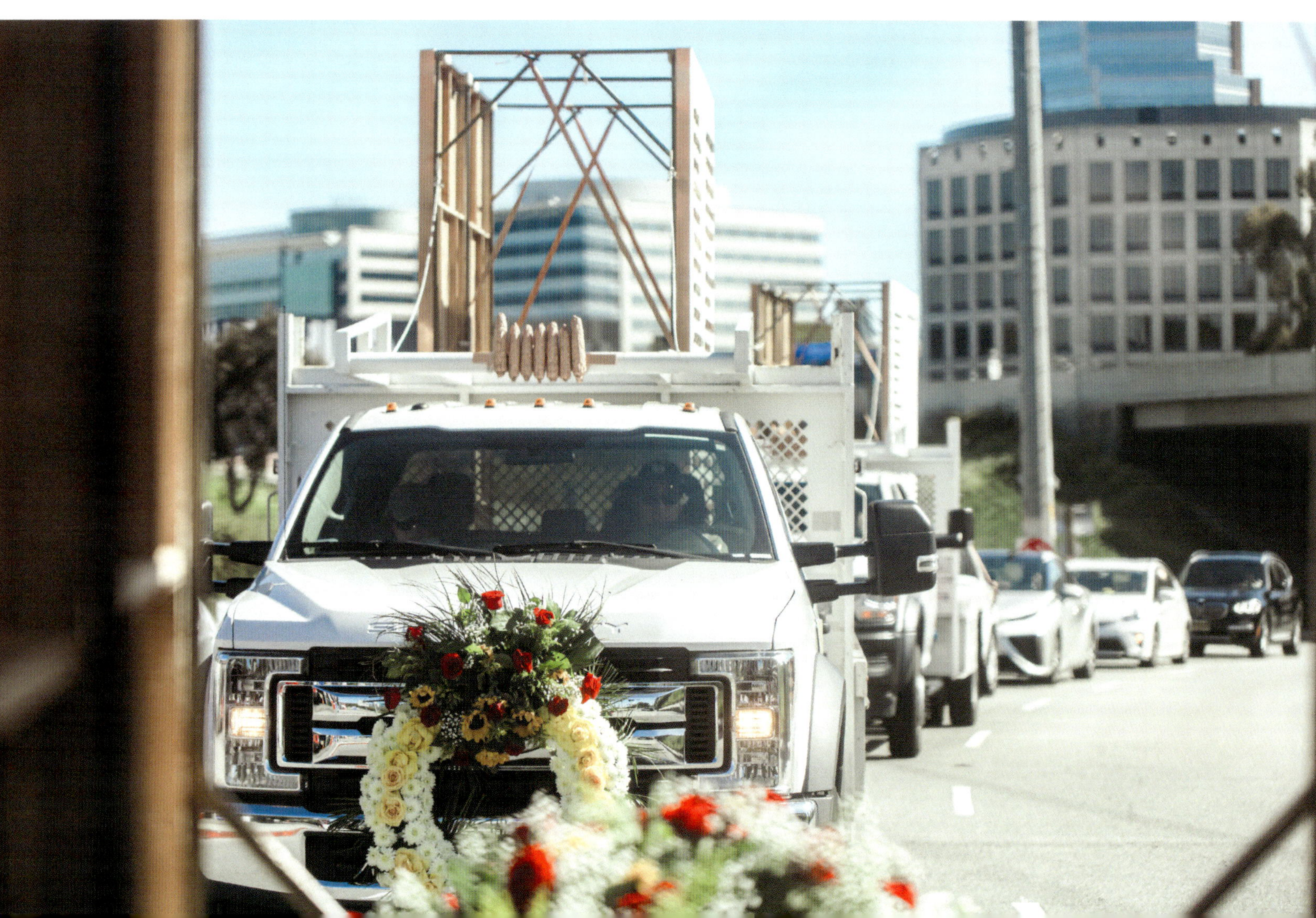

26B

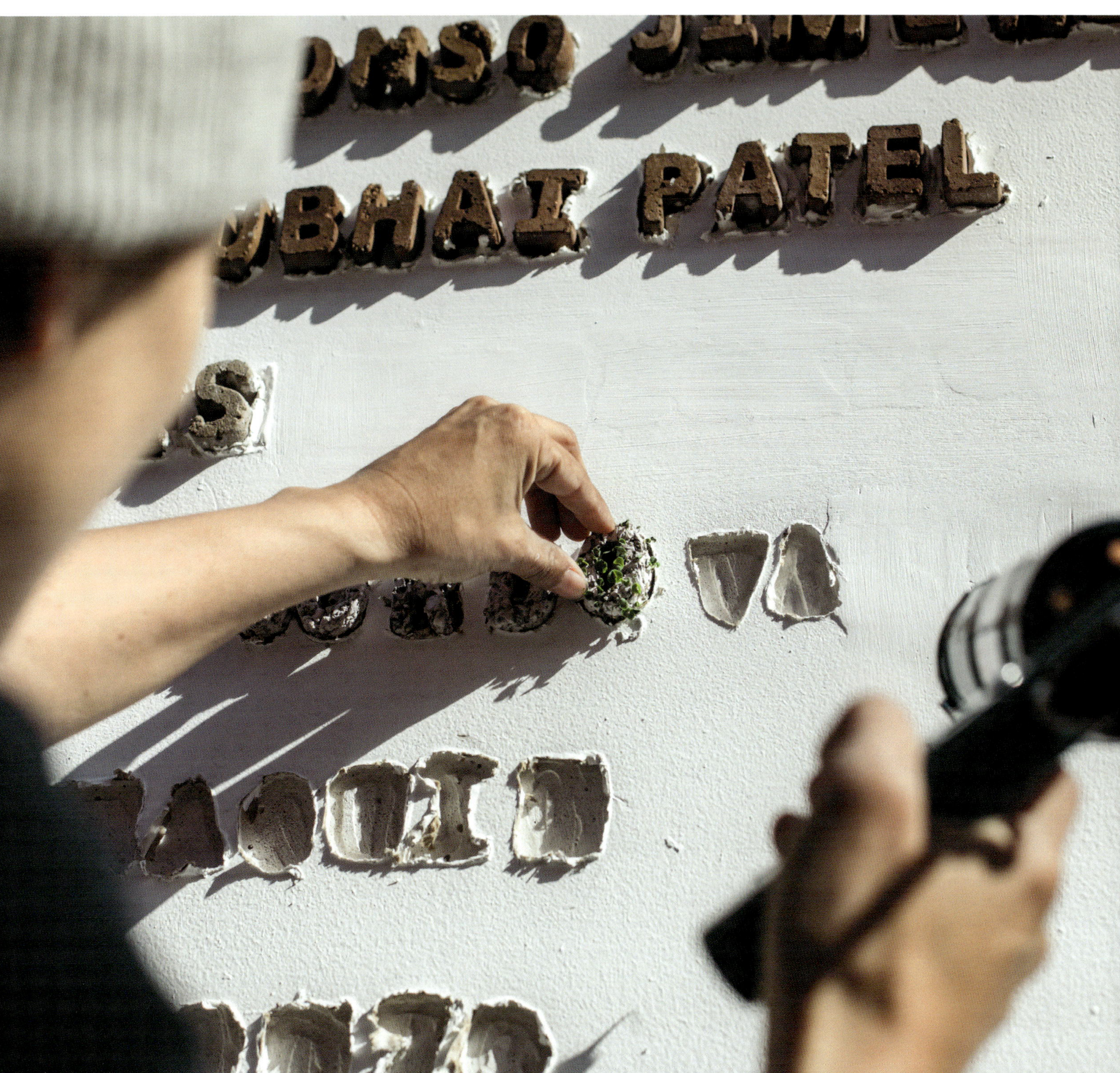

26C

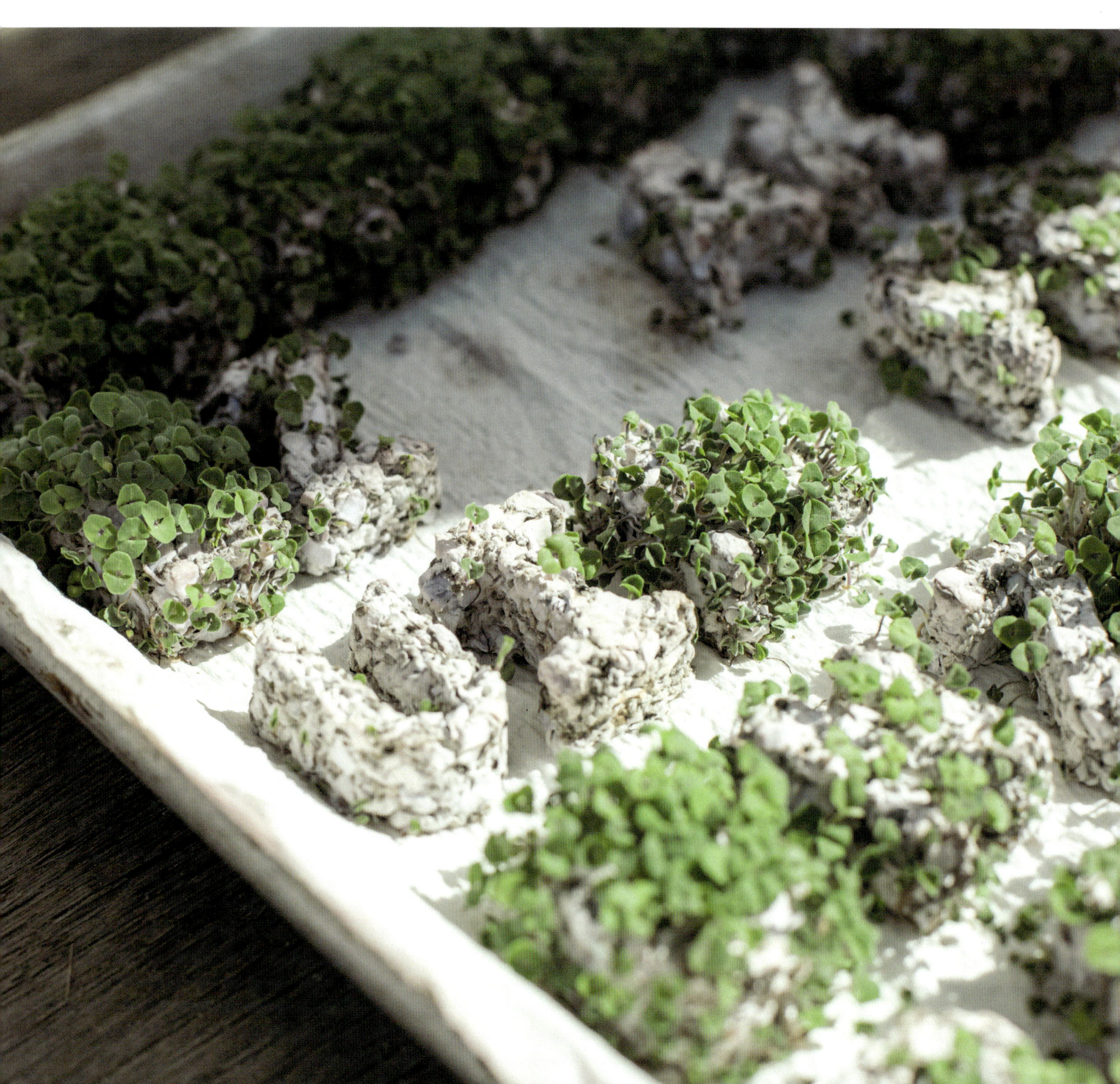

On March 25–26, 2023, the work transcended into political art action as the artist activated the slabs in a procession that wound its way through Los Angeles County—co-produced by Los Angeles Contemporary Exhibitions (LACE) and Los Angeles Nomadic Division (LAND).[44] She began by updating the list of names to include those who died in ICE custody in 2022–23; then rode in a caravan led by three trucks, each transporting four wooden panels recounting the death toll of two decades (2003–23).[45] A row of cars followed the trucks in what felt like a funerary procession. This political art action highlighted the ever-growing public death list produced by the Department of Homeland Security. Over the course of two days, the caravan ceremoniously visited various detention centers and pro-immigrant mutual aid organizations, bringing attention to the institutions that perpetuate the systemic oppression of immigrants in Los Angeles and those who work against this oppression. *Gemidos de la Tierra* sheds light on the many deaths forgotten by the overt bureaucratization of ICE. The artist and her co-conspirator spoke the names of the undocumented individuals who had lost their lives in ICE detention centers, gently holding space for community mourning, allowing members of the undoc+ spectrum,[46] undocumented diaspora,[47] and even the host society to participate in a shared grieving ceremony that highlighted the quotidian realities of undocumented immigrants.

The artist, who is a member of the undoc+ spectrum (as a formerly undocumented immigrant herself), confronted the Detainee Death Report and the Detainee Locator System—both released by the U.S. Department of Homeland Security—during her family's asylum-seeking process. For weeks, she endlessly scrutinized these lists, trying to ascertain the whereabouts of her missing family members after they had crossed the border. *Gemidos de la Tierra* honored the humanity of people on the death lists, in stark contrast to their mere reduction to statistics. While emphasizing the precarity of immigrants' lives in the U.S., the artist also invited new modes of resistance against systemic oppression and exploitation.

Re-indigenization

"Como se atreven a 'descubrir' nos cómo se atreven a clamar nuestro hogar soy pata rajada poque mis pies encarnan la tierra y mi resistencia esta firme."[48]

Tiemperos del Antropoceno: Tenixclanetis Mopayo (FIG. 27) is an intervention in the collection of the Fowler Museum. The artist was smuggled into the U.S. from México. As a cultural bearer away from his ancestral home, he has been deemed illegal, labeled undocumented, and called alien. Today, he is a cultural nomad who smuggles the Nahua ancestral ethos into the new geographical lands he calls home. His installation, inspired by the Carnaval de Huejotzingo, delineates migration and displacement while visually smuggling self-preservation, rematriation (a term used by Indigenous women to describe the process of restoring balance to the world and sacred relationships between Indigenous people and their ancestral land), and resistance into the Fowler Museum. In the artist's words "Somos alienígenas ilegales de otro mundo nómadas culturales contrabandistas, contrabandeados, contrabandeando la re-indigenización. (We are illegal aliens from another world, cultural nomads, counterfeiting, smuggled, smuggling a re-indigenization.)"[49] The work conceptually excavates the museum's holdings to create a responsive installation unique to the Fowler Museum and to think through the re-Indigenization of collected cultural objects that, like the artist himself, exist beyond their ancestral lands. This work converges Nahua cosmology with the folk traditions of Coapan (Cholula-Puebla)—the artist's place of birth—colliding futurity with ancient customs and contemporary artisanal crafts. As this undocreative explains, "you cannot think of futurity without acknowledging the past because we need to build a future where we see ourselves thriving beyond surviving."[50] In this artist's body of work, futurity becomes blurred with the past and the present because time exists beyond a Western lens; it is atemporal and indigenized.[51]

Existing simultaneously in two places and dimensions of time is an immigrant's experience: many of the artist embody a transborder life; navigate the past, present, and future simultaneously; and transcend time and space to reclaim a new dimension that must exist in-between the past and the future, and between identities.

27 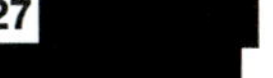

(b.1991, San Francisco Coapan, Cholula, Puebla, México)

Coyotl-Intergalácticx (foreground),
Xochipitzahuatl-Nova (background), 2024
Foreground: mixed media and
intervened found object
213 × 152 × 107 cm
Background: three-channel video
10 minutes
Courtesy of the artist

Coyotl-Intergalácticx (background), *Xochipitzahuatl-Nova* (foreground) smuggles acts of self-preservation, re-Indigenization, rematriation, and resistance—an axis of Nahuatl Indigenous Mexican traditions—into the museum space to spark a conversation about the colonial displacement of Indigeneity in México and displaced undocumented Mexicans in the United States. The project's title roughly translates as "Timekeepers of the Anthropocene: lend me your shawl." The subtitle is often used colloquially in the artist's immediate community to signal a protective gesture of support for one another.

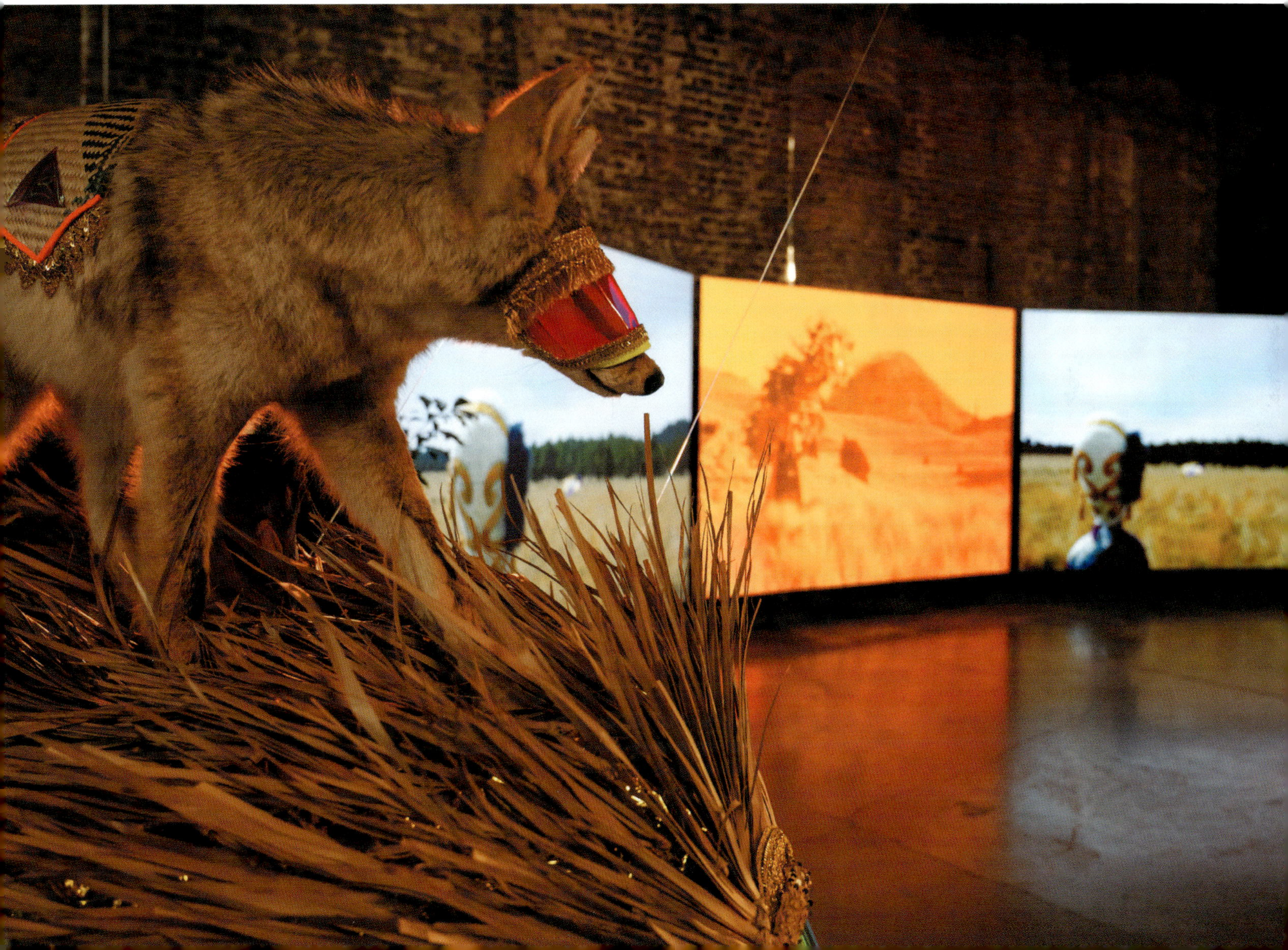

Healing

"The sheer mental, emotional, and spiritual anguish motivates me to "write out" my/our experiences."[52]

Immigrant trauma can affect the mind, body, and soul, and lead to a heightened sense of not belonging, alongside a plethora of other intense physical manifestations. *Alivio y Asilo's Mobil Botanica* and *Echos of Tlaloc* (FIG. 28) focus on healing the undoc+ community through art that is combined with curanderismo. A curandera enters a heightened consciousness in a soul-retrieval ceremony, harvesting soul fragments from the spirit realm. This artist, a curandero himself, spiritually undertakes a soul retrieval, and uses the results to render portrait limpias of his sitters in order to heal their sustos (scares / fears) resulting from woundings, traumas, racism, and other kinds of violations "que hacen pedazos de nuestras almas" (that shred apart our souls)—that split us, scatter out energy, and haunt us.[53] He creates from within nepantla—a space between imagination and physical existence.[54] The same spiritual anguish that motivated Anzaldúa to write, motivates this artist to work with the undoc+ community. His portrait limpias depict members of the undoc+ community. A *Mobil Bonatica* consists of a cart holding a fraction of the objects typically found in a botanica (spiritual goods and services store), so the user can partake in a limpia à la carte. This work is meant to be a play-as-you-go soul retrieval, self-guided by the user's intuition. To engage with the work, the user must gather the objects that speak to their soul, after which a pre-made recording of a soul retrieval by the artist leads the user to a series of prompts and instructions on how to self-perform a soul retrieval. This innovative healing modality is the artist's effort to heal people in the undoc+ community with whom he does not share physical proximity.

Mija, or the things we carry (FIG. 29) also centers on immigrant healing. It uses textiles and a series of found objects to depict mijas[55]—in this case, doll-like figures fashioned of yarn and other found materials that are suspended from a grid-like structure whose fringe holds what a mija carries (physically and psychologically). This work visualizes the internal weight on undocumented immigrants' shoulders and serves as a placeholder for what weighs heavily on an immigrant's soul. Spiritual healing is but one of the many forms of recuperation that the artists in this publication yearn for and hope to extend to every member of their communities.

28 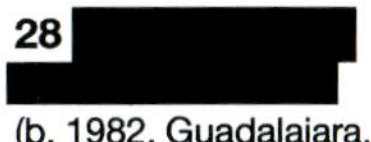

(b. 1982, Guadalajara,
Jalisco, México)

Alivio y Asilo: Mobil Botanica
(foreground), *Echos of Tlaloc*
(background), 2024
Mixed media and intervened
found object
Foreground: 250 × 182 × 152 cm
Background: 304 × 487 cm
Courtesy of the artist

Alivio y Asilo: Mobil Botanica (foreground) consists of a cart that
holds a selection of objects typically found in a botanica (spiritual goods and serves convenience store), inviting the viewer to
take part in a limpia a la carte. Limpia is a ritual performed by a
curandera who seeks to heal the client of ailments plaguing their
mind, body, and soul. It generally uses natural materials, such as
incense and flowers, including rue, basil, marigolds, and rosemary.

This play-as-you-go limpia is to be guided by the user's intuition, with
the help of the artist. To engage with the work, the user must gather
the objects that speak to their soul, after which a pre-made recording
of a limpia meditation by the artist will lead them through a series
of prompts and instructions on how to self-perform this ritual. The
innovative healing modality is the artist's effort to heal people in the
undoc+ community with whom he does not share physical proximity.

Echos of Tlaloc (background) is a spiritual portal made of imi-
tation cobijas San Marcos (Mexican fleece blankets). The mural-like
structure is meant to open toward the West, the realm of the water.
With this work, the artist seeks to gather the healing properties
of Tlaloc (the water deity in Mexica cosmology). These works are
offerings the artist provides as gifts to the spirit realm in return for
guidance and healing of his community.

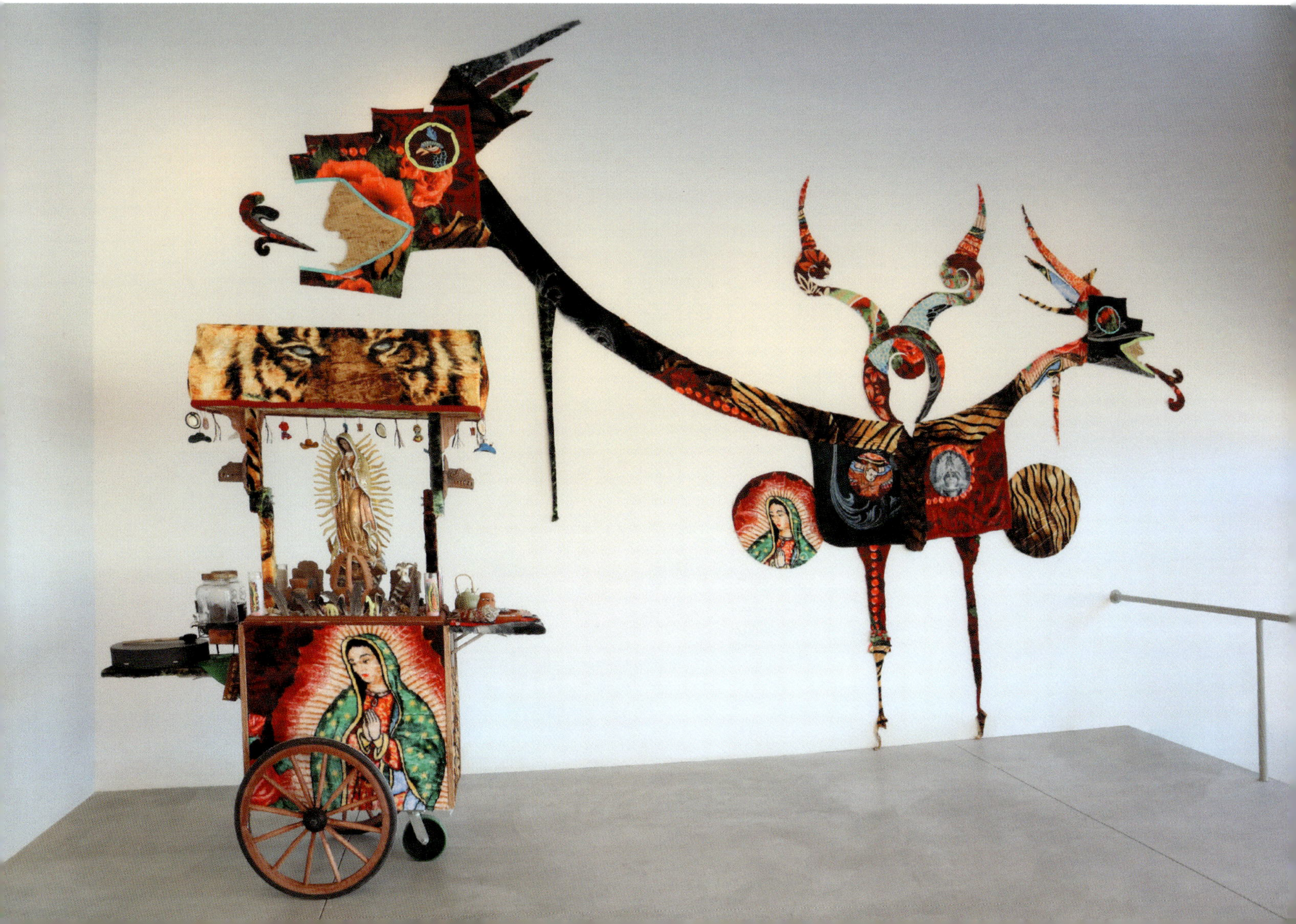

29 ████████████
(b. 1992, Nuevo Laredo,
México)

Mija, or *The Things We Carry*, 2025
Nylon cord, hardwood dowel, rosaries,
yarn, gold wire, found objects, beads
182 × 121 × 15 cm
Courtesy of the artist

Mija or *The Things We Carry* centers on immigrant healing. Mija is a term of endearment by which elders refer to females in Spanish. This artwork uses textiles and found objects to depict mijas—in this case, doll-like figures fashioned from yarn and other found materials and suspended from a grid-like structure that holds them in place. That same structure's fringe holds several small found objects that point toward that which a mija carries. This work makes visible the internal weight on undocumented immigrants' shoulders and serves as a placeholder for that which weighs heavily on a mija.

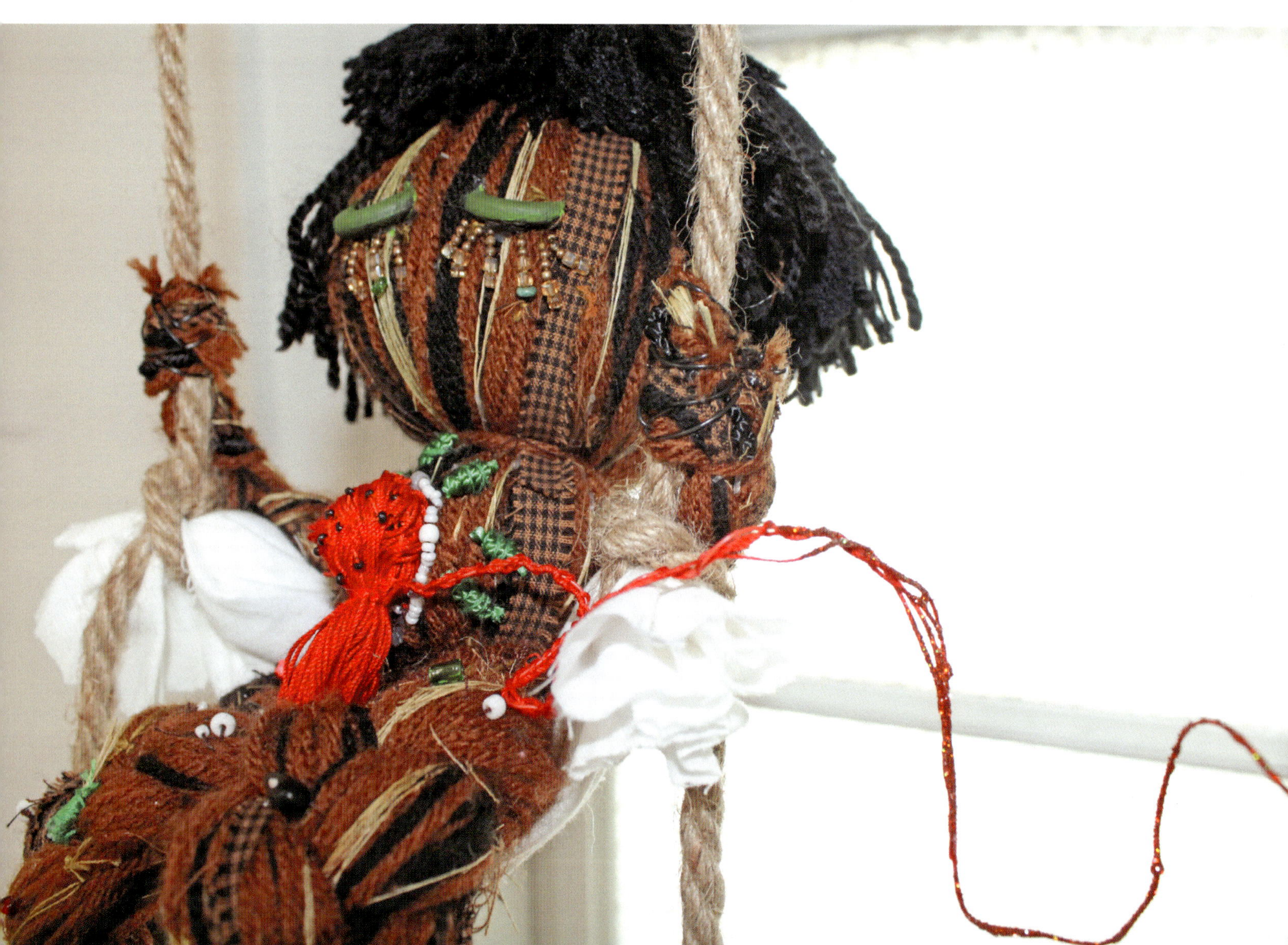

Imperfect Solidarities

"Exile is neither aesthetically not humanistically comprehensible."[56]

This component is anchored by the works of an artist who is a triple exile from Shiraz, Iran, having left his family and motherland over 14 years ago.[57] His work simultaneously signals the basis of his ancestral faith (peace, harmony, tolerance, ethical conduct, and unity through art) and visually challenges Said's quote above. With *Door of Exile* (FIG. 30), *Untitled* (water vessel on oil vessel) (FIG. 31) and *Untitled* (citizenship game) (FIG. 32), this artist aesthetically conveys that which, for Said, was not comprehensible. *Untitled* (citizenship game) invites viewers to play "American." On top of a Persian rug, he places the Monopoly game (United States Army edition), toy soldiers, and the United States Naturalization Test flashcards.[58] Playfully, he problematizes the "American" construct as people are encouraged to quiz each other on the history and civic components of the U.S. or just enjoy Army Monopoly.[59]

What collides in these artworks are decades of political conflicts between Iran and the United States, complicated by the U.S. role in the overthrow of a once democratic Iranian government for economic gains (the decades after the 1953 Iranian coup d'état were marked by the lack of socio-political autonomy for Iranian people). In this artist's words, "there is no place more distant, politically, geographically, and metaphorically, than the place I now call home, which is also responsible for my exile."[60]

30 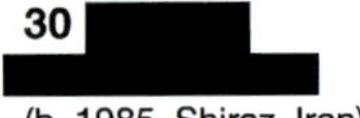

(b. 1985, Shiraz, Iran)

Door of Exile, 2024
Persian handmade carpet, steel oil
barrel, resin, photo paper, and
medium-density fiberboard
304 × 234 × 101 cm
Courtesy of the artist

Door of Exile is a conceptual portal: a black metal arch fabricated
from flattened oil drums that have been riveted together. Behind it
we see a partly obscured Persian rug in shades of red with intricate
designs. The artist, an exile from Shiraz, Iran, left his family and
motherland many years ago. The rug was a gift from his sister (who
lives in exile in the Netherlands) and holds footprints from their
home and family memories of the time before their departure from
Shiraz. Resin drips from the flat pedestal that serves as an entry-
way into the sculpture; this blackish-red liquid alludes to spilled
blood and histories of exiles.

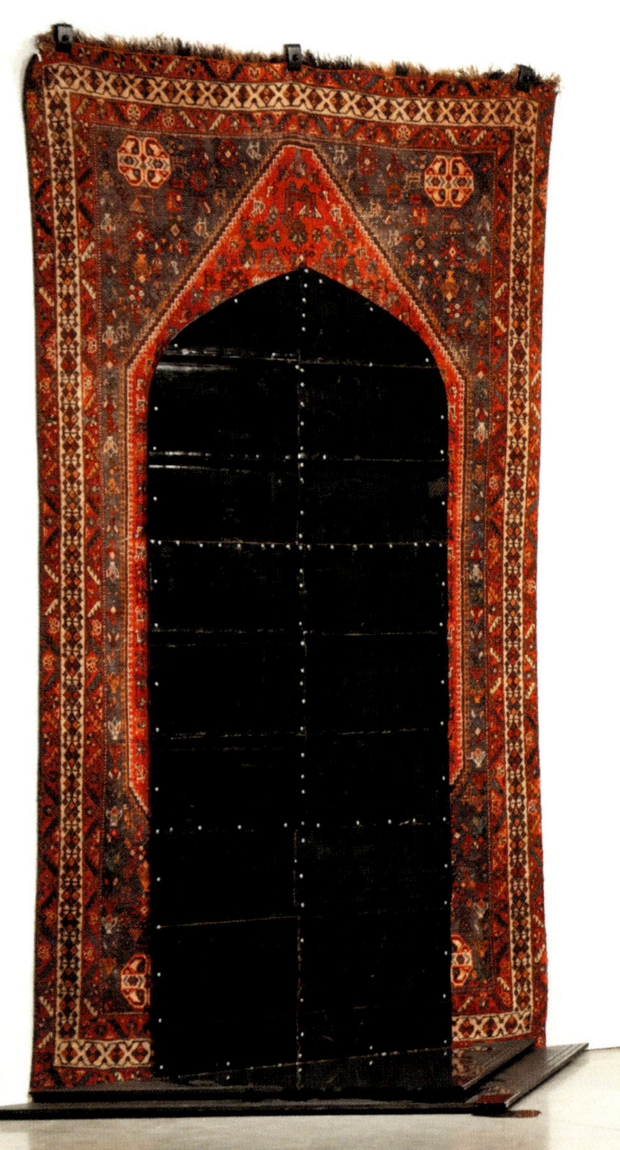

31 ████████████████
(b. 1985, Shiraz, Iran)

Untitled (water vessel on oil
vessel), 2023
Clay, steel oil barrel, and CIA
documents (related to 1953
Iran coup)
158 × 61 × 61 cm
Courtesy of the artist

Untitled (water vessel on oil vessel)
comprises a hand-built clay arch the
color of the artist's flesh; a freestand-
ing rusted oil barrel; and a ceramic
water jar above it made of clay that
has the same color as the arch.
Inside the ceramic vessel are shred-
ded documents related to the Iranian
coup d'état of 1953, orchestrated by
the CIA, which removed a democrat-
ically elected prime minister and the
first Middle Eastern leader to attempt
to nationalize their country's oil. The
coup set in motion political events
that led to the artist's life in exile.

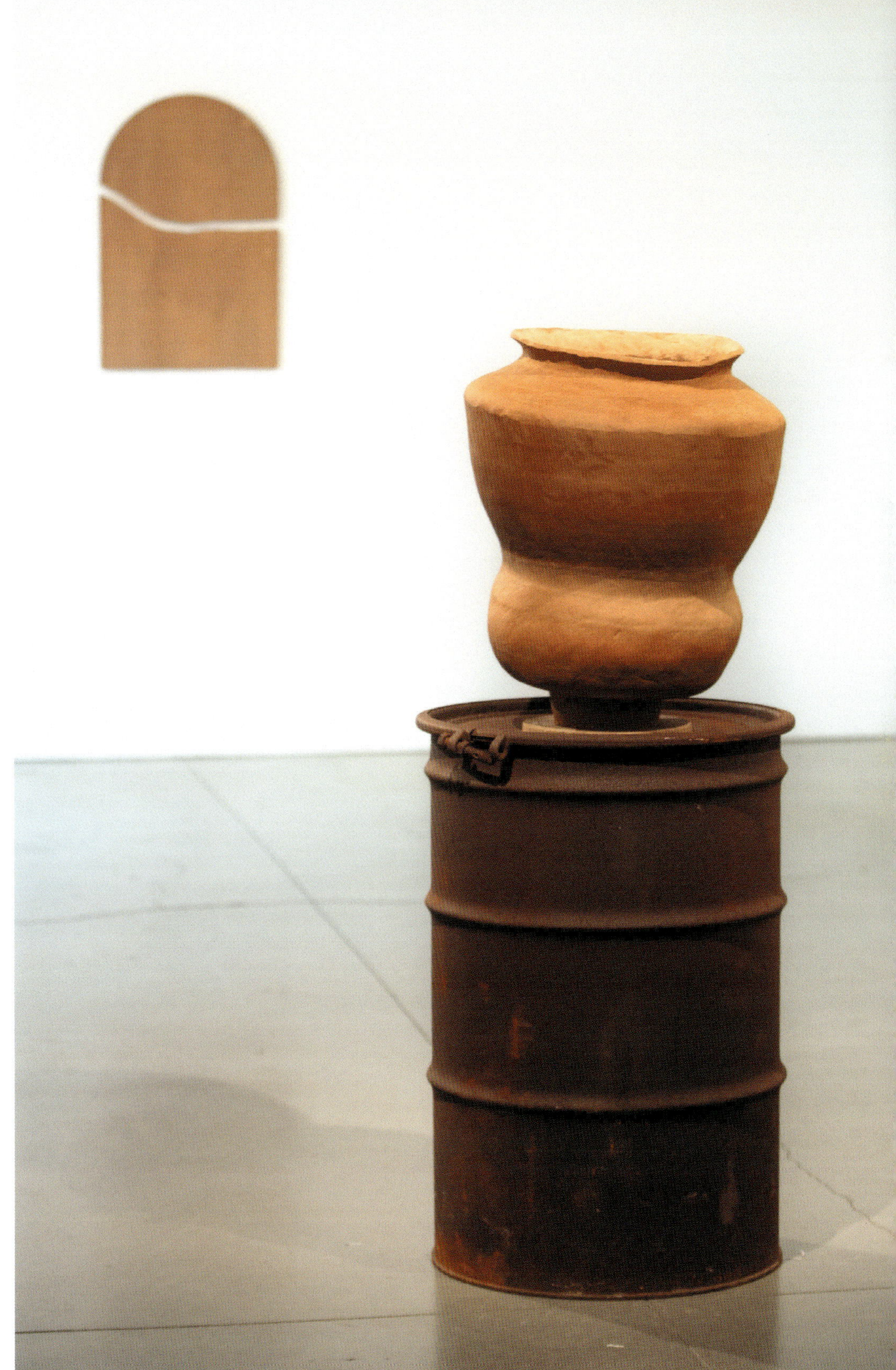

32 ███████████████
(b. 1985, Shiraz, Iran)

Untitled (citizenship game),
2023
Persian carpet and found
object (board games and
citizenship test cards)
144 × 245 × 30 cm
Courtesy of the artist

Untitled (citizenship game) turns
Americanness into a game. On top
of a Persian rug, the artist placed a
Monopoly game (United States Army
edition), toy soldiers, and the United
States Naturalization Test flashcards.
Playfully, the artist problematizes
the construct of an "American" by
encouraging people to quiz each
other on U.S. history and civics; or
they can just enjoy the Army Monopoly, playing with toy soldiers, tanks,
and other war machinery.

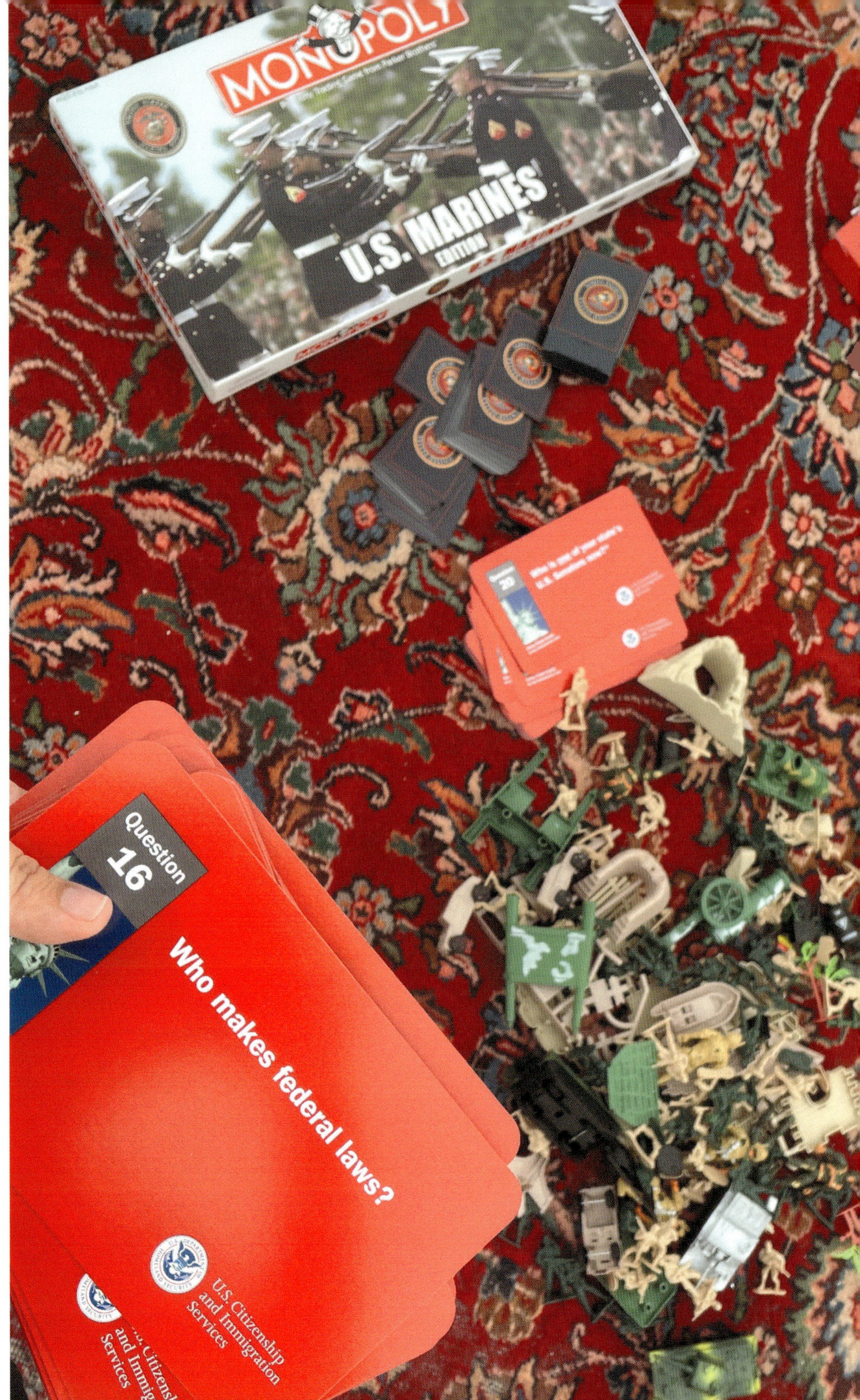

Conclusion

"The right to opacity stands in opposition to Western ontology's demand for transparency."[61]

D'Souza proposes understanding the world beyond binaries, where political solidarity can exist and embrace human interconnectedness as defined by a respect for opacity—an opacity that for Glissant was emancipatory and for D'Souza stands in opposition to the Western demand for transparency. The exiles, refugees, and undoc+ artists joined together in *(in)visibility* communally decided to conceal their identities to protect those who are legally powerless against the U.S. government—to stand together in imperfect solidarity. All these individuals have a complicated relationship with their place of birth and the country they now call home. They share a deep connection through longing, remembrance, and hope for a future free of assimilation, hyperdocumentedness, and the heaviness of immigrant trauma carried by those who live beyond their ancestral lands.

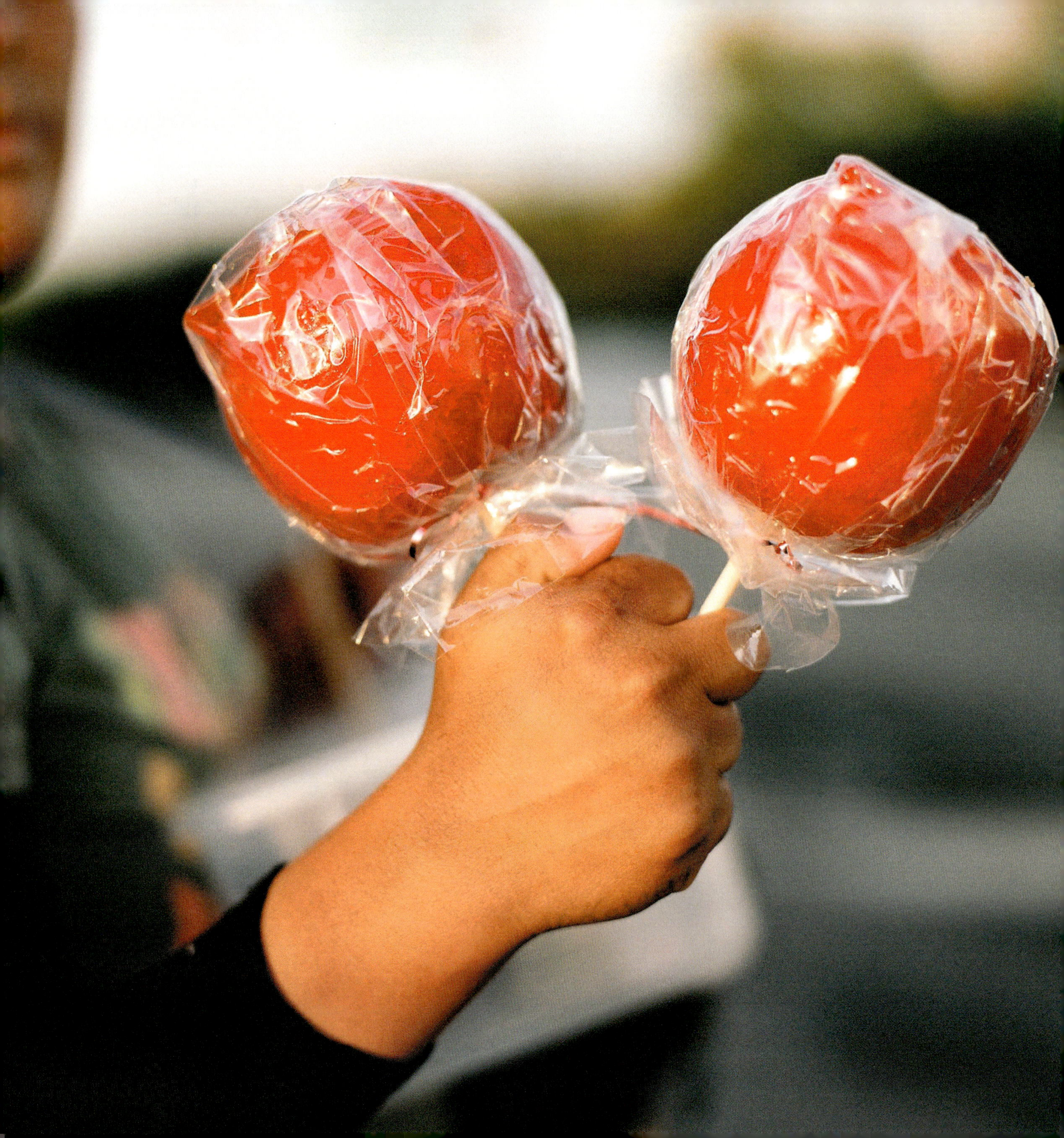

For Once I Do Not Feel Like an Outsider AUTHOR

Untitled (Candied Apples Vendor), 2024
Archival ink-jet print
40.5 x 51 cm
Courtesy of the artist

When I first encountered the works presented in *(in)visibility*, I was reminded of Félix González-Torres' "Untitled" (Portrait of Ross in L.A.), a conceptual composition of candy piled many feet high.

Guests were instructed to partake of the sweets, which represented the declining health and weight of González-Torres' beloved who was dying of AIDS. The installation featured in this volume and titled *Mantel que cruzo la frontera de ida y vuelta, y mi hermana no* (FIGS. 3 AND 33)—centered on a tablecloth created by the artist's sister in México and imbued with the sweetness of its bright polychrome embroidery—evokes in me a similar response: an intensity of feeling brought out by the seemingly innocuous nature of the work. The tablecloth's cheerfulness belies the sorrow imbued in each stitch: it had been shipped to the U.S. to be used in

33 ▮▮▮▮▮▮▮▮▮▮▮
(b. 1981, Atotonilco El Grande,
Hidalgo, México)

*Mantel que cruzó la frontera, de ida y
vuelta, y mi hermana no* (Tablecloth
that crossed the border back and
forth, but my sister didn't), 2020
(SEE ALSO FIG. 3, P. 25)
Video on embroidered tablecloth
Video: 9 minutes 18 seconds
Artwork: 340 × 183 cm
Courtesy of the artist

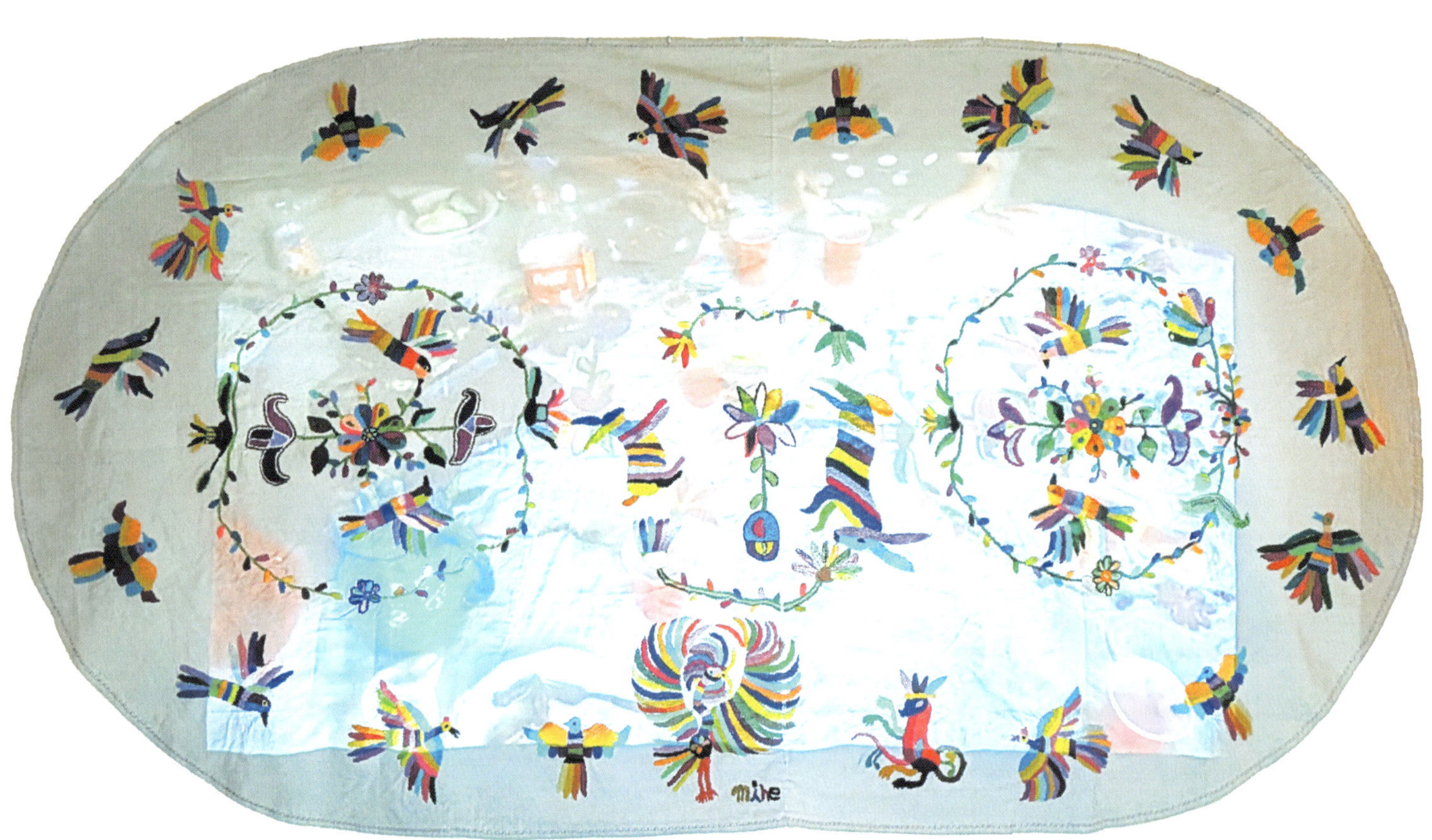

an installation, while its maker was not allowed to join her family here. Families separated by borders, mine included, always experience this two-fold pain: one of the absence itself and another when the mechanism of the border prolongs it.

The first time I was able to return to México and come back, I brought with me things that could have been shipped. But upon returning, I brought something I could have never imagined. A cousin whose father passed after my leaving, whom she had not seen in decades, held me and held me longer because she said I had held him and still carried his touch. She wanted to touch a memory of her father through the brief interaction I had with him. Maybe one day she will at least get a chance to visit his grave. For some, the only way to return is in a casket.

And so, this begs the question: what does it mean that objects are free to move between borders, unburdened by the violence of the state, while people (those still alive) cannot? *Mantel que cruzo la frontera de ida y vuelta, y mi hermana no* expands the definition of touch that extends beyond the body. The sister, unable to cross the border herself, is both present and absent through every saturated color thread she has carefully chosen, and every shape she has laboriously embroidered.

The U.S. can permit work by artists from countries they deem as "other" to enter, but often not the artists themselves (as in the case of the tablecloth) because the capital involved in global trade receives priority over people, and creations are severed from the (dehumanized) creators. While the tablecloth was allowed to cross the border, the artist's sister could not because the state, as it always does, tears things apart.

Such is the logic of relics, of objects that are infused with a sacredness not because of their own physical nature, but because of what they touched, because of their context and associations. We understand a relic to be a bridge—a border we can cross—to the touch of the body that was holy or personally dear to us. To eat at a table covered by this tablecloth is, for her loved ones on the U.S. side of the border, the closest thing to sharing a meal and a space with a beloved sister whose labor is permanently embedded in the cross-stitched patterns that now bespeak both family love and wreckage. Were you to sit down with the artist's family and share a dinner set on that tablecloth, the food (although served from the same pot) will always taste different in your mouth than in the family's, whose every bite will be tinged with grief.

There are certain things that we, the undocumented who have been hurt, would rather not share with the public, things that we need to keep private. And it is this privacy that both holds together and isolates us.

Recently, I participated in a short Zoom writing/creating session for undocumented artists of all kinds. I was at a loss for words to describe the feeling of being in community with other people who knew exactly what I have gone through, for whom I did not have to contextualize or justify anything because they all understood my suffering. The moment was so precious, it almost felt fragile, as if a small breeze could blow it away. It made me almost want to hold my breath so as not to scare away that precious sense of belonging.

A therapist once told me that I had a tendency to sabotage good fortunes that came to me because, even when rightly earned, such prospects were rare and unfamiliar. She told me that I did this because it was my body's way of aligning the patterns that I knew best from experience: dismay. It's how I brace myself for the inevitable disappointments that befall me at the hands of the institutional powers of government documentation. Maybe I have been too alone in my thoughts, racked by the fears that come with being undocumented, to find comfort even in the blessing of community. But if I could compare this Zoom gathering to anything, it would be akin to the dinner the artist performed with his family once the tablecloth had made it to their side of the border. We knew that, even on Zoom, our words were laced with the sense of distance from those we loved who always felt both present in spirit and absent in reality.

There must be a word for the feeling you get when you recognize in a work of art a part of yourself that you have buried not only from others but yourself. You could call it sublime, or surreal but these are inadequate. The word must be a synonym for the verb that both holds your body together when looking in a mirror and parcels your likeness into unrecognizable pieces. Such is the trouble with words: they always fall short.

As someone with a range of experiences on the undocumented spectrum, to hear someone else voice something that you could not say for fear of the real legal consequences behind such a confession, or to encounter the visual object that conveys that absence, is almost like staring at something too bright to see. Once, when I was driving in the car with my mother, a song came on the radio that my father used to sing before he was deported. I quickly turned it off but not before it made its presence known and so, there was nothing to do but to cry as we felt the brief touch of his hand on our shoulders. And then it was gone. It is difficult not to want to avoid those moments of acute longing, so I can only imagine what the ritual of breaking bread over an object made by the inaccessible loved one, which conveys the bittersweetness of their touch, feels like. Outside of the family unit, those moments are rare.

So rare are these spaces of shared experiences that when you enter them, they almost do not feel real. Even as a writer and editor who engages often with others' artistic representations of their experiences of being undocumented, I still find that I retreat into what I know best: hiding the parts of myself that hurt, the ones that are easiest to hurt.

Because so much of our lives is spent in hiding, in not saying more than what is necessary, in isolation, when we at last feel ourselves seen, *really seen* and in the presence of each other, it is easy to retreat into

(b. 1966, Toluca, México)

Untitled (detail), 2025
Embroidery thread, sequins,
and beads on found object
121 × 152 cm
Courtesy of the artist

ourselves because that isolation is so familiar, so habit-
ual. I do so after every publication I release, after every
editorial endeavor I thrust myself into—because being
undocumented has meant approaching things from the
outside, not from the center. I am comfortable orbiting
on the periphery because that is the only place where
I have some chance to control what others see and
know about me. But such works as those collected in
this volume move experiences like mine to the center,
to the kitchen table, among those who understand. For
once I do not feel like an outsider.

Someone said that my own work felt unresolved.
And in my head, it did not occur to me that that was the
point; that my family's travails and junctures of departure are not, and perhaps cannot be formally "finished"
in a way in which we normally understand the concept
of "finished." It feels like there is no end in sight. I know
that this art piece—this tablecloth—is not an end point, a
culmination. It is not a recollection after the fact, because
the pain is ongoing, sometimes never to be resolved.

A mentor of mine said that art is always larger
than our definitions of it. I do not know how to define
the feeling I had when I faced the tablecloth and the
installation. But I know it is powerful because it contin-
ues to work its way inside me long after I have left its
presence. Which is to say that such art is as much a
process as it is a presence.

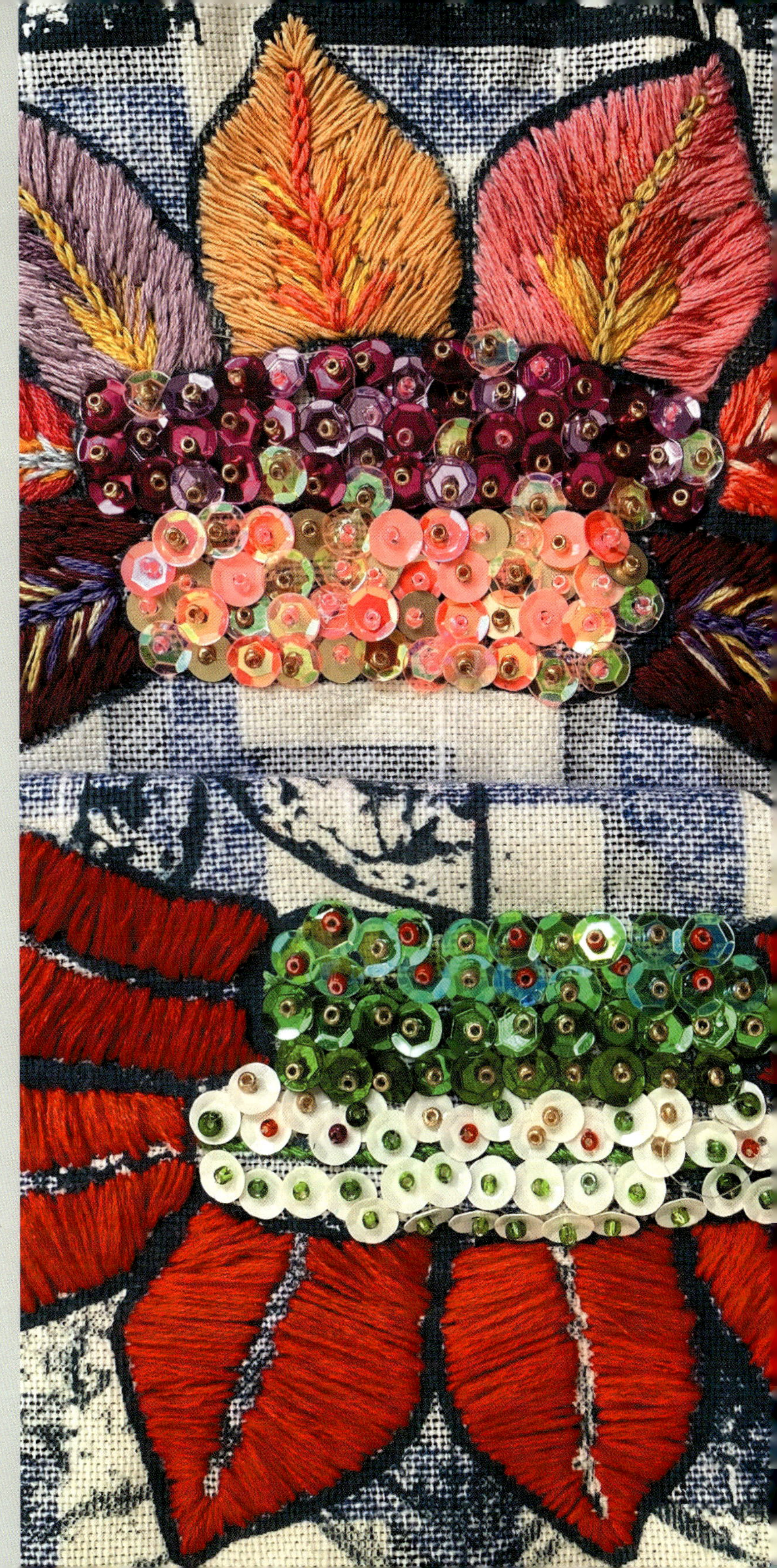

What Does it Mean to Be Documenting the Undocumented? AUTHOR

An undocumented person is, in fact, a strangely documented individual. On that experience, some clarification is necessary.

If this essay is being read by someone who is on the undoc+ spectrum, a term coined by the curator and an artist in the *(in)visibility* project to define those in close relationship to undocumentedness, you may know the following concepts intimately; agree, disagree, cease reading here, or indulge me for a bit. If you are outside of the undoc+ spectrum, you may have heard of what follows from close friends or applied to the undoc+ community by strangers. To this day, I still find people surprised by the bi-annual fee one must pay to remain safe from deportation, known as TPS (Temporary Protected Status). I hope that the reflections below will be equally relevant to those who are aware of the struggles of undoc+ people and others who happen upon them by chance. While I seek to communicate one specific viewpoint, I will attempt to encompass many experiences and make them clearer to a broad audience. I will share my own path to "becoming undocumented;" address the interstitial status of undoc+ people and surveillance / countersurveillance as the undoc+ reality; and discuss "othered cinema" and Third World Film movement. The artworks in this book are informed by these concepts.

When I was just beginning to experience the benefits of schooling under the DREAM Act and received my approved Deferred Action for Childhood Arrivals (DACA), along with an opportunity to use a work permit, I was supposed to go to San Diego, California. Many people urged me not to put myself in danger by being so close to the border—even though the ports of entry and Immigration Customs Enforcement agents would be far from my intended destination. At that time, I also did not know how the world post-DACA worked and was concerned about many things: Should I reveal my status? Does the school have a way to support students like me? Would I be able to meet people in the same situation? Such uncertainty plagued my immediate community, all the more so as rumors of many types circulated among us: they're actually cancelling DACA; they will round up the immigrants on campuses; they're stopping buses and asking people about their immigration status, etc. These worries may have spread some misinformation, but they could also have been a reality. I certainly had no verifiable way of knowing what my next steps might or should be. This long-winded preamble leads to a topic with which many of us are intimately familiar: surveillance.

Entre ciudadano y otra cosa (between citizen and another thing)

The undocumented experience is based on surveillance. When rumors like those I mentioned above spread, people like me feared that some enforcement agent might cast his eye malevolently upon us, a monstruous beast like El Cucuy (mythical ghost-like creature equivalent to the boogeyman); or a curse like el mal de ojo (evil eye) would set in motion a separation or a deportation. I thought, "and who would stop them? I don't know the law, I'm not a citizen, anything could happen." Since the beginning of the policy affecting me when I applied for a work permit and DACA, the label "undocumented" marked me as different from a citizen. Prior to that, I carried the name of illegal alien as a self-directed epithet, funny only to friends and family. Once the United States Citizenship and Immigration Services (USCIS) decided my paperwork was sufficient, I became something between a citizen and non-citizen. The Italian philosopher Giorgio Agamben has argued that from the earliest treatises on political theory, especially Aristotle's discussion of man as a political animal, and over the course of Western thinking about sovereignty (whether that of the king or the state), a notion of sovereignty as power over "life" has been implicit. It remains implicit because the idea of sacrality has been indissociable from the idea of sovereignty. Agamben defines the sacred person (homo sacer) as one who can be killed and yet not sacrificed——a paradox he sees as operative in the status of the modern individual living in a system that exerts control over the collective "naked life" of all individuals.[1] An undocumented person may be likened to Agamben's "homo sacer": existing outside of the rule of law and therefore deprived of its protections.[2] This being, living outside of a sovereign power's jurisdiction, is especially vulnerable because having been reduced to a stateless/less-than-human status, they have no nation to defend them.

Following Agamben's logic, refugees, asylum seekers, and people on the undoc+ spectrum fall outside the state and its protections to varying degrees. Being undocumented also means they cannot leave the country, as they would not gain re-entry, so they remain in limbo, although some have opted for self-deportation to have a say in their fate. A person on the undoc+ spectrum possesses a natural right to exist, just as any living being, but access to the fullness of opportunities can only be bestowed by the sovereign power, at its discretion. Someone on the undoc+ spectrum may, of course, venture outside their immediate surroundings and visit different states in the U.S. and its territories of Puerto Rico, Guam, American Samoa, and Palmyra Atoll, but further movements are problematic.

Agamben's thinking is useful for understanding how an undocumented person dwells in a state of exclusion, inhabiting an unstable terrain because they are caught in that interstitial space between citizen and non-citizen. While such immigrants have few powers, they are perceived as an active threat by a segment of the American population that claims that undocumented migrants intend to take jobs from citizens and thus steal their income. People on the undoc+ spectrum either stay undocumented to the fullest extent or receive additions to their status, such as DACA or Green Card, though their mobility remains unguaranteed. Yet Agamben's concept of bare life can be nuanced: while the undoc+ person may exist between statuses, they are ever-present in the legal sphere and civic life. Sylvia Gonzalez-Gorman counters Agamben's rigidly binary view of a sovereign state as an enforcer of an immutable status quo, noting that "undocumented youth and unaccompanied children do influence federal policy and are not necessarily in a complete state of exception or *homo sacer*."[3] Gonzalez-Gorman found that unaccompanied children and undocumented youth in particular were instrumental in inspiring legal changes in the U.S., especially in bringing into being four statutory documents: the Flores Settlement Agreement (FSA), the Homeland Security Act of 2002, the William Wilberforce Trafficking Victims Protection Reauthorization Act (TVPRA), and Deferred Action for Childhood Arrivals (DACA).[4] Still, many undocumented immigrants find themselves in a precarious and exploited position: they contribute to the economy in a manner equal to citizens, yet receive no corresponding benefits, and remain in danger of surveillance and deportation.

Visible / invisible (visible / ______)

One section in the *(in)visibility* project is titled "Hyper-documentedness." It points to the efforts necessary to obtain legal status—through mountains of paperwork. Another section, "In/visibility," reflects on the predicament of being simultaneously invisible and surveilled. The latter has particular resonance for trans people, who seek acknowledgment and respect through Transgender Day of Visibility, yet encounter risks through it, as visibility makes them targets of violence. I felt some of that anxiety myself when, as I started school, I worried whether visibility would endanger my life in the U.S. and, at the same time, whether I would find other undoc+ students or DACA students specifically who would give me a sense of community and belonging. The question for many is whether the benefits of connection outweigh the dangers of exposure. And what about the role of allies who might be willing to stand with the undoc+ people and even put their bodies between the immigrants and the law enforcement? While visibility can be dangerous, it is also important and impactful. This book, for example, has created a space in which undoc+ artists shed light on their predicament and experiences, making the broader public aware of their humanity and need for understanding and support.

Francisco J. Villegas adds further to these reflections: "It must be said that regardless of the strategy used by… migrants, suspicions about immigration status will arise when they bear markers or signifiers that accord with the current discourse regarding undocumented migrants."[5] Villegas notes that migrants use strategic invisibility: there are times when one should not be in physical proximity to the dangers of protests.

Similarly, any marginalized community practices strategic visibility, one steeped in gestures and summarized well by Juana Maria Rodriguez: "As Latin@s and as queers, we are often represented, if not identified, by our seemingly over-the-top gestures, our bodies betraying—or gleefully luxuriating in—our desire to exceed the norms of proper corporeal containment."[6] The *(in)visibility* represents the interplay of in/visibility by simultaneously highlighting the work of undoc+ artists and concealing their identities for safety.

In keeping with the curator's message of emancipatory opacity, as I discuss the artists in this book, I will assign to them a made-up alien registration number consisting of digits taken from the date they produced their featured artwork. I apologize if the numbers become a distraction, but I wanted to experiment with a form of identification that many people might not recognize. The non-legal usage of "alien" might implant thoughts of (green, grey, or any color) extraterrestrial beings whose reputation may have been tarnished by countless cinematic portrayals of alien abductions, invasions, infiltrations, or destructions. According to the USCIS, an alien number is "a unique seven-, eight- or nine-digit number assigned to a noncitizen by the Department of Homeland Security."[7] Some may find this fact strange or insulting, for a person receiving this number has been de-humanized. But, looking at the naming uncritically may also yield a silly response, or draw comparison with terms such as nerd or queer, which were once seen as insulting but have become common markers readily applied by people to themselves, ironically or otherwise.

Supervision o vigilancia (surveillance)

Alán Pelaez Lopez is another scholar/poet/activist whose work offers useful intellectual food for thought in connection with this project. Their book, *Intergalactic Travels: poems from a fugitive alien*, details the use of self-abjection in fashioning oneself as an alien; and comments on engaging with one's identity as a critique of the U.S. attitudes toward undocumented people. Pelaez Lopez's book is divided into chapters titled: "Unknown," "Undocumented," "Hyper-documentation," "Post-Documents," and "A Future, Elsewhere." Throughout the volume, they weave together origin stories, maps, diagrams, old photographs, collages, newspaper clippings, redacted email exchanges, poetry of various kinds—especially blackout and found poetry. The visual variety comprising each poem—the dynamism of varying font sizes, handwritten scripts, verses that mimic the shape of something described in words, photographs, and drawn artworks—brings the pages to life. The "Hyper-documentation" section in the book presents valuable lessons for undocumented folks and those around them. Pelaez Lopez' journey from childhood in México to adult undocumentedness in the U.S., understanding their body through government-sanctioned paperwork, queer explorations of love and self, and sickness in a country whose CEOs make millions off the denial of healthcare to untold numbers of people, is a magnum opus on the perils faced by individuals on the undoc+ spectrum. The resounding "I AM MORE THAN POLICY" and "Papers will not protect us" stamped in projected words over the artist's body in the book's photographs are powerful and loud messages the artist seeks to deliver despite the need to remain vigilant about dangers posed by ICE, USCIS, FBI, etc. Collectively, artists in the *(in)visibility* project serve as beacons of solidarity; they show us the complex realities of being undocumented, and ways to protest such dehumanizing treatment.

Tools of surveillance and oppression manifest themselves in various ways. Migrants need documents to show that they are sanctioned to cross an established border—papers that mark them as acceptable or trespassing; most migrants are placed into an archive of surveillance by the U.S. governing bodies or escape it and craft their own un-documenting. Facial recognition software has long been used to bolster criminalization (preceded by other forms of visual surveillance in the pre-internet era of carceral archiving and colonial capture); today, its deployment by the police state is accelerating at a frightening pace. Virtual reality and AI are further enhancing these capabilities. But even simpler methods are readily available, be they scrutiny of selfies posted on social media or open hostility by the police state.

In 2013, Steve Mann developed the notion of the Veillance Plane, proposing eight modes of "veillance"—from the French word "veiller" ("to watch"). He wrote that, "(1) sousveillance (undersight) is necessary to a healthy, fair, and balanced society whenever surveillance (oversight) is already being used; and (2) sousveillance has numerous moral, ethical, socioeconomic, humanistic/humanitarian, and practical justifications that will guarantee its widespread adoption, despite opposing sociopolitical forces."[8] Sous/sur are opposites in French and Mann plays on the contrast, for when surveillance gets excessive, sousveillance is necessary to balance it with such actions as, for example, filming the police arresting someone—if you feel safe enough to do so. The undoc+ subjects must constantly deal with being watched and tracked, whether in the workspaces or in public life. The documents they carry have numbers linking them to certain possibilities of status. I have an alien number designating me as an outsider who cannot leave the country that defined me as an alien: my movements are watched and limited to the territories controlled by the U.S. government. These documents are tools of surveillance. Sousveillance, in Mann's view, is justified in a society where surveillance is overused: perhaps through the destruction/rupture of the documents that define and limit immigrants' lives. With these concepts in mind, what does this look like materially? For one, by displaying the type of scrutiny the undoc+ community is under—through vast amount of paperwork—we raise awareness of surveillance we know intimately.

Papeleo (paperwork)

Many artists in this volume engage in gathering papers both as the material of their artworks and their substance, with documents referencing their lives and status. Documentation proving our existence is often gathered in some container (in my house, it is a dusty accordion folder in the corner of a room); and paper is a readily accessible medium for artists (think of how much art and political material is simply a slogan or an image on a piece of paper). As Robb Hernandez and Tatiana Reinoza note, "More than a discursive text, paper is an expressive agent, a social mediator, an exteriorization of latinidad concretized in printed matter."[9] Several creators in this book work with paper, depict "papers" (the colloquial shorthand for legal documentation), and reflect on hyperdocumentedness.

The artist who made *Social Security Card (un) Documented* (2018) (**FIG. 34, SEE ALSO FIG. 4, P. 26**), whom I will designate as A-218-218-218, recreated this highly recognizable object using craft paper and thread, fashioning a replica of a Social Security card, though only its border: there is no number, name, or anything else legible beyond the official letterhead. The potential possessor of this piece becomes (un)documented, thwarting or suspending surveillance. A real Social Security card represents important benefits guaranteed by law to U.S. citizens and each one is assigned a number, which serves as an identification proving that money taken out of one's paycheck will be returned upon retirement. Certain DACA recipients get this card, but with a fine print denying full citizenship and its benefits. What are we to make of a document with the entirety of its official content defaced, effaced, lacking, gone, as if it never existed? This simple but subversive gesture rebuts tracking and the possibility of being seen. At the same time, the artwork gestures toward those who do not have this document at all. The absence of Social Security information where it should be becomes symbolic of something the undoc+ spectrum people experience all the time: a lack of social security. The use of identification forms to track subjects has been traced by scholars to the colonial era and especially to British and Dutch imperialist practices in their subject territories. The dawn of photography further helped to capture criminals visually and store their likenesses as archival records, first in filing cabinets, later in computers. The non-document that prevents legibility is, therefore, a strong statement of resistance.

34 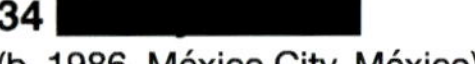
(b. 1986, México City, México)

Social Security from *the (Un)documented* series, 2024
(SEE ALSO FIG. 4, P. 26)
Embroidery thread on Lokta paper
6.35 × 9.5 cm
Courtesy of the artist

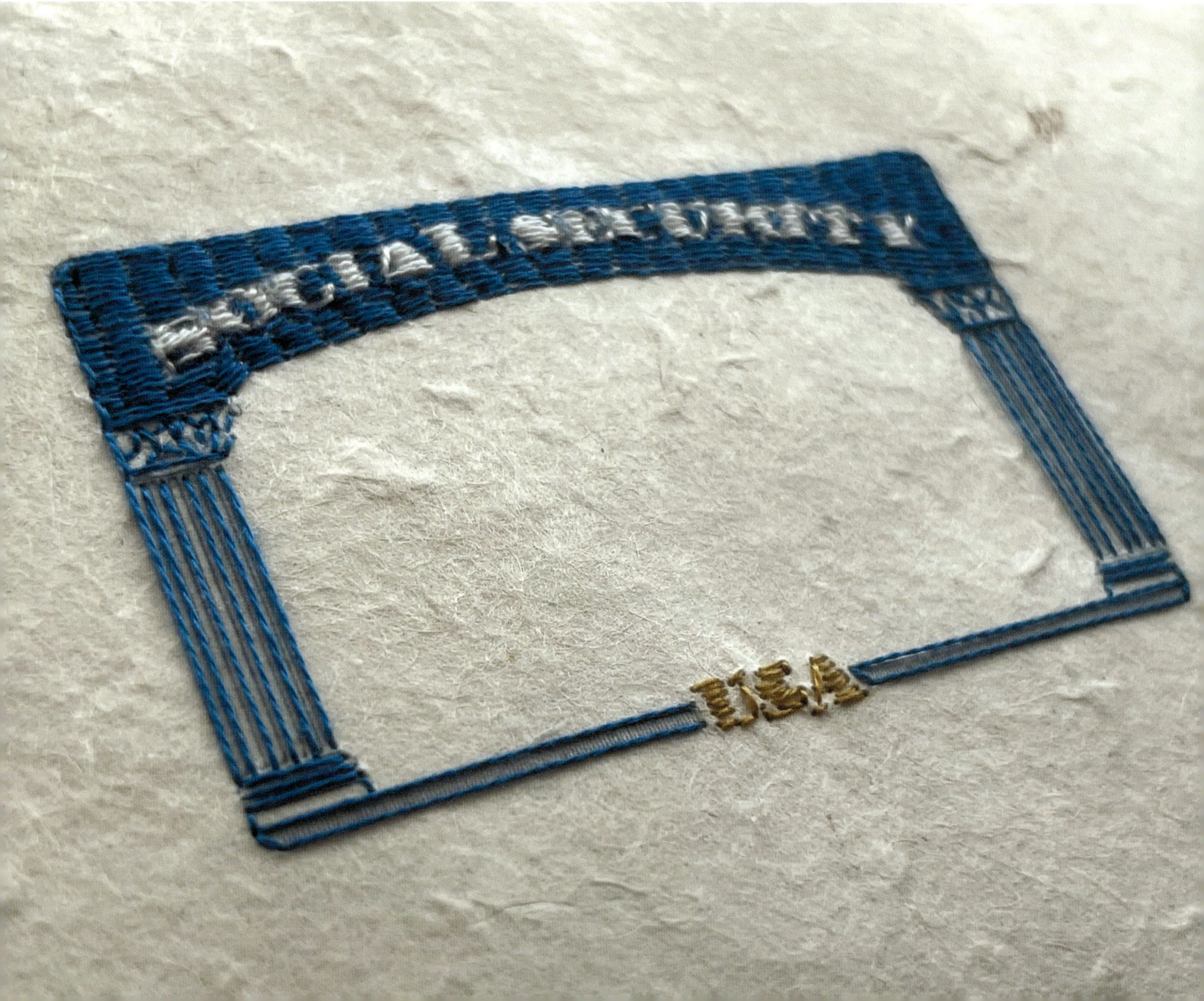

A-217-217-217's *Reoccurence One Liner* (2017) (FIG. 11, P. 50), similarly focuses on a form well familiar to immigrants: I-797 Notice of Action. The layering of documents in this work causes the viewer to shift between the multiple items being represented, while the repetitions in screenprint recall the Pop Art of the 1960s. An invocation of the I-797 form sparks dread in people like me, for I receive this paper in its thinly pressed envelope every two years, from the same processing center. The Notice of Action can carry a wide variety of statements, and at the same time say nothing concrete. It informs the recipient that the form they previously submitted is being processed, or maybe insufficient, or potentially accepted, or possibly denied. While the presence of a $20 bill might mean abundance, when combined with the aforementioned form, the repetition of the money symbol echoes my dread at: 1) the amount of money I send in to renew my DACA documents, and 2) a possibility that my next letter might contain a different message from the ones I have received for the past 12 years. One day, the work permit might cease and my application for renewal might end up in denial. To display the I-797 form in this repeated way conveys to the viewers the experience of the undoc+ people who must engage with it on the government agency's whims.

My own collection of applications and back-and-forth correspondence with USCIS remains in the accordion folder in the corner of my room, but others have more creative modes of record-keeping. Blending playful expression and serious legal documentation, *10-Year-Old Book* (2007–17) (FIG.12, P. 51) is displayed in a recycled wooden box adorned with a metallic creature handle given to A-207-000-217 as a gift. This found-object installation presents a notebook filled to the brim and a gathering of documents ranging from a Social Security card, to a nondescript card decorated with a marijuana leaf, to a fake Resident Alien card. These papers constitute a serious commitment to years-long documentation of a life; meanwhile, the artist playfully turns them into a collage. A series of cut magazine pages features models dressed in haute couture strutting down catwalks toward the viewer; they take up 80 percent of the page while the remaining 20 percent shows where they seemingly descend from: a Mexican pyramid. The artist thus juxtaposes two unrelated realities. Though one might potentially find tourists in similar garb visiting beautiful destinations, their descent from atop a pyramid in heels and blazers would likely be met with frustrated yelling from caretakers and visitors of the place. Collage allows the artist to humorously connect such disparate images. The bulging notebook packed with several unseen collages turns the installation into a snapshot of the total collection of items in the artist's life, some of them serious, others whimsical.

Homeland Insecurity (2023) (FIG. 35, SEE ALSO FIG. 1, P. 17) presents a bleak view of home and its comforts. This installation by A-223-223-223 represents a bedroom that might seem like a sweet time capsule of the artist's youth, but on closer inspection, it is riddled with pages of DACA documents. The artist has covered the repeated wallpaper with cute animal stickers that create a feeling of a cartoon-like space; yet the interplay between the dull lighting and the yellow and pink birds and butterflies induces a nauseating nostalgia. On one side of the installation, we see a chest of drawers covered in pink papers; atop it stands a small CRT/box television, an empty picture frame, and a found object—a cherub statuette. In the center, a small bed assembled from red milk crates and covered with a floral-patterned cloth holds plush animal toys. At right, a small drawer covered in DACA documents holds a wicker lamp whose pale-yellow bulb shines through the slits. At the base of the bed lies a suitcase. In some versions of this installation, it is open, revealing its contents; in others a rope dangles from it; or it is positioned as if just dropped off.

The potentially benign title, *Homeland Insecurity*, is belied by the profusion of DACA documents through which migrants seek to make a home in the U.S. As lovely as this little room might seem—a safe space of comfort—further inspection highlights a lack of a safe feeling typical for people on the undoc+ spectrum residing in the United States. The title's play on words and the cozy-seeming room, which actually reflects profound unsettledness, invites reflection on whether the domestic space (and the institution of Homeland Security) delivers security. This tension between safety and insecurity is highly present in domesticana art practices, a term coined by artist Amalia Mesa-Bains to define Chicana feminist altar- and home-building practices—as a specific departure from the use of found objects and home goods dubbed rasquachismo by scholar Tomas Ybarra-Frausto. "Characterized by accumulation, display, and abundance," Mesa-Bains notes, "the altars allow a commingling of history, faith, and the personal."[10] While there is no uniformity in making altars, something in the artist's wording approximates this room as a personal space of comfort. As the curator of the *(in)visibility* project commented, "Many thoughts crossed my mind, but one that always stayed was, no me quieren aquí (they don't want me here). Even though I tried to escape my life's realities, I always ended up hiding in my room. My childhood room was a safe space, my home away from home."[11] The installation is caught between the insecurity of being a child away from one's birthplace, or wherever home is, and the safety of the newly formed space. I am inclined to call this installation an altar due to its front-facing position vis-à-vis the viewer; a few relics (both the cherub and

35 ████████████████   *Homeland Insecurity*, 2023
(b. 1990, Veracruz, México)   **(SEE ALSO FIG. 1, P. 17)**
          Mixed media on found object
          250 × 130 × 250 cm
          Courtesy of the artist

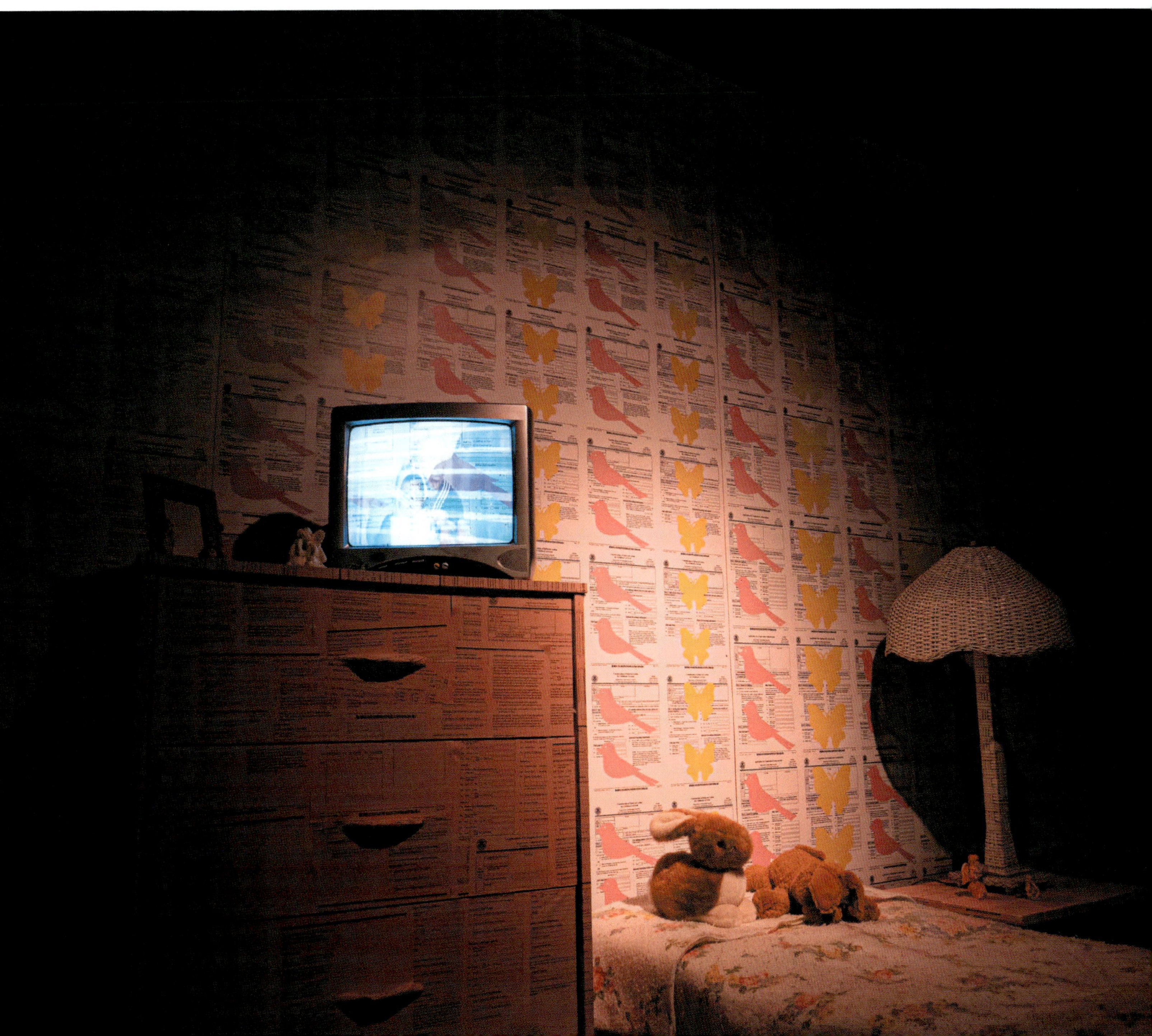

the TV can be counted in this category); and the space of comfort it suggests, with personal belongings, such as photographs of the artist's family, laid out beside the suitcase. In this publication, Mesa-Bains' domesticana sensibility expands beyond Chicana artists to show that this home scene with its mix of government documents and intimate, personal touches conveys the undocumented person's suspension between home and newly crafted space, between what was known long ago and what we must learn to love. Seen from the perspective of Mann's veillance plane, this installation signals the surveillance of immigrants through DACA documents plastered on the walls, the television set with the same documents, and the suitcase that implies an uncompleted journey.

Sácale video (take a video)

Videos in museums and galleries often get overlooked in favor of other artworks that claim more immediate attention. Videos demand more time and patience: one might encounter them midway through their running time and need to wait for them to restart, to follow the narrative. Some people never enjoy them in their totality, put off by their length. I would urge visitors to give those videos a second chance, to increase their attention span and fully take in the content, be it weird, educational, or moving.

Film scholar Erika Balsom speaks about videos in art museums as "othered cinema," a term coined by Raymond Bellour after viewing installations at the 2001 Venice Biennale and finding it difficult to fit them into fixed categories of cinema versus plastic art, and seeking something between those poles.[12] In her book *Exhibiting Cinema in Contemporary Art*, Balsom describes "an othered cinema" as an installation that differs from film yet retains some of its qualities; "boundaries between media are both articulated and blurred."[13] "Othered cinema" has been a subject of debate among certain scholars who wish to maintain the purity or clear demarcation between "art" and "film."

According to Jonathan Walley, "Avant-garde cinema is personal and artisanal, while artists' cinema is collaborative… Modes of distribution espoused are different… Avant-garde [film prefers] rental-based model to the limited edition that dominates the art world."[14] Walley summarizes the different boxes created to separate art and film into even further categories: avant-garde, experimental, limited, art world, etc. The scholars involved in these debates and distinctions are too numerous to address in this essay, but it is useful to know how divided the study of video-based work has become. The artists on the undoc+ spectrum have further complicated these discussions as their art travels between formal cinema, art practice, and everything in-between, prompting scholars to create other, othered, and tertiary terms to define this unruly output.

By "tertiary" I mean the wave of 1960s Third Cinema movements by filmmakers from African and Latin American countries. The works in this genre featured in this volume follow in their footsteps. The Argentinian filmmakers Octavio Getino and Fernando Solanas originally published their manifesto, "Hacia un tercer cine: Apuntes y experiencias para el desarrollo de un cine de liberación en el tercer mundo (Towards a Third Cinema)," in 1969 in a Cuban magazine *Tricontinental*. The authors defined film as the art of the masses and urged people to use cinema not as mere entertainment but as an active tool for liberation; they argued that the alternative to cinema of the bourgeoisie is "making films that the System cannot assimilate and which are foreign to its needs, or making films that directly and explicitly set out to fight the System."[15] "System" with the capital S may refer to different things: in the context of this project, it may be the U.S. government that blocks the path to citizenship for undoc+ spectrum folks, or ICE and the border patrol that thwart people escaping dictatorial regimes or gang violence in their home countries.

For Getino and Solanas, "The capacity for synthesis and the penetration of the film image, the possibilities offered by the living document, and naked reality, and the power of enlightenment of audio-visual means make the film far more effective than any other tool of communication."[16] For us today, YouTube videos and social media valorize the audio-visual medium. Many artists in the *(in)visibility* publication blend media and use personal material to educate or memorialize, inviting viewers to spend time with this othered cinema. Like the Third World cinema, they offer a glimpse from the undercommons, or a view from below, including from the state of sousveillance.

A-202-020-202's installation *Mantel que cruzó la frontera, de ida y vuelta, y mi hermana no* (2020) (FIGS. 3, P. 25 AND 33, P. 86) is equally personal, collaborative, and artisanal: the artist worked with their family members on both the video and the material it depicts. At the center of the work is a white tablecloth colorfully embroidered by the artist's sister who remained in México while her creation crossed the border. Birds of resplendent hues surround the edges, some of them real, others mythical, ranging from hummingbirds feeding on flowers to alebrijes—invented, multi-colored creatures fashioned by Mexican artisans—spreading their plumage; two rabbits prance in the center, flanked by flora and fauna. The tablecloth is a marvel of intricate design as well as a screen for video projection. The artist has asked family members to record short clips describing their lives; one video collage shows the embroidery process; others capture gatherings, parties, landscapes of home, and previous performances by the artist.

The full film details the installation's making, a self-referential and self-reflective engagement in cross-border solidarity. Photos of the family eating around the table covered with the embroidered tablecloth highlight its special place in their lives. Eluding the distinctions between "art" and "film," this collaborative and multilayered work turns the tablecloth into a living object, infused with personality, and the video as a whole into a journey that unites family members separated by the border. This combination of collaborative, documentary, and artistic elements defy precise characterization.

A-215-000-215's film (FIG. 24, P. 68) opens with a view of a cold, gray hallway; the sound of men shouting out playfully is punctuated by a call to "play it." The interspersed bangs and hits are later revealed to be a game of football taking place in an empty warehouse several floors up in the air. Prior to the game, men dressed similarly in white shirts of varying styles sit in a circle and the camera moves around to capture their comments. Seventeen time cards sit in a slot board near a time recorder, as the participants have punched in for their shift; the title card "PROLE" punctuates the start time. Conversations in Spanish, subtitled in English, address such topics as being paid extra for working quickly and efficiently, the differences between Latino and white American bosses, workplace accidents caused by hasty work, and collaborative efforts to unionize with other Latinos (the discussant says "Hispano," but the translation says "Latino"). Between pauses in conversation, the video captures people running around and kicking a ball.

The tone becomes heated when an older man declares that he works like an American and has his papers already, having learned from "this country" (referring to the United States); he proclaims that "we come alone, and no one will help us." The counterpoint is presented by at least three speakers who prioritize the need for union formation for Latino workers, calling out the older speaker for sounding egotistical and like an American (to which the man responds with the only moment of English in the video, saying "yeah!"). A third voice supporting the objection to the older speaker introduces the potential that all workers have, and questions why someone should be exploited because they don't know how to work—an allusion to workers who migrate for jobs and end up performing unskilled labor.

While the video focuses on the speaker with the unpopular mindset of individualism sitting silently and facing downward, the final point in the conversation posits that if Hispanic/Latin American workers do not unionize (both formally and informally in solidarity while working together), they are worth nothing. A man nods as the video fades out. The final shot shows men working together to put all the metal desks back to the center of the warehouse—their last collaborative effort before the screen fades to black. The underlying theme of the film is collaboration, whether in playing sports, engaging in a discussion, or moving furniture. Even the men's shirts are emblazoned with a union logo; the camera focuses on their shirts and the uniformity of their visual presentation.

Only one person in the video is a proponent of individualism that rubs the others the wrong way. By the end of the video, the majority opinion prevails. While different perspectives are given similar weight, eventually, the pick-yourself-up-by-the-bootstraps mentality is rejected by those who propose mutual aid and proletarian union, intimated by the shortened use of that word in the title. As Getino and Solanas remind us, "The decolonization of the filmmaker and of films will be simultaneous acts to the extent that each contributes to collective decolonization. The battle begins without, against the enemy who attacks us, but also within, against the ideas and models of the enemy to be found inside each one of us."[17] The dissenting opinion in the film stands for the type of internal enemy the Argentinian filmmakers warned against in their manifesto.

The collaborative approach advocated by *Prole* dovetails with a call for collaboration across species, particularly between bees and migrant women, proposed by A-223-000-223, whose work is itself a product of a group effort between the artist and two other women in her family. In the following description of the film, Speaker 1 refers to the interviewer, Speaker 2 to the first interviewee, and Speaker 3 to the second one. The film *Con miel en la boca* (2023) (**FIG. 36, SEE ALSO FIG. 23, P.67**) opens with a view of a beehive, its occupants buzzing around. Speaker 1 asks in Spanish, "In what year did you arrive in the United States?" Speaker 2 responds in a slight rasp, "in 1985, in August," her answer followed by a delightful, almost playful oboe riff, which seems to musically represent the meandering flight of a bumblebee moving from flower to flower. Speaker 3 recounts the crossing of the border while pregnant, due to visa denial (interspersed with another jazzy riff); later, she talks about a family member being abused by a man in Colombia where she saw violent cartels, unemployment, and lack of opportunities for upward social mobility. Speaker 2 details her crossing experience, noting the dismal food she had along the way and the boat struggling to keep afloat during her passage in Tijuana, the instructions to not answer the door for anyone (presumably issued by a coyote)—all while the bees' buzzing slowly increases.

The two-channel video bounces back and forth between the artist's two family members recounting their migration paths and fears of abandoning children along the way, the melancholy melody, and the droning of bees. While the bees fly around and the camera follows them now and then, the rest of the time it holds

36 ███████████
(b. 1976, Bogotá, Colombia)

Con Miel en La Boca
(With honey in the mouth), 2023
(SEE ALSO FIG. 23, P. 67)
Two-channel video: 13 minutes
24 seconds
Courtesy of the artist

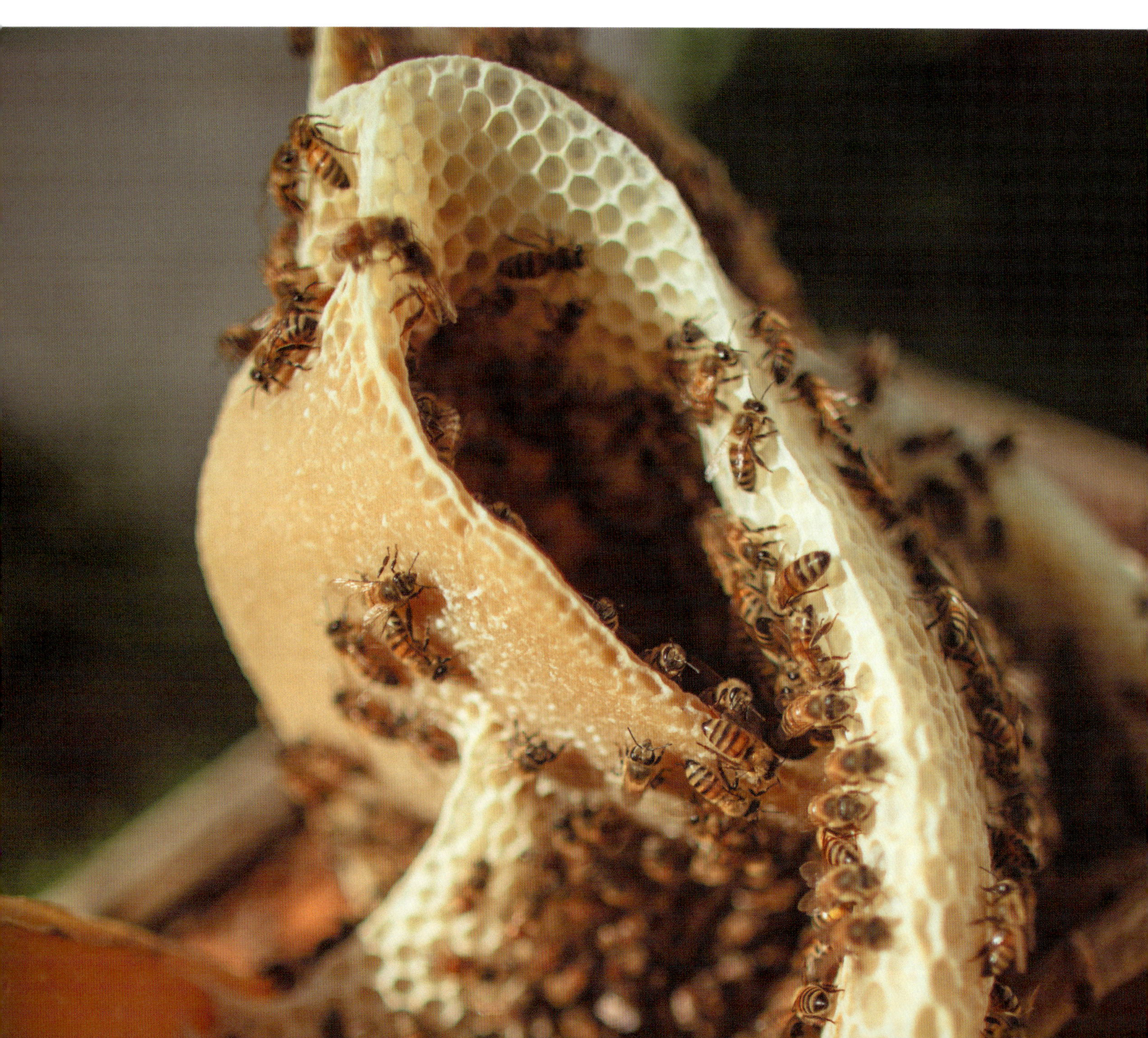

still so that the viewer can focus on the conversation. Midway through the video, soft percussion kicks in as Speaker 3 describes her brief and scary encounter with border patrol: her coyote alerted the group to its presence, and she crammed herself into a car full of migrants stuffed inside like sardines. The woman's journey to Los Angeles reaches its climax after this encounter, as she learned that she would be reunited with her children. Speaker 2 discusses labor opportunities in the U.S., such as working in a factory, packing food, after finding that job listed in a *Pennysaver* magazine; travelling on a bus without knowing if it would take her to her workplace; and noting that her bus trip was guided by compassionate people. Speaker 1 asks, "Do you think you've lived the American Dream in those 31 years [you've been here]?" Speaker 2 responds, "Yes because this country gave my kids what I couldn't give them there." Later, she details the horrifying stories of undocumented migrants getting caught or dying while trying to cross the border, which causes her to cry in mourning for them. The interviewee acknowledges that although she loves her own country, she would not return there. (A similar moment occurs in *Prole*.)

Up to this point, the conversation is held in Spanish. Toward the end of the film, the interviewer asks Speaker 2 if she is American and she replies, "yes, I'm the first one." Then, switching language, Speaker 1 asks, "do you speak English?" The response is a resounding "I know it really well." The difference between this conversation and the one captured in *Prole* is that although Speaker 2 asserts her new American identity, she does not abandon her solidarity with other migrants, mourning those who have died en route and wishing others

safety. Lastly, Speaker 3 discusses her job at McDonald's, where she would take leftovers at night upon the manager's behest. Like the other interviewed migrant, she declares her love for her two countries, Colombia and the United States, noting the humiliation she had suffered, the struggle and honor of working hard and not doing bad things—all while on the screen, beekeepers protected from stings move the honeycombs into boxes for transport. The imagery, the women's stories, the honeycombs, and the sculptures made from beeswax all result from various collaborations.

Con miel en la boca engages with the vital pollinator to tell the story of women who have travelled from place to place in order to establish a better life despite their love for their birthplace and the place where their family began. The film's use of bees as an allusion to migrants echoes the adoption of butterfly imagery by undoc+ folks as a symbol of long-distance migration spanning the Americas. Even the champions of these insects can be as endangered as the animals, as the murder of conservators of the Monarch Butterly in México, Homero Gomez Gonzalez and Raul Hernandez Romero in 2020, demonstrates. A-223-000-223's piece offers a hopeful view of cross-species work. The *(in)visibility* volume similarly conveys not only the hardships of people on the undoc+ spectrum, but also their hopes, particularly for unity, solidarity, and productive life in the U.S.

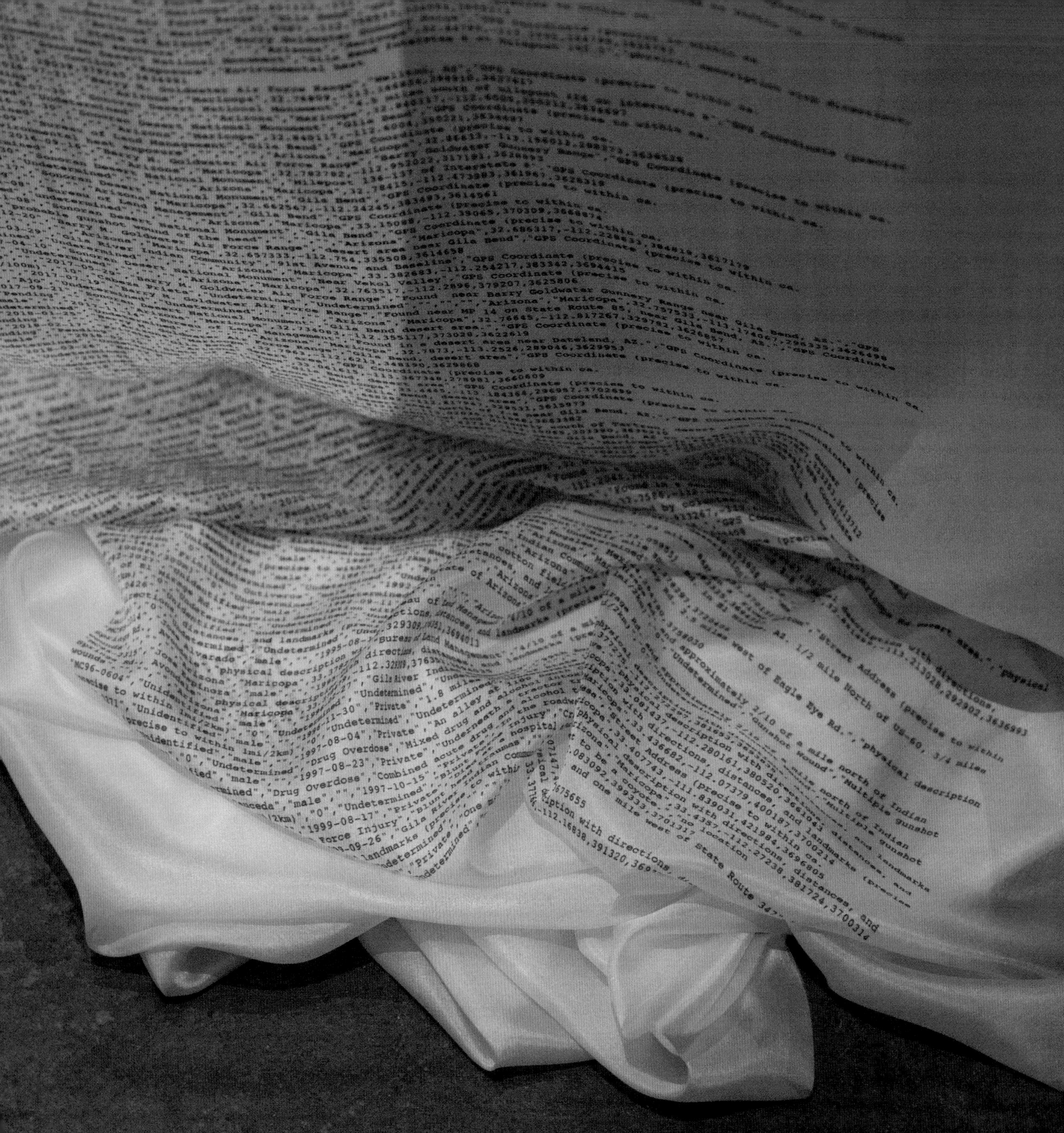

Detainee Death Reporting 2003–2024

Names of people who died while in ICE detention

Reverencia: mapeo de muertes migrantes en Arizona (Reverence: Arizona Migrant Death Mapping), 2023
Archival pigment on habotai silk
508 × 71 cm (each of 10)
Courtesy of the artist

Jakelin Caal Moquin

Felipe Gomez Alonso

Carlos Gregorio Hernandez

Mariee Juarez

Wilmer Josue Ramirez

Juan de Leon Gutierrez

Darlyn Cristabel Cordova-Valle

Sergio Adrian Hernandez- Guerecol

Kataria, Pankaj Karan Singh

Sanchez-Castro, Jose Manuel

Bamaca-Zacarias, Brendy Yohana

Quintana, Jhon Benavides

Boror-Urla, Hugo Roberto

Dennis, Cambric

Farias-Farias, Edixon Del Jesus

Singh, Jaspal

Daniel, Charles Leo

Ba, Ousmane

Chirino Peralta, Julio Cesar

Shrestha, Subash

Juan Francisco, Carlos

Okpu, Frankline

Mendoza, Melvin Ariel Calero

Dumitrascu, Cristian

Rosales-Vargas, Salvador

Rocha-Cuadra,
 Ernestosanchez-Gotopo, Pablo

Gonzalez-Soto, Benjamin

Vial, Kesleyjones, Anthony

Montes, Felipe

Dean, Jesse

Gallego-Agudelo, Diego Fernando

Centeno-Briones, Elba Maria

Abienwi, Nebane

Hernandez-Diaz, Roylan

Akinyemi, Anthony Oluseye

Mavinga, Samuelino

Owen, Ben James

Hernandez-Fundora, Alberto

Hernandez-Colula, David

Ochoa-Yoc De Ramirez, Maria Celeste

Carcamo-Navarro, Orlan Ariel

Hernandez-Ibarra, Ramiro

Baten-Oxlaj, Santiago

Perez-Montufa, Onoval

Sanchez-Perez, Luis
 (Aka Hernandez-Cabrera, Mauricio)

Hill, James Tomas

Lee, Kuan Hui

Guillen Vega, Jose Freddy

Sabonger-Garcia, Fernando

Chavez Alvarez, Cipriano

Jally, Romien

Padron, Wilfredo

Amar, Mergensana

Volkov, Guerman

Reyes-Clemente, Abel

Singh, Simratpal

Balderramos-Torres, Yimi Alexis

Arriago-Santoya, Pedro

Rodriguez-Espinoza, Roberto

Mirimanian, Gourgen

Romero, Ronal Francisco
 (Aka Cruz, Ronald)

Hernandez, Jeffry
  (Aka Hernandez, Roxana)
Tran, Huy Chi
De La Rosa, Efrain Romero
Ramirez-Arreola, Augustina
Caceres-Maradiaga Vicente
Patel, Atulkumar Babubhai
Jiminez-Joseph Jean Carlos Alfonso
Lopez Sergio Alonso
Gonzalez Gabda Osmar Epifanio
Rayson Roger
Calderon-De Hidalgo Raquel
Campos Wenceslau Esmerio
Joshua-Toyin Olubunmi
Tino-Lopez, Moises
Carela, Santo
Fino Martinez, Luis Alonso
Boch-Paniagua, Juan Luis
Zyazin, Igor
Leonardo Lemus Rajo, Jose
Barcenas-Padilla, Rafael
Saengsiri Thongchay
Banegas-Guzman, Saul Enrique
Azurdia, Hernandez, Jose Manuel
Garcia-Hernandez, Juan
Nguyen, Nho Thi
Navarrette-Quintana, Marcos
Deniz-Sahagun, Jose De Jesus
Funez Ochoa, Carlos
Morales-Ramos, Raul Ernesto
Umana-Martinez, Jorge Alberto
Garcia-Huezo, Welmer Alberto

Hernandez-Valencia, Jose Javier
Rockwell, Peter Geroge Carlysle
Bell, Marjorie Annmarie
Carlos, Tiombe Kimana
Mponda, Clemente Ntangola
Rodriguez, Leslis
Mendez-Hernandez, Federico
Garcia-Maldanado, Jorge
Guadalupe-Gonzales, Elsa
Tomanek, Oldrich
Smith, Glaston
Ortiz-Matamoros, Pablo
Cota-Domingo, Manuel
Flores-Segura, Juan Pablo
Mandza, Evalin-Ali
Dominguez-Valivia, Fernando
Sarabia-Ortega, Miguel Angel
Rojas-Martinez, Ricardo
Gracida-Conte, Pablo
Rivera-Romero, Mauro
Ramirez-Ramirez, Anibal
Ramirez-Reyes, Victor
Bamenga, Irene
Hernandez, Miguel Angel
Militec, Amra
Guo, Qi Gen
Aguilar-Espinoza, Jose
Palomo-Rodriquez, Juan
Segundo, Jose Manuel
Sterling, John

Hernandez-Gomez, Jose
Antonio
Reyes-Zalaya, Jose Nelson
Holowienko, Kazimierz
Cogle-Del Pino, Julian
Rodriguez-Solis, Arnulfo
Obey, Evelyn
Gomez-Vasquez, Ernesto
Padilla-Perez, Sebastian
Tavarez, Pedro Juan
Jimon Tiniguardo, Rolando
Negusse, Huluf
Stojka, Vera
Cruz -Silva, Arnoldo
Martinez Medina, Roberto
Jimenez-Rojas, Sergio
Coronado-Gabriel, Claudio
Martinez, Julio
Alvarez Gomez, Jose
Newborough, Guido
Saylab, Hadayatullah
Santos Maidiqui, Alberto
Baires, Juan
Owusu, Emmanuel
Barnett, Edwin
Ng, Hiu Lui
Dawood, Nail Yoursef
Canales Baca, Rogelio
Valasquez, Ambrocio
Joseph, Valery
Dubegel-Paez, Luis

Suares-Almenares, Arturo

Diaz-Salgado, Alejandro

Gumayagay, Pedro

Gonzalez_Baez, Cesar

Guevara-Lazaro, Alejandro

Contreras-Dominguez, Rosa Isela

De Araujo, Edimar

Arellano, Victor

Bah, Boubacar

Romero, Nery

Rodriguez-Torres, Felix

Chavez-Torres, Mario Francisco

Abdeulaye, Sall

Cervantes-Corona, Jesus

Martinez-Rivas, Antonio

Carlos-Cortez, Raudel

Lopez-Gregorio, Jose

Singh, Jamer

Kim, Young Sook

Castro-Jimenez, Rene

Osman, Yusif

Lazano-Blanco, Jorge

Rodriguez-Gonzalez, Miguel

Rodriguez Castro, Walter

Inamagua-Mercha, Maria

Polanco-Molina, Angel

Garcia-Mejia, Geovanny

Garcia-Sanchez, Felipe

Murphy, Vincent

Kenley, Sandra Marina

Salazar-Gomez, Juan

Ledesman-Guerreo, Roberto

Marrero-Abreo, Domingo

Sanchez-Rodriguez, Sergio

Prado-Arencilia, Reinaldo

Delapaz, Eduardo

Ahmad, Tanveer

Alvarez-Esquivel, Walter

Cruz Garcia, Rene

Vargas, Nhung

Tunon-Abeal, Jose

Lazo Reinoso, Silvio

Belbachir, Hassiba

Heo, Sung Soo

Nand, Maya (Aka Narid, Maya)

Correoso-Jay, Conrado

Rosell Sierra, Jose

Sarabia-Vallasenor, Ignacio

Lopez Ruelas, Elias

Herrera-Limas, Pedro

Anache-Campos, Luis

Fils-Aime, Yvel

Dantica, Joseph

Zarou, Jose

Lopez-Lara, Jose

Reyes-Altimirano, Simon

Ruiz-Tabares, Ervin

Ayala-Garcia, Antonio

Singh, Bhupinder

Soca-Ros, Otalio

Mejia Vicentes, Sebastian

Enriquez-Betancourt, N

Alonso, Juan

Martinez, Jose Alberto

Herrera-Teran, Jose

Mendez, Enrique

Figueredo-Lopez, Juan

Rust, Richard

Fankeu, Samou

Satkunes-Waran, Kandiah

Mendez-Bacca, Carlos

Perez-Ayala, Manuel

Alvarez Arias, Jose De La Concepcion

Solis-Perez, Maria

Hernandez, Wilfredo

Rodriguez, Jose Rangel

Mosley, Hector

Rioz-Martinez, Cezar

Popoola, Adetunji

Gutierrez, Ramiro

Leyva-Arjona, Argelio

Linde-Cepero, Alberto

Jorrin-Miller, Daniel

Verdecia-Carrillo, Heriberto

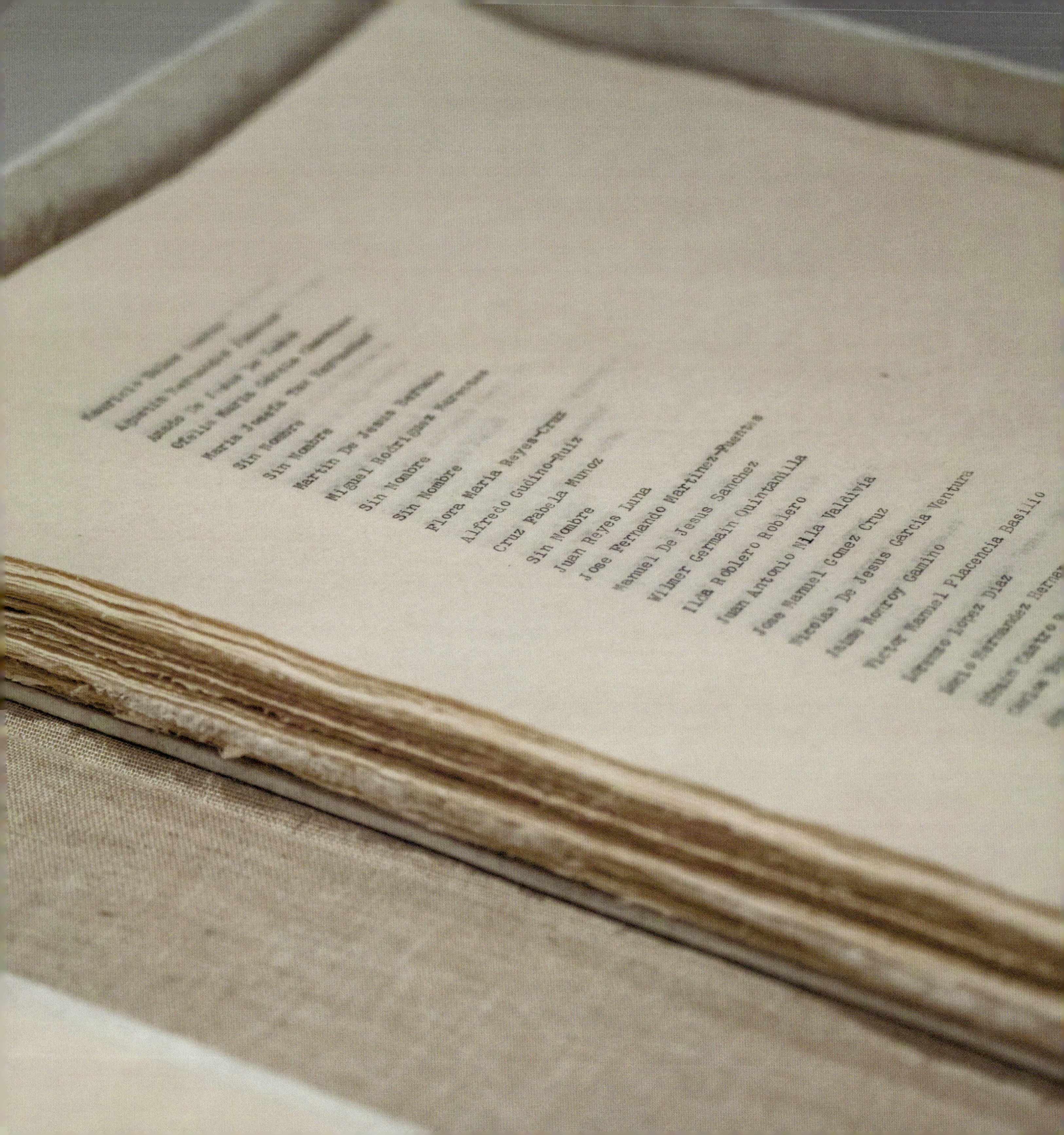

María Josefa ...
Sin Nombre
Sin Nombre
Martín De Jesús ...
Miguel Rodríguez ...
Sin Nombre
Sin Nombre
Flora María Reyes-Cruz
Alfredo Gudiño-Ruiz
Cruz Fabela Muñoz
Sin Nombre
Juan Reyes Luna
José Fernando Martínez-...
Manuel De Jesús Sánchez
Wilmer Germaín Quintanilla
Ilca Roblero Roblero
Juan Antonio Nila Valdivia
José Manuel Gomez Cruz
Regina De Jesús García Ventura
Monroy Gamiño
Víctor Manuel Placencia Basilio
... López Díaz
... Hernández Hern...

APPENDIX 2

Arizona Migrant Death Mapping

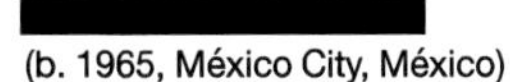

(b. 1965, México City, México)

Un Libro De Familia: Una reescritura del proyecto de mapeo de muertes de migrantes (A family book: a rewriting of the Migrant Death Mapping Project), 2023
Handmade corn-husk paper, clamshell box, natural book cloth, and amate (bark) paper
40.6 × 31.75 × 7 cm
Courtesy of the artist

Migrant Death Mapping by Humane Borders (Fronteras Compasivas), based out of Tucson, Arizona, was founded in 2000 in partnership with the Pima County Medical Examiner's Office. This effort maps out undoc+ migrant deaths in their region to bear witness to the death toll of Prevention Through Deterrence.

Their Migrant Death Map (formally known as Arizona Open GIS Initiative of Deceased Migrants) records the exact location where each migrant body has been found, alongside (when available) name, gender, date of discovery, and cause of death. The information is updated monthly by the Pima County Medical Examiner.

As of today (March 12, 2025), their database includes 4366 deaths, with more added monthly. If you are trying to find a loved one who crossed the desert and has gone missing, visit humaneborders.org.

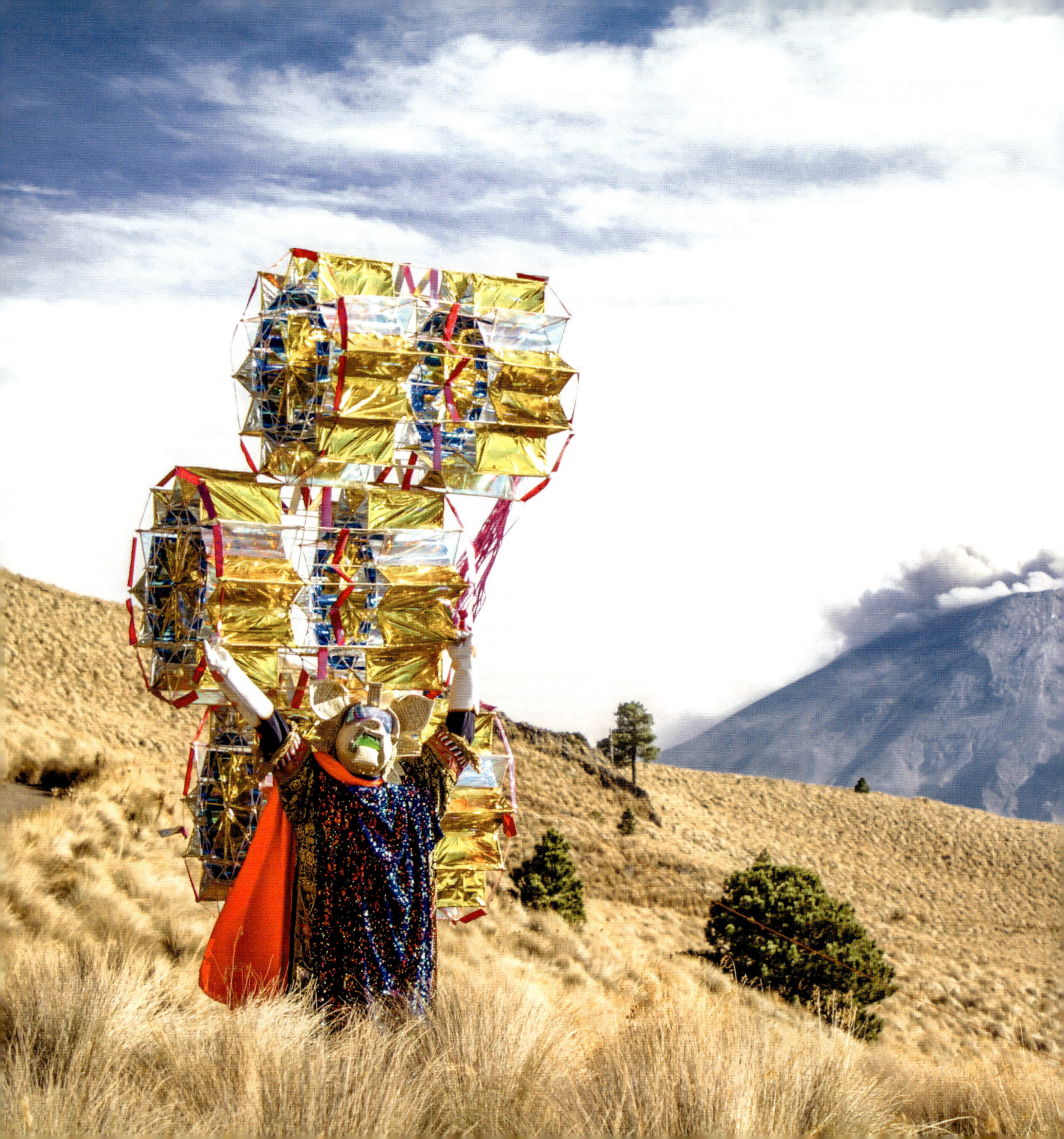

APPENDIX 3   **In Hope**

[redacted]
(b.1991, San Francisco Coapan,
Cholula, Puebla, México)

Xochipitzahuatl-Nova, 2024
Still from a three-channel video
10 minutes
Courtesy of the artist

This page serves to acknowledge every undoc+ immigrant whose life has been lost and whose remains have yet to be found; every undoc+ immigrant whose name has yet to be codified in a list like the ones on preceding pages; every undoc+ immigrant whose story has yet to be spoken; and every undoc+ immigrant being forcibly removed from home.

While this publication may give a voice to many, it can never truly capture the immeasurable grief carried by the undoc+ community.

Notes to the Text

Solidarity through Opacity

1. El Comité Clandestino (1994). Roughly translated: "We are nothing walking alone; we become everything walking alongside dignified steps."
2. D'Souza (2024, 57).
3. Glissant (1997, 192).
4. D'Souza (2024, 57).

Aesthetics of Undocumentedness

1. Villavicencio Cornejo et al. (2020).
2. People on the undoc+ spectrum are currently or formerly undocumented. A need for linguistic opacity is prevalent in this community in order to shield its members from legal ramifications.
3. D'Souza (2024, 81).
4. Glissant (1997, 192).
5. Glissant (1997, 190).
6. This was not the single choice of any one individual. The artists and the curator of *(in)visibility* communally decided to stand in solidarity with one another and protect those most vulnerable in this project.
7. Cohen (2009, 5).
8. Cohen and Ghosh (2019, 16).
9. Chomsky (2014).
10. Chomsky (2014).
11. Vargas (n.d.)
12. Baker (2021).
13. Some hid their gender, others their body. Some hid their age, others their nation. Some will hide forever.
14. Many journeys I cannot begin to comprehend or fathom.
15. U.S. Customs and Border Protection, "1924: Border Patrol Established."
16. Southern Border Communities Coalition, "Operation Gatekeeper."
17. Wiland et al. (2022).
18. [redacted] "Migratory Land Knowledges" (2024).
19. Anzaldúa *Borderlands* (1987).
20. [redacted] "Ceremonia" (2023).
21. [redacted] "Ceremonia" (2023).
22. Chang "Undocumented to Hyperdocumented" (2011, 509).
23. Chang "Undocumented to Hyperdocumented" (2011).
24. "Resident Alien" cards were paper documents laminated in plastic; they granted individuals the right to live and work permanently in the U.S. On January 30, 2023, they were changed from "resident alien" to "permanent resident" cards. The new document is fully made of printed plastic.
25. Artist received his B.F.A. degree at this university and is currently employed by it.
26. [redacted] "Donde Esta" (2023).
27. [redacted] "Donde Esta" (2023).
28. Schum et al. (2021).
29. [redacted] *Children of the Land* (2020, 10).
30. [redacted] *Children of the Land* (2020, 13).
31. Park and Burgess (1921). In problematizing assimilation as a general concept, other, more specific assimilation theories (such as segmented assimilation or downward assimilation) become absorbed within the main arguments presented here.
32. Park and Burgess (1921); Alba and Nee (1997).
33. Feldmeyer (2018).
34. "American" is a social construct invented to speak of a set of characteristics available exclusively to citizens of the United States. Every individual on the American continent can be American; therefore, this designation is also a linguistic misnomer. FOB (derogatory), short for "Fresh of the Boat," is one of the terms of immigrant abuse.
35. [redacted] *Children of the Land* (2020, 4).
36. Villavicencio Cornejo (2020, 13).
37. This is especially the case around the time of presidential elections.
38. Some Braceros became citizens through direct sponsorship from their employer.
39. USCIS stopped taking in new applications into the DACA program as of July 16, 2021 (it started on August 15, 2012). As of today, individuals who have applied for DACA before July 16, 2021 can continue to renew their application, but no new applicants can join the program.

40. Individuals lacking employment authorization can still work as independent contractors, consultants, and freelancers. Any immigrant can start a business using an individual taxpayer identification number (ITIN) or a Social Security Number (SSN). As mandated by the Immigrant Reform and Control Act (IRCA), the employer is not required to inquire about the legal standing of independent contractors.

41. Mitchell (2024).

42. Rivera Garza (2020, 9).

43. Villavicencio Cornejo (2020, 53).

44. ▮▮▮▮ "Gemidos de la Tierra" (2023).

45. ▮▮▮▮ "Gemidos de la Tierra" (2023).

46. ▮▮▮▮ "Pertenecer" (2023b, 15).

47. ▮▮▮▮ "Pertenecer" (2023b, 15).

48. ▮▮▮▮ *Tiemperos del Antropoceno* (2022). The phrase roughly translates as: "How dare they discover us, how dare they claim our homes, I am a scarred leg (pejorative toward indigenous folx in Spanish) because my feet embody earth and my resistance is firm."

49. ▮▮▮▮ *Tiemperos del Antropoceno* (2022).

50. Undoc+ individual who is a member of the creative industries.

51. Curator in conversation with the artist on August 12, 2022.

52. Anzaldua *Borderlands* (2015).

53. Anzaldua *Borderlands* (2015).

54. Anzaldua *Borderlands* (2015).

55. Term of endearment used for females in Mexican communities.

56. Said (2002, 174).

57. Triple exile because he was born into a Bahá'í family after the Islamic revolution in Iran, left the country as an exile, and has been in a precarious position as a Middle Eastern refugee in post 9/11 sociopolitical landscape of the U.S.

58. This test is one of the last steps toward naturalization. Successful completion gains one citizenship.

59. The first time I encountered this artwork, I quizzed a U.S. citizen on the same questions I had to study to pass my citizenship exam. Other naturalized individuals as well as citizen joined the lengthy game (of 100 questions). Despite being triggered, the naturalized immigrants gained a higher score than the citizens.

60. Artist, "Unhealable Rift" (2024).

61. D'Souza (2024, 52).

What Does it Mean to Be Documenting the Undocumented?

1. I am grateful to ▮▮▮▮ ▮▮▮▮ for this summary of Agamben's work.

2. Agamben (1998, 83).

3. Gonzalez-Gorman (2023, 18).

4. Gonzalez-Gorman (2023, 26).

5. Villegas (2010, 157).

6. Rodriguez (2014, 4).

7. U.S Citizen and Immigration Services, "A-Number" (n.d.).

8. Mann (2013, 1).

9. Hernandez and Reinoza (2017, 130).

10. Mesa-Bains (1999, 161).

11. ▮▮▮▮ "Caption" (2023a).

12. Balsom (2013, 15).

13. Balsom (2013, 17).

14. Balsom (2013, 21).

15. Solanas and Getino (2014, 238).

16. Solanas and Getino (2014, 239).

17. Solanas and Getino (2014, 249).

Reference Cited

Alba, Richard, and Nee, Victor
1997   "Rethinking Assimilation Theory for a New Era of Immigration." *International Migration Review* 31, no. 4: 826-74.

Agamben, Giorgio
1998   *Homo Sacer: Sovereign Power and Bare Life*. Stanford: Stanford University Press.

████████████
2023   "Gemidos de La Tierra." https://██████████.com/gemidos-de-la-tierra/ (accessed September 4, 2023).

Anzaldúa, Gloria
1987   *Borderlands / La Frontera: The New Mestiza*. San Francisco: Aunt Lute Book Company.

Anzaldua, Gloria
2015   *Light in the Dark: Rewriting Identity, Spirituality, and Reality*, edited by Analouise Keating. Durham: Duke University Press.

Balsom, Erika
2013   *Exhibiting Cinema in Contemporary Art*. Amsterdam: Amsterdam University Press.

Baker, Bryan
2021   "Estimates of the Unauthorized Immigrant Population Residing in the United States: January 2015–January 2018," https://ohss.dhs.gov/sites/default/files/2023-12/unauthorized_immigrant_population_estimates_2015_-_2018.pdf

████████████
2024   "Unhealable Rift." ████ M.F.A. thesis." April 4, 2024.

Chang, Aurora
2011   "Undocumented to hyperdocumented: A jornada of protection, papers, and PhD status." *Harvard Educational Review* 81, no. 3: 508–20.

Chomsky, Aviva
2014   *Undocumented: How Immigration Became Illegal*. Boston: Beacon Press.

Elizabeth F. Cohen
2009   *Semi-Citizenship in Democratic Politics* (Cambridge: Cambridge University Press.

Cohen, Elizabeth F. and Cyril Ghosh
2019   *Citizenship (Key Concepts in Political Theory)*. 1st ed. Newark: Polity.

El Comité Clandestino Revolucionario Indígena-Comandancia General del Ejército Zapatista de Liberación Nacional
1994   "Comunicado a Las organizaciones que forman la Coordinación Nacional de Acción Cívica para la Liberación Nacional (ConacLN)" (Ejército Zapatista de Liberación Nacional, February 14, 1994), https://palabra.ezln.org.mx/comunicados/1994/1994_02_14.htm.

D'Souza, Aruna
2024   *Imperfect Solidarities*. Critic's Essay Series. Berlin: Floating Opera Press.

Feldmeyer, Ben
2018   "The Classical Assimilation Model." In *Routledge Handbook on Immigration and Crime*, edited by Holly Ventura Miller and Anthony Peguero, 35–48. London: Taylor and Francis.

Glissant, Édouard
1997   *Poetics of Relation*. Translated by Betsy Wing. Ann Arbor: University of Michigan Press.

Gonzalez-Gorman, Sylvia
2023   "Disrupting Agamben: Beyond undocumented children as 'Homo Sacer.'" *Human Geography* 16, no. 1: 17-30.

████████████████
2020   *Children of the Land: A Memoir*. New York: Harper Perennial.

Hernández, Robb, and Tatiana Reinoza
2017   "Introduction: The People of Paper/La Gente de Papel." *Aztlán: A Journal of Chicano Studies* 42, no. 1: 129-38.

████████████████
2023a "Caption." *Instagram*, September 29, 2023.

████████████
2023b *Pertenecer / Encarnar: Aesthetics of Undocumentedness*. Los Angeles: Lulu.com.

2024 "Migratory Land Knowledges: ███████████"
CuratorLove. http://www.███████.com/csusm (accessed
November 16, 2024).

Mann, Steve
2013 "Veillance and Reciprocal Transparency: Surveillance versus
Sousveillance, AR Glass, Lifeglogging, and Wearable Computing."
Paper presented at the *2013 IEEE International Symposium on
Technology and Society (ISTAS)*, June 27–29.

Mesa-Bains, Amalia
1999 "Domesticana: The Sensibility of Chicana rasquache."
Aztlán: A Journal of Chicano Studies 24, no. 2: 157-67.

Mitchell, Sophia M.
2024 "Domestic Workers in the United States." U.S. Department
of Labor, United States Women's Bureau.

████████████████
2023 "Donde Està Mi Hogar?" Chicago.

Park, Robert Ezra, and E.W. Burgess
1921 *Introduction to the Science of Sociology*. Chicago:
University of Chicago Press.

███████████
2023 "Ceremonia en la Tierra Sagrada." Arizona.

Rivera Garza, Cristina
2020 *Grieving: Dispatches from a Wounded Country*. Translated
by Sarah Booker. New York: The Feminist Press at CUNY.

Rodriguez, Juana Maria
2014 *Sexual Futures, Queer Gestures, and Other Latina Longings*.
New York: New York University Press.

Said, Edward W.
2002 *Reflections on Exile and Other Essays*. Cambridge, MA:
Harvard University Press.

Salazar Moreno, Rafael, and Ava Wiland
2020 "Tanya Aguiñiga." PBS, Episode 3: Borderlands (Art 21:
Art in the Twenty-First Century, Season 10).

Schum, Matthew, ed.
2021 *Rodrigo Valenzuela: Journeyman*. Milan, Italy:
Mousse Publishing.

Solanas, Fernando, and Octavio Getino
2014 "Towards a Third Cinema: Notes and Experiences for the
Development of a Cinema of Liberation in the Third World (Argen-
tina, 1969)." In *Film Manifestos and Global Cinema Cultures: A
Critical Anthology*, edited by Scott MacKenzie, 238–50. Berkeley:
University of California Press.

Southern Border Communities Coalition
n.d. "Operation Gatekeeper and The Birth of Border Militarization."
https://www.southernborder.org/operation_gatekeeper (accessed
August 26, 2022).

Vargas, José Antonio
n.d. "If There Are an Estimated 45 million Immigrants Living in
America, Then There Are 45 Million Ways of Being an Immigrant in
America. Like All Groups, We Are Not a Monolith." https://twitter.
com/Joséiswriting/status/1524837404649017345 (accessed May
14, 2022).

Villavicencio Cornejo et al.
2020 "Portland Institute for Contemporary Art - PICA," February
13. https://www.pica.org/events/WeDidntArriveHereAlone.

Villegas, Francisco J.
2010 "Strategic In/Visibility and Undocumented Migrants."
Counterpoints 368: 147-70.

U.S. Citizenship and Immigration Services.
"A-Number/Alien Registration Number/Alien Number (A-Number
or A#)." https://www.uscis.gov/glossary-term/50684 (accessed
January 14, 2025).

U.S. Customs and Border Protection.
"1924: Border Patrol Established | U.S. Customs and Border
Protection." https://www.cbp.gov/about/history/1924-border-
patrol-established (accessed August 26, 2022).

**Wiland, Ava, Rafael Salazar Moreno, Rafael Lozano-Hemmer,
Richard Misrach, Tanya Aguiñiga.**
2022 "The Postcommodity collective." PBS, Episode 2:
Borderlands (Art21: Art in the Twenty-First Century).

Artists and Contributors

█████████████ **(b. 1995, México City, México)** is an undocumented (since 2007) human/alien hybrid currently living in █████████, CA. Their videos expose the absurdity of institutional and societal beliefs about migrants, places of power, and nations. As someone with a status of an "alien" according to the U.S. government, they experience many limitation, but through a dgaf attitude they have grown to make fun of things as a coping mechanism. Their work mainly exists on YouTube and Vimeo, with other musings on Instagram. They are currently a Ph.D. student at University of California ████████, focusing on modern and contemporary Latin American and Latinx art, especially new/digital/virtual media.

████████████ **(b. 1976, Bogotá, Colombia)** is an artist living in ███████████ CA. She participates in movements of immigrant rights, anti-gentrification, socio-economic equity, and ecology. Her artistic practice is characterized by a collaborative and narrative-driven approach; and integrates elements of nature, land, place, and people as both mediums and layers in her installations and public art pieces. She creates immersive experiences that invite viewers to engage with the interconnectedness of the environment and human stories. Her ability to weave together diverse elements results in artworks that resonate deeply with audiences, fostering a sense of connection and reflection on the relationships between people, place, and their surroundings. Her work contributes to the historical memory of the collective and facilitates placemaking within communities of color. The artist has received grant from California Arts Council as an Established Artists Fellow, and from 18th Street Arts Center as a Creative Corps Fellow. She has held residencies at Grand Central Art Center, funded through a grant by The Andy Warhol Foundation; and a Community Engagement Residency in Akumal-México. She is the director and co-founder of the ████████ Community Artis(a) Coalition, whose mission is to connect artists to their communities in a collaborative process and to create public art focused on anti-gentrification efforts. She is also a founding member of the City of ████████ arts steering committee and a participant in the Occupy movement.

(b. 1993, Michoacán, México) is a recipient of the Bay Area Fellowship at Headlands Center for the Arts and a recipient of a regional Emmy award for her feature She was named a Eureka Fellow by the Fleishhacker Foundation and was a finalist for the SECA Award through the San Francisco Museum of Modern Art. Her work was featured in Focus at The Armory Show, curated by the executive director and chief curator of Forge Project. She had a solo exhibition at the Trout Museum of Art in Appleton, Wisconsin. Another at the Benemérita Universidad Autónoma de Puebla in México generously sponsored by The ANT Project. MCA Gallery in Ontario, Canada—was her first major international solo presentation. She was featured in exhibitions at the Pacific Northwest College of Art, Oregon; San Francisco Arts Commission; Lower Manhattan Cultural Council in New York City; and Alfred University, New York. Her work is currently featured in BAN9: Bay Area Now 9 at Yerba Buena Center for the Arts. She had solo exhibitions at the Bolinas Museum and the Utah Museum of Fine Arts. Her work is held in the permanent collections of the Cantor Arts Center at Stanford University; Crocker Art Museum; Utah Museum of Fine Arts; Nerman Museum of Contemporary Art; Grand Valley State University Museum of Art; Ulrich Museum of Art; and 21c Museum Hotels. Based in Napa Valley, CA, she has been represented by Gallery. She received her M.F.A. from College of the Arts. One of four children originally from Arteaga, Michoacán, México, she is a beneficiary of DACA (Deferred Action for Childhood Arrivals) and is on a path to becoming a naturalized U.S. citizen. Her family fled to the U.S. in 1997, finding home in California's Valley.

(b. 1966, Toluca, México) is a multidisciplinary artist and educator interested in performance, photography, video, textiles, serigraphy, and social practice. Her projects have focused on the interactions between Mexican and American cultures. As a Latina artist, she addresses the marginalization and inequality faced by women in the immigrant community. Originally from México, she earned her degree in communication sciences at the Technological Institute of Monterrey and studied photography at the University of Wisconsin–Stout. She studied advertising at the Autonomous University of the State of México, where she subsequently taught photography courses for several years and coordinated different programs at the University Extension. She left México in 2002 for , CA.She earned a Certificate in Museum Studies from Community College; and an M.F.A. from San Diego State University with an emphasis on painting and printmaking. She has lectured, taught, performed, and exhibited at universities, community colleges, and museums in Los Angeles, San Diego, and Tijuana; and currently lectures at State University.

██████████ (b. 1989, San Francisco Coapan, Cholula, Puebla, México; d. 2017) lived and worked in the U.S. A lover of tacos al pastor and atole de calabaza, he wanted to be a boxer at an early age. He received his B.F.A. from Ball State University and his M.F.A. from Pennsylvania State University.

██████████ (b. 1965, México City, México) is an emerging artist based in ██████, AZ. Her work explores issues of home, identity, belonging, erasure, and the tragedy of migrant deaths in the Arizona desert. Drawing on her own immigrant experience, she speaks visually of community, touching on language barrier, culture, and society. She has earned her M.F.A. in photography from ██████ State University.

██████████ (b. 1985, Shiraz, Iran) was born and raised in Iran and is currently living and working in ██████, CA. He received his B.A. from the University of California, ██████ and M.F.A. from the University of California, ██████. His work has been featured at the New Wight Gallery, Los Angeles; Guest House, Inglewood; ADVOCARTSY, Los Angeles; San Diego Art Institute; UCI Room Gallery, Irvine; A Ship in the Woods, Escondido; The Front Art Gallery, San Ysidro; and the Museum of Contemporary Art, San Diego, among other venues. He has upcoming exhibitions at LA Artcore, Los Angeles; the San Diego International Airport; and forthcoming residencies at MASS MoCA in Massachusetts and Radio 28 in México City.

██████████ (b.1991, San Francisco Coapan, Cholula, Puebla, México) is currently based in ██████, VA, and is an associate professor in the Department of Art at the University of ██████. His work addresses Nahua Indigenous immigration, social art practice, and cultural sustainability. Building on his own experience as an undocumented immigrant and DACA holder, his creative practice brings together Indigeneity and immigration. At the core of his most recent research and artistic production is the intersection of transborder Indigeneity, migrant Indigenous diasporas, and Nahua futurisms. His independent films have been screened at national and international film festivals and exhibitions. As a co-founder of ██████+Collective and the founder and director of the ██████ Artist Residency in Puebla, México. He is actively involved in socially engaged works and binational endeavors.

██████████████████ **(b. 1976, San Salvador, El Salvador)** is a transdisciplinary visual artist, choreographer, and healer. At the age of eight, he was part of the first wave of unaccompanied, undocumented children to arrive at the U.S. border (in the 1980s) as a result of the Salvadoran Civil War. Upon becoming a U.S. citizen he adopted his current name in solidarity with his undocumented father who uses that name. As an acknowledgment of his past, the artist grounds his practice in both historical and contemporary contexts, including those of belonging to the undocumented and cancer communities. He currently lives in ████████, New York. His work is in the permanent collections of the Museum of Modern Art; The Guggenheim Museum; the Whitney Museum of American Art; Museo Nacional Centro de Arte Reina Sofía, Madrid; and the Institute of Contemporary Art, Miami. Additionally, he has performed and presented his work at the Whitney Museum of American Art, MoMA, Metropolitan Museum of Art, Institute of Contemporary Art Miami, Queens Museum, Bronx Museum of the Arts, and many more.

██████████████████ **(b. 1981, Atotonilco El Grande, Hidalgo, México)** is a borderless artist living in ████ ██, CA. He uses various artistic media, drawing on his perspective as a formerly undocumented migrant and a campesino urbano. After more than 20 years of living as an undocumented immigrant in the U.S., he has received his U.S. residency and quit his job in a furniture-making factory to pursue his B.F.A. at ██████ and M.F.A. at the University of California, ████████. His thesis artwork was awarded the David Antin Prize from UCSD and the Graduating Artist Award from ICA San Diego. He was recently named a California Arts Council Established Artists Fellow grantee. His work with maguey plants was featured in a special project at the U.S. Library of Congress. His artwork has been shown at The Cheech Marin Center for Chicano Art and Culture, ICA San Diego, the University of Virginia, Agnes Scott College, and California State University San Marcos, among other venues.

████████████ (b.1985, Quetzaltengo, Guatemala) lives and works in ███████, CA. She is an artist with a multidisciplinary practice. Her research is articulated through the use of materials and forms associated with pre-Columbian cultures. She creates public performances, installations, and objects that fuse Indigenous mythologies with contemporary community engagement. She received her M.F.A. from the University of California, ████████, and her B.F.A. from ████████ College of Design. She has exhibited at the Hammer Museum; LACE (Los Angeles Contemporary Exhibitions); LAND (Los Angeles Nomadic Division); 18th St Art Center, CA; The Armory Center of the Arts, CA; Vincent Price Art Museum, CA; The Annenberg Space for Photography CA; Human Resources Los Angeles, CA; and MAD (Museum of Art and Design), NY. She is the recipient of the Mohn Public Recognition Award, Mohn Land Award, Andy Warhol Foundation for the Arts, Los Angeles Art Fund, and National Performance Network Fund. She has been featured in the *Los Angeles Times*, *ARTnews*, *The Art Newspaper, LA Weekly*, *Hyperallergic*, and the Walker Art Center magazine.

████████████ (b. 1973, Ibagué, Colombia) is an interdisciplinary artist who explores the intersection of history, research, Indigenous spirituality, and ancient beliefs. His art includes paintings, sculptures, and installations that serve as a commentary on colonialism, mysticism, labor, and ceremonial gatherings. His work has been featured in major outlets, such as *Hyperallergic*, CNN, *New York Magazine*, *The Observer*, *Newsweek*, *The Daily Beast*, Yale University radio WYBCX, NTN24 (TV interview), Good Day New York (TV interview), Fox News (TV interview), *Whitehot Magazine*, *Whitewall Magazine*, and other venues. He has exhibited at the Queens Museum, Petzel Gallery, Anna-Maria and Stephen Kellen Gallery at the New School, 601 Artspace, Penn State University, Spring Break Art Show, Collar Works, Galerie Richard, Whitebox NY, The Gabarron Foundation, Flowers Gallery, and all over the world. His artwork is included in the permanent collections of the Marina Tsvetaeva Museum in Moscow, Russia; The Acuity Brands Corporate private collection in NYC; The Gabarron's Foundation collection in New York and Spain; Foursquare headquarters in NYC; and other private collections.

████████████ (b. 1992, Leon, Guanajuato, México) is a multi-disciplinary artist based in ██████, GA. His work primarily focuses on identity; he is currently exploring the migrant experience in the American South. He is the recipient of the MINT + ACP Emerging Artist Fellowship, is one of three awardees of the Atlanta Artadia Awards, and a Working Artist Project winner at MOCA GA. His work is part of the permanent collections of the High Museum of Art, the Virginia Museum of Fine Art, and the Michael C. Carlos Museum. His clients include *Rolling Stone*, *TIME Magazine*, and *The New York Times.*

[redacted] (b. 1993, Acámbaro, Guanajuato, México) in a Mexican-born and Chicago-raised artist whose work frequently highlights immigration issues, unseen labor, and social disenfranchisement. As a DACA recipient and artist, he depicts the nuances of existing with a politicized identity in both the U.S. and the art world. Colliding art preparator gestures with minimalism and conceptualism, he fossilizes the unseen labor of undocumented art preparators who support the operations of many industries in the U.S. as they work in the shadows of great institutions but are rarely recognized. Through his practice, he also communicates and questions the parallels between the bureaucratic processes and spaces he inhabits. He holds a B.F.A. and is currently the assistant director of exhibitions and staff advisor of [redacted] Galleries and [redacted] at the School of the Art [redacted]. He has exhibited in the Chicago Latinx Art Now Biennial, National Museum of Mexican Art, and debuted a series of new and ongoing work in a solo show titled [redacted] at the Chicago Art Department. He has been co-organizing Undocumented Projects and was selected as one of the eight Breakout Artists by *Newcity* Chicago magazine and the Chicago Artists Coalition. He created a temporary graphite mural through "Mind Map," a bi-monthly program at MANA Contemporary Chicago. He was selected as an artist for the Center Program at the Hyde Park Art Center, where he also exhibited. His artwork can be found in the collections of the National Museum of Mexican Art and the Illinois State Museum in Springfield.

[redacted] (b. 1992, Nuevo Laredo, México) (ella/e/she/they) is a visual artist and language justice worker in [redacted]. Born in México and raised in Southeastern Louisiana, they create work that challenges conventional depictions of migration by exploring (im)migrant experiences beyond linear narratives, documentation, and borders. Their art practice includes painting, illustration, soft sculpture, assemblage, and embroidery, and is a part of various collections, including the Hood Museum and UC San Diego's Undocumented Student Center. Their illustrations have been featured in various publications, including The *L.A. Times*' "Latinx Files," *United We Dream*'s "Immigrant Made" zine, and *Antigravity Magazine*'s tarot column. They received the Define American Immigrant Artist Fellowship and served as an Artist-in-Residence at the Joan Mitchell Center. They are a member of various collectives in [redacted].

(b. 1961, México City, México) career spans more than 20 years. While in México, he formally trained under the muralist Mario Orozco Rivera and collaborated with him on the restoration of the Polyforum Siqueiros. After arriving in the U.S., he discovered printmaking and lithography, which are now integral parts of his professional practice. After a short period at Self Help Graphics, he became a Master Printer at Cirrus Editions, working closely with artists like John Baldessari and Denis Hollingsworth. He challenges image destabilization, net aesthetics, and digital expression through his printmaking oeuvre, while defragmenting collages and blending multiple processes into each configuration, be it drawing, painting, lithography, or watercolor. He explores color abstraction, collage, figure, geometry, and printmaking. He currently lives and works in ██████, CA. His work has been exhibited in various museums and galleries in the U.S. and México.

(b. 1982, Guadalajara, Jalisco, México) is a material-based artist whose practice weaves traditional Mexican crafts, curanderismo, and contemporary art, reimagining ancestral rituals as acts of healing and transformation. His work honors the resilience of undocumented laborers and Indigenous communities, underscoring the potential of art to repair the spiritual, cultural, and historical wounds of colonization. His creations have been exhibited at such venues as the Museum of Contemporary Art Chicago, Latchkey Gallery in New York City, Charlie James Gallery in Los Angeles, Arvika Art Gallery in Sweden, the National Museum of Mexican Art in Chicago, EXPO Chicago, NADA Art Fair in New York City, and the Chicago Cultural Center. His practice has been featured in *Artforum*, *Hyperallergic*, the *Los Angeles Times*, the *Chicago Tribune*, and *The Latinx Project* at New York University. Additionally, he has been spotlighted on national television for receiving the 3Arts Award and awarded the United States Artists Fellowship.

████████████████ (b. 1961, Tijuana, Baja California, México) received his law degree from the Universidad Autonoma de Baja California. In 1983, he immigrated to the U.S., where he worked in the construction industry. While still in that sector, he became active in the visual arts, and since then has participated in residencies, lectures, and different individual and collective exhibitions in Argentina, Brazil, México, Canada, Chile, China, Colombia, Cuba, France, Germany, Poland, Portugal, Puerto Rico, Russia, Spain, Sweden, and U.S.A. His work was shown at InSite94, InSite97, the VI and VII Havana Biennials, the Whitney Biennial, the second Moscow Biennial, the San Juan Poly/Graphic Triennial, the Sao Paulo /Valencia Biennial, the California Biennial, the Zero One Biennial, The Site Santa Fe Biennial, Made in California, Mexico Illuminated, From Baja to Vancouver, "Politica de la Diferencia, *Arte Iberoamericano de fin de siglo*," Human/Nature, ECO Contemporary Mexican Art, and the Centro Reina Sofia Museum in Spain. He received a United States Artist Fellowship and has been a fellow member of México National System of Art Creators.

████████████████ (b. 1990, Veracruz, México) is an interdisciplinary artist born in México and raised in Chicago, IL. She started her art career after graduating with a B.A. in cinema and photography, and a M.F.A. in sculpture from the School of Art and Design at Southern Illinois University, ████████. She has collaborated on various community projects, installations, and video performances. Her current work focuses on her first-generation immigrant experience and DACAmented status.

████████████ (b. 1986, México City, México) is a Mexican American visual artist and arts administrator living and working in ████████, Utah. Through photography and mixed media, she explores the interplay between migration and hybridity as part of an evolving practice that investigates notions of identity, belonging, and citizenship. She has exhibited nationally in a variety of traditional and nontraditional venues, including Spring/Break Art Show in Los Angeles; Ruffin Gallery at the University of Virginia in Charlottesville; ████ Museum of Contemporary Art in Salt Lake City; and Granary Arts in Ephraim, Utah. Her work is part of private and public collections, such as the Center for Creative Photography, the Utah Museum of Fine Arts, and the State of Utah Alice Merrill Horne Art Collection. She is an alumna of the National Association of Latino Arts and Cultures (NALAC) Leadership Institute and has served as a guest lecturer, juror, and board member for institutions such as 516 Arts, Brigham Young University, the Utah Museum of Contemporary Art, and the Salt Lake City Arts Council. She received the CENTER Jay and Susie Tyrrell Excellence in Works by Hand Award. As the director of planning and programs at the Utah Museum of Fine Arts, she oversees the programmatic initiatives, including exhibition planning in support of the institution's mission and core values.

[REDACTED] **(b.1990, Oaxaca, México)** sees the term "alien" as a pivotal point in their practice. As Suzanne Kite (Lakota) points out, the cultural and political use of the word reflects the complex and contradictory experiences of Indigenous peoples in the U.S. While 47 percent of Americans believe in extraterrestrial life, many view Indigenous peoples and immigrants—referred to as "illegal aliens"—as invaders. This juxtaposition speaks to a broader narrative about who is included and excluded from the national identity. In their work, the artist looks to the untold and suppressed stories of Indigenous peoples, their technologies, and knowledge systems to challenge and reshape these narratives. Their practice fuses Indigenous mythologies, Oaxaquene and Yaqui epistemologies, science fiction, and rituals, all of which coexist with the Amerindigenous subconscious. The artist's work merges site-specific sculptures, themes of time travel, and future archaeologies. They received a B.F.A. from the University of California, [REDACTED] School of the Arts and Architecture, after which they attended the [REDACTED] School of Painting and Sculpture. They are currently an M.F.A. candidate at the University of California, [REDACTED]. Their work has been exhibited at Clemente NYC, Der Greif (Munich, Germany), and Latinx Project NYU.

[REDACTED] **(b. 1977, Rach Gia, Vietnam)** is a [REDACTED]-based artist and educator with a practice encompassing drawing, painting, public art, and community engagement. Her work explores cultural perceptions and representations. She challenges beauty standards by constructing images of the Asian female body vis-à-vis plastic surgery to unpack how contemporary cosmetic surgery can whitewash cultural and racial identity. Her drawings and prints on pink donut boxes explore the complexities of assimilation and cultural negotiation among Cambodian and Vietnamese refugees who have resettled in the U.S. She has had solo exhibitions at Gagosian Gallery in Beverly Hills and the Sweeney Art Gallery at the University of California, Riverside. Her paintings and drawings have been exhibited nationally and internationally, including at the U.S. Embassy in Phnom Penh, Cambodia. She has also completed public art commissions for the Metro Orange Line, Metro Silver Line, the Los Angeles Zoo, and the Los Angeles County + USC Medical Center through the Los Angeles County Department of Arts and Culture. She has served as Chair of the Public Art Commission for the city of South Pasadena and Chair of the Prison Arts Collective Advisory Council, which supports arts programming in California state prisons. She has served on the Board of Directors for LA Más, a non-profit organization that serves BIPOC working-class immigrant communities in Northeast Los Angeles. She completed her undergraduate coursework at the University of Southern California, received a B.F.A. with distinction from the ███████ College of Design, and M.F.A. from ███████ University. She is a recipient of the City of Los Angeles Individual Artist Fellowship, the California Arts Council Individual Established Artist Fellowship, the California Community Foundation Visual Artist Fellowship, and the Marciano Art Foundation's Artadia Award. She is an assistant professor of art at California State University, ███████ and is represented by ███ ███████ Los Angeles.

███████████████ **(b. 1982, Santiago, Chile)** received his M.F.A. from the University of ███████, Seattle; a B.A. in philosophy from ███████ State College, and a B.F.A. from the University of Chile, ███████. He has presented solo exhibitions at the New Museum, New York; Lancaster Museum of Art and History, CA; Orange County Museum of Art, CA; and Portland Art Museum, OR; and has participated in group exhibitions at the Phillips Collection, Washington, DC; the Drawing Center, New York, NY; Frye Art Museum, Seattle, WA; Museum of Fine Arts, Houston, TX; and Henry Art Gallery, Seattle, WA. He was awarded residencies at Light Work, Syracuse, NY; MacDowell Colony, Peterborough, NH; Core program, Houston, TX; Bemis Center for Contemporary Art, Omaha, NE; Kala Art Institute, Berkeley; and Skowhegan School of Painting and Sculpture, ME. He was awarded a Guggenheim Fellowship and a Smithsonian Artist Research Fellowship. He received a Joan Mitchell Painters and Sculptors Grant, and an Arts innovator Award. His work is included in the collections of LACMA, Los Angeles, CA; Whitney Museum of American Art, NYC, NY; Museum of Fine Arts, Houston, TX; Nelson-Atkins Museum of Art, Kansas City, MO; Frye Art Museum, Seattle, WA; as well as numerous private and corporate collections. He lives and works in ███████, CA.

████████ **(b. 1974, Oceanside, CA, U.S.A.)** is an artist whose practice engages space as both a concept and a material. Often produced with materials associated with construction, his works expose the ideological and broader sociopolitical and economic relationships that facilitate the way spaces we inhabit and move through are assembled. His work has been the subject of various solo exhibitions at the Museum of Contemporary Art, San Diego, the Atheneum Museum of Art, Hartford, CT, the Locust Projects, Miami, FL; the Museum of Contemporary Art, San Diego, CA; and Site Santa Fe, Santa Fe, NM; among others. His work has also been included in many group exhibitions, most notably: at the Smithsonian American Art Museum, Washington D.C.; the Museum of Contemporary Art, Detroit, MI; at Denver Art Museum, Denver, CO; at Perez Art Museum, Miami, FL; at the Hammer Museum, Los Angeles, CA and Menil Collection, Houston, TX; at Nasher Sculpture Center, Dallas, TX; *The Future Generation Art Prize Exhibition* at Venice, Italy; at the Museum of Contemporary, Los Angeles, CA; at LACMA, Los Angeles, CA; and at the Whitney Biennial, New York, NY. In addition to his exhibitions, he has completed various public art projects. His creations are included in the collections of the Perez Art Museum, the Hammer Museum, LACMA, the MCA San Diego, MOCA, the Phoenix Art Museum, the Smithsonian Museum of Art, the Orange County Museum of Art, and the Whitney Museum of American Art. He is the recipient of numerous awards, including a California Community Foundation Fellowship and a Guggenheim Fellowship. He received his B.F.A. from ██ College of Art and Design and his M.F.A. from the University of California, ████. He lives and works in ████████, CA, and is represented by ██████████ Los Angeles.

████████ **(b. 1984, México City, México)** is an interdisciplinary artist specializing in sculpture and community-based art practices. Born in México City and raised along the U.S.–México border in Baja California, she is a fronteriza, which informs her exploration of borderland dynamics. Immigrating to the U.S., she established her practice in Los Angeles after transitioning from her studio in Tijuana. Her technical expertise spans traditional and contemporary sculpting, mold-making, casting, and work with diverse materials: clay, resin, bronze, and found objects. Her educational foundation includes apprenticeships in sculpting and bronze casting, a B.F.A. focused on integrating art and disability; and studies in neuroscience, art history, and fashion design. Her work is deeply rooted in community engagement and education. She has led art initiatives in México and the U.S., collaborating with institutions like USAID, CONACULTA, and LAUSD to support underrepresented populations, including immigrants, individuals with disabilities, and communities affected by systemic inequities. Her projects foster inclusive spaces for creative expression, connecting diverse generations through meaningful artistic experiences. Inspired by her early exposure to collaborative environments—shaped by her mother's ceramic practice and mentorship from Baja California's pioneering women artists—she prioritizes accessibility and community in her artistic and educational endeavors.

████ **(b. 1999, San Salvador, El Salvador)** is an interdisciplinary artist whose work emphasizes the memories of migration, childhood in El Salvador, and growing up queer in Los Angeles; and explores the in-betweens of the past and present. They use their childhood foods, such as marañones, mangos, and banana leaves, to navigate themes of connection and create a future of belonging where memories correlate with symbols of lived experiences. They received their B.F.A. from the School of Museum of Fine Arts at ███ University and currently live and work in ████.

████████ **(b. 1983, Guadalajara, Jalisco, México)** is a formerly undocumented, first-generation, transnational, Japanese Mexican immigrant. She holds an M.A. in art business from the ████████ Institute of Art. She also has an M.A. in Chicanx studies, an M.Phil. in contemporary aesthetic theory, and a B.A. in art history from the University of California, ████████, with minors in Chicano/a studies and Mexican studies. She is currently a teaching fellow and doctoral candidate of the same university, where she epistemologically braids the aesthetics of undocumentedness to challenge immigration and migration policy and politics. She is the founder of ████████; co-founder of the ██████+Collective; the executive director at ████; and a professor at various colleges. She has been awarded the Arts for LA Fellowship, NALAC NLI Fellowship, DAICOR Fellowship, and CCI Catalyst. As a Getty and Kress Foundation Fellow, she has developed curatorial statements at museums across México and the U.S. After being a public art curator for the Department of Cultural Affairs in Los Angeles, she became the curatorial director of the Ronald McDonald House Charities, leading various galleries. She has curated exhibitions for galleries and museums across the globe, and her written work has been published internationally. She is currently inhabiting ████████, CA—the unceded land of the Tongva, Tataviam, Serrano, Kizh, and Chumash peoples.

████████████████ **(b. 1988, Zacatecas, México)** is the author various publications; and is the co-editor of an anthology. His work has been long listed for the California Book Award, the Foreword Indies Prize, and the Lambda Literary Award, among other recognitions and citations. He is a founding member of the Undocupoets, which eliminated citizenship requirements from all major poetry book prizes in the U.S.; was recognized with the Barnes and Noble Writers for Writers award; and was the first undocumented student to graduate from the Helen Zell Writers Program at the University of Michigan. He served as distinguished fellow for the Marshall Project's Art for Justice initiative from the University of Arizona, which advocates for prison reform; and is an inaugural winner of the Writing Freedom Fellowship from Haymarket books and the Mellon Foundation. He currently serves as faculty in the M.F.A. program at ████████ College of California and the ████████ University low-res M.F.A. program.

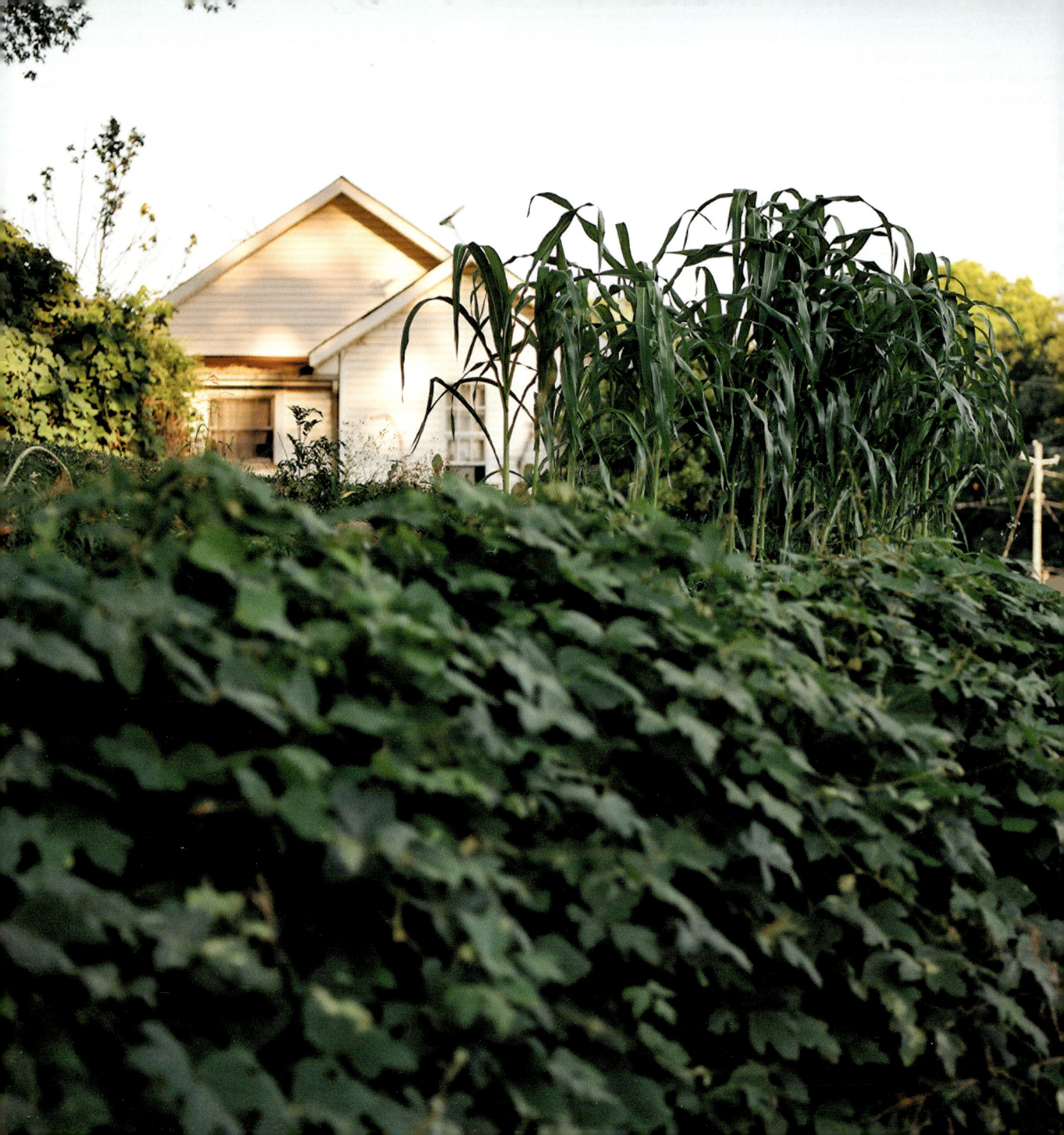